WILLIAM ROY
IN VITRO

Life Drawn

William Roy
Story & Art

•

Benjamin Croze
Translator

•

Jonathan Stevenson
US Edition Editor

Amanda Lucido
Assistant Editor

Vincent Henry
Original Edition Editor

Jerry Frissen
Senior Art Director

Fabrice Giger
Publisher

Rights and Licensing - licensing@humanoids.com
Press and Social Media - pr@humanoids.com

IN VITRO.
This title is a publication of Humanoids, Inc. 8033 Sunset Blvd. #628, Los Angeles, CA 90046.
Copyright © 2020 Humanoids, Inc., Los Angeles (USA). All rights reserved.
Humanoids and its logos are ® and © 2020 Humanoids, Inc.
Library of Congress Control Number: 2019910142

Life Drawn is an imprint of Humanoids, Inc.

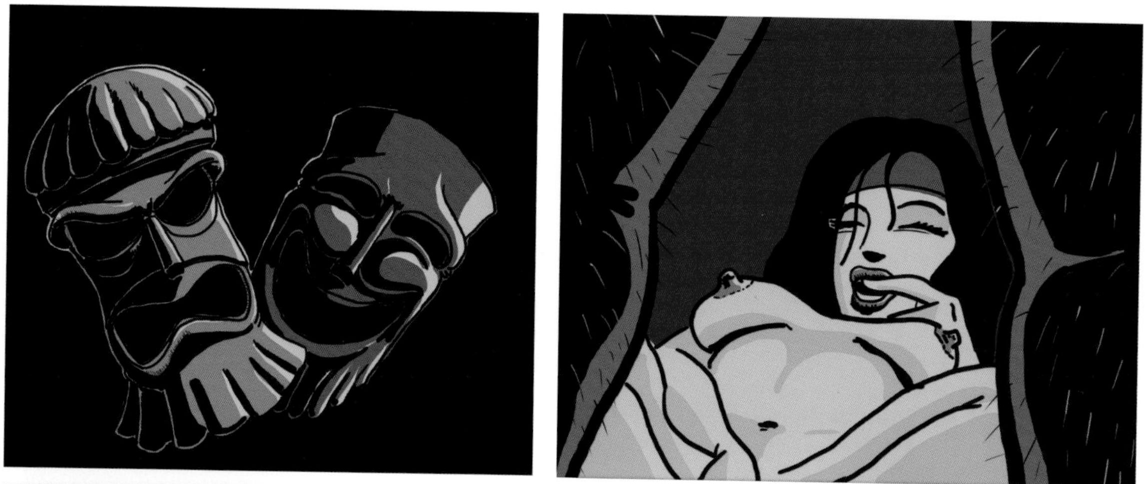

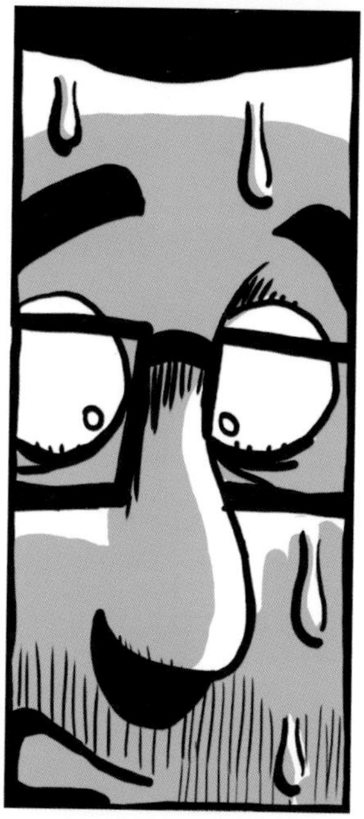

1. DEAD-END DAD

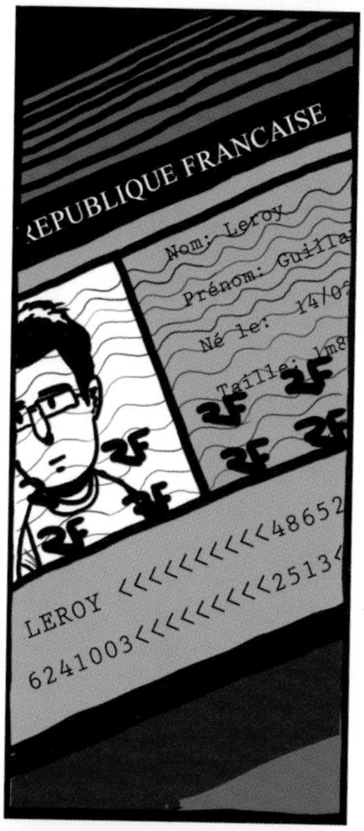
REPUBLIQUE FRANCAISE
Nom: Leroy

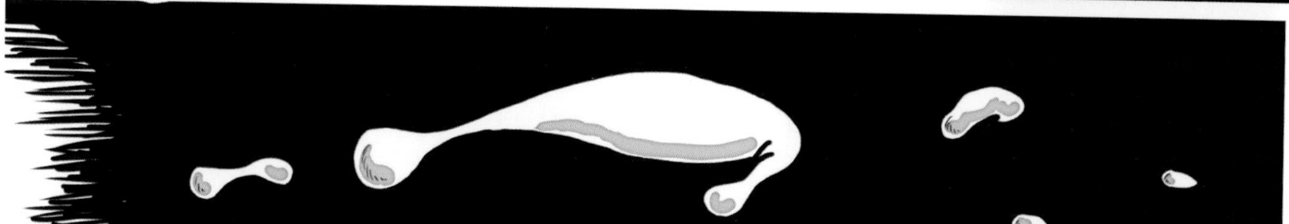

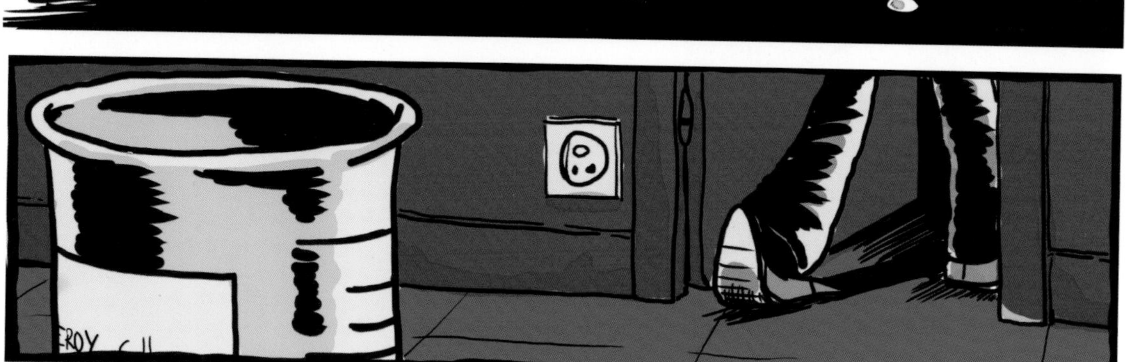

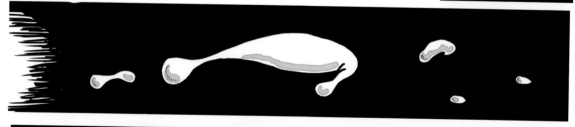

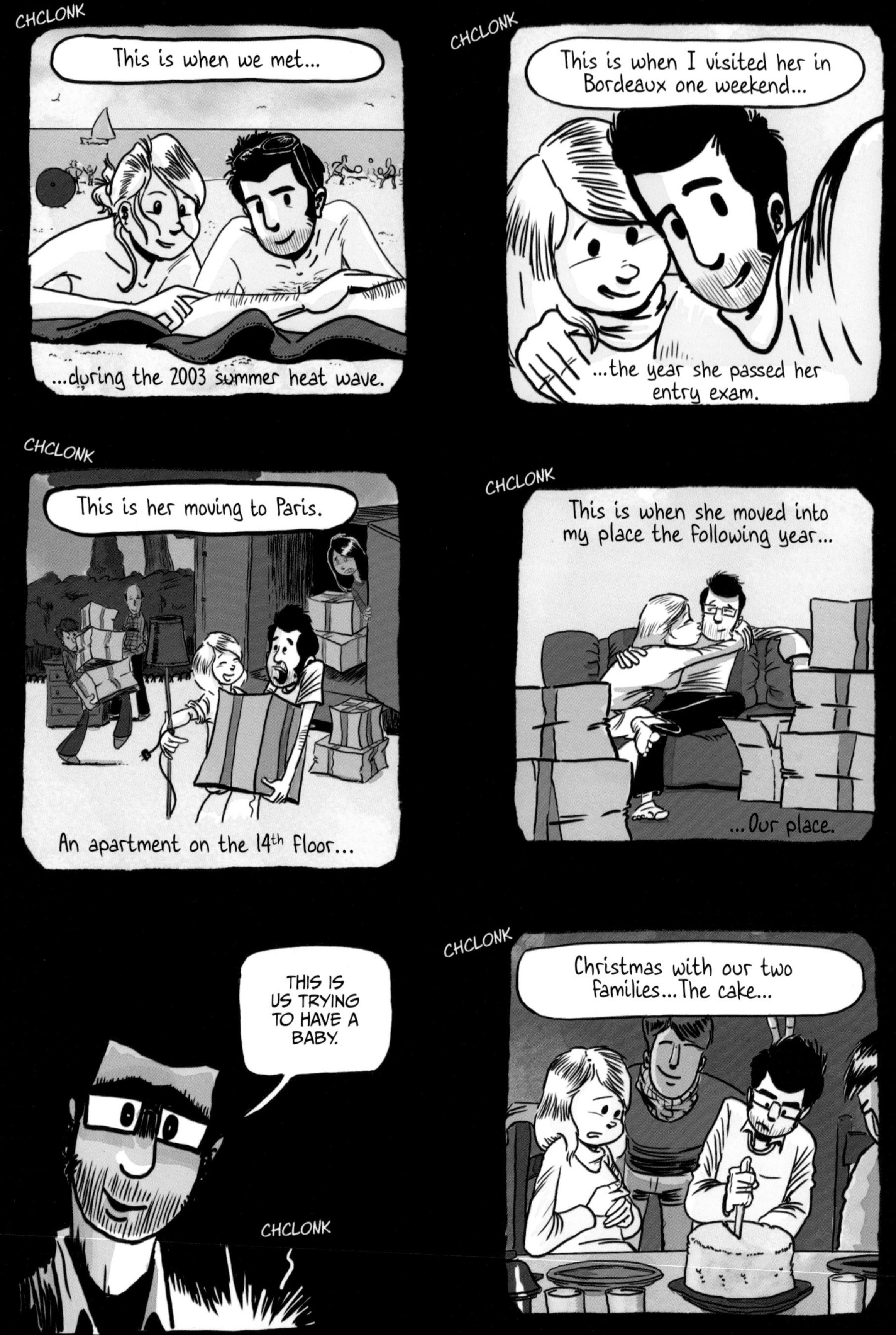
CHCLONK
This is when we met...
...during the 2003 summer heat wave.
CHCLONK
This is when I visited her in Bordeaux one weekend...
...the year she passed her entry exam.
CHCLONK
This is her moving to Paris.
An apartment on the 14th Floor...
CHCLONK
This is when she moved into my place the following year...
...Our place.
THIS IS US TRYING TO HAVE A BABY.
CHCLONK
CHCLONK
Christmas with our two families...The cake...

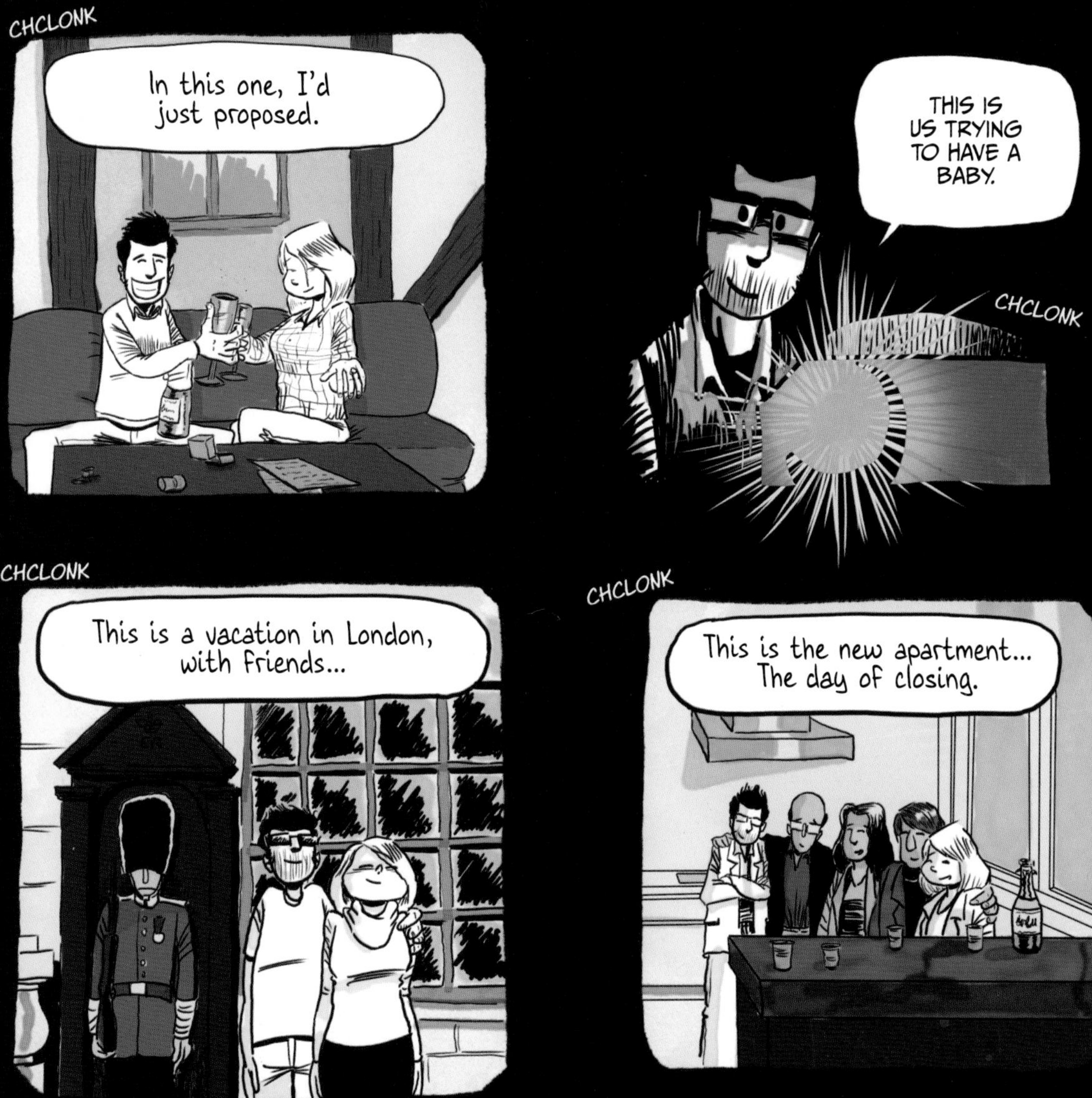
CHCLONK
In this one, I'd just proposed.
THIS IS US TRYING TO HAVE A BABY.
CHCLONK
CHCLONK
This is a vacation in London, with friends...
CHCLONK
This is the new apartment... The day of closing.

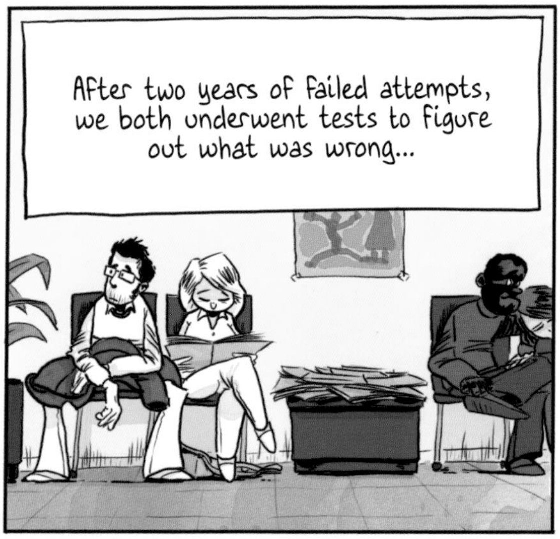
After two years of failed attempts, we both underwent tests to figure out what was wrong...

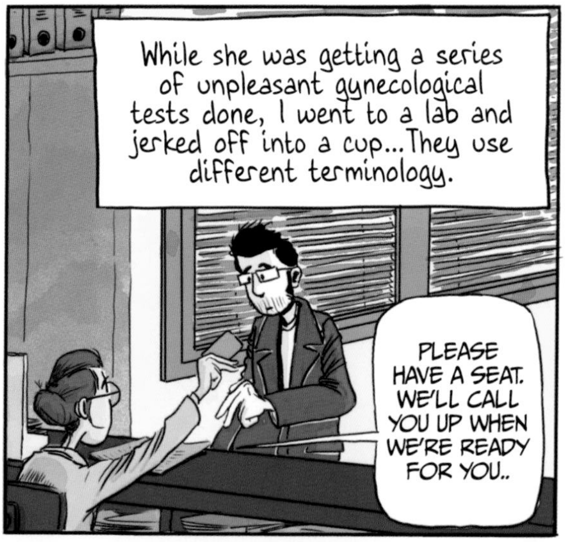
While she was getting a series of unpleasant gynecological tests done, I went to a lab and jerked off into a cup...They use different terminology.
PLEASE HAVE A SEAT. WE'LL CALL YOU UP WHEN WE'RE READY FOR YOU..

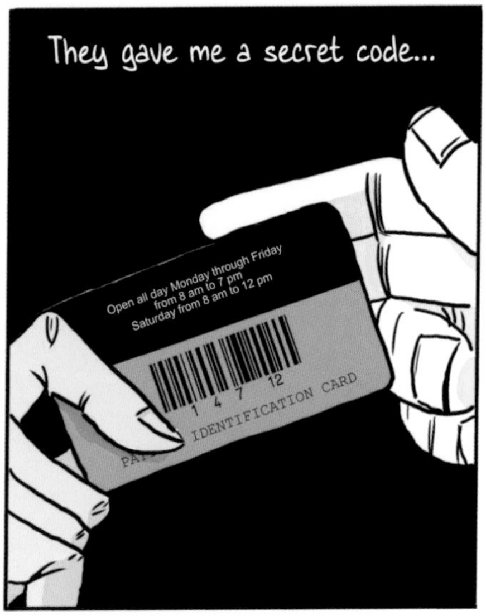
They gave me a secret code...
Open all day Monday through Friday
from 8 am to 7 pm
Saturday from 8 am to 12 pm
1 4 7 12
IDENTIFICATION CARD

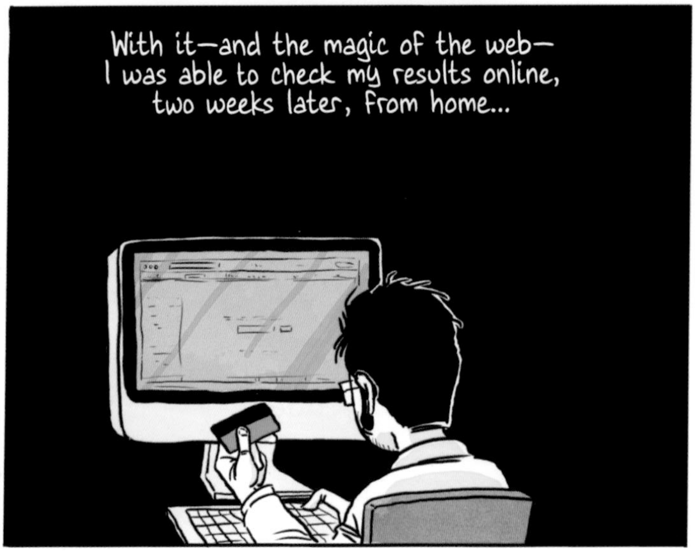
With it—and the magic of the web—I was able to check my results online, two weeks later, from home...

...Alone...

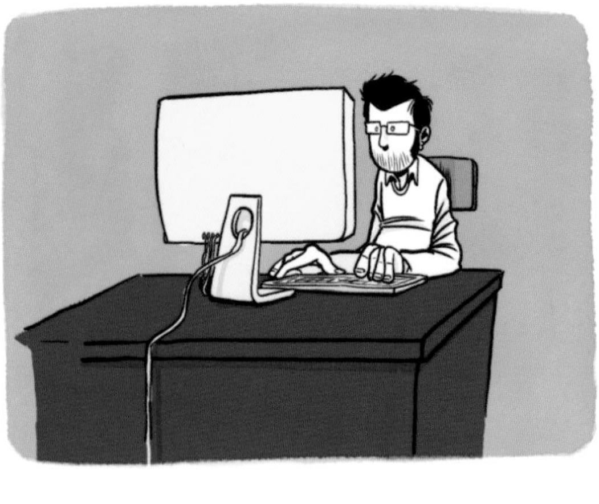

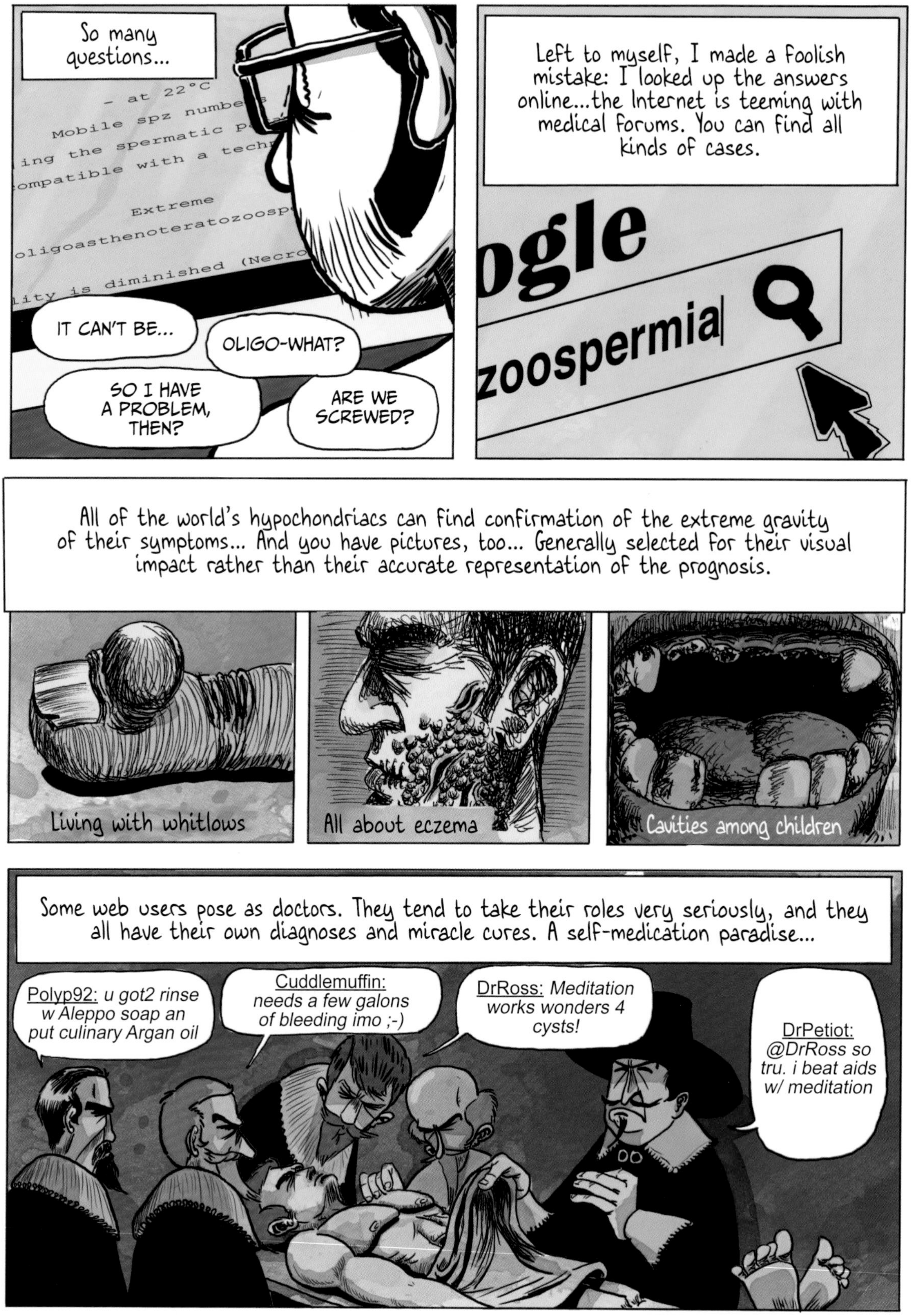
So many questions...
- at 22°C
Mobile spz numbe
ing the spermatic p
ompatible with a tech
Extreme
oligoasthenoteratozoosp
ity is diminished (Necro
IT CAN'T BE...
OLIGO-WHAT?
SO I HAVE A PROBLEM, THEN?
ARE WE SCREWED?
Left to myself, I made a foolish mistake: I looked up the answers online...the Internet is teeming with medical forums. You can find all kinds of cases.
ogle
zoospermia
All of the world's hypochondriacs can find confirmation of the extreme gravity of their symptoms... And you have pictures, too... Generally selected for their visual impact rather than their accurate representation of the prognosis.
Living with whitlows
All about eczema
Cavities among children
Some web users pose as doctors. They tend to take their roles very seriously, and they all have their own diagnoses and miracle cures. A self-medication paradise...
Polyp92: u got2 rinse w Aleppo soap an put culinary Argan oil
Cuddlemuffin: needs a few galons of bleeding imo ;-)
DrRoss: Meditation works wonders 4 cysts!
DrPetiot: @DrRoss so tru. i beat aids w/ meditation

Today, the odds and ends of the web bring you:

OLIGOASTHENOTERATOZOOSPERMIA!

Presented by
Professor Beuaârr

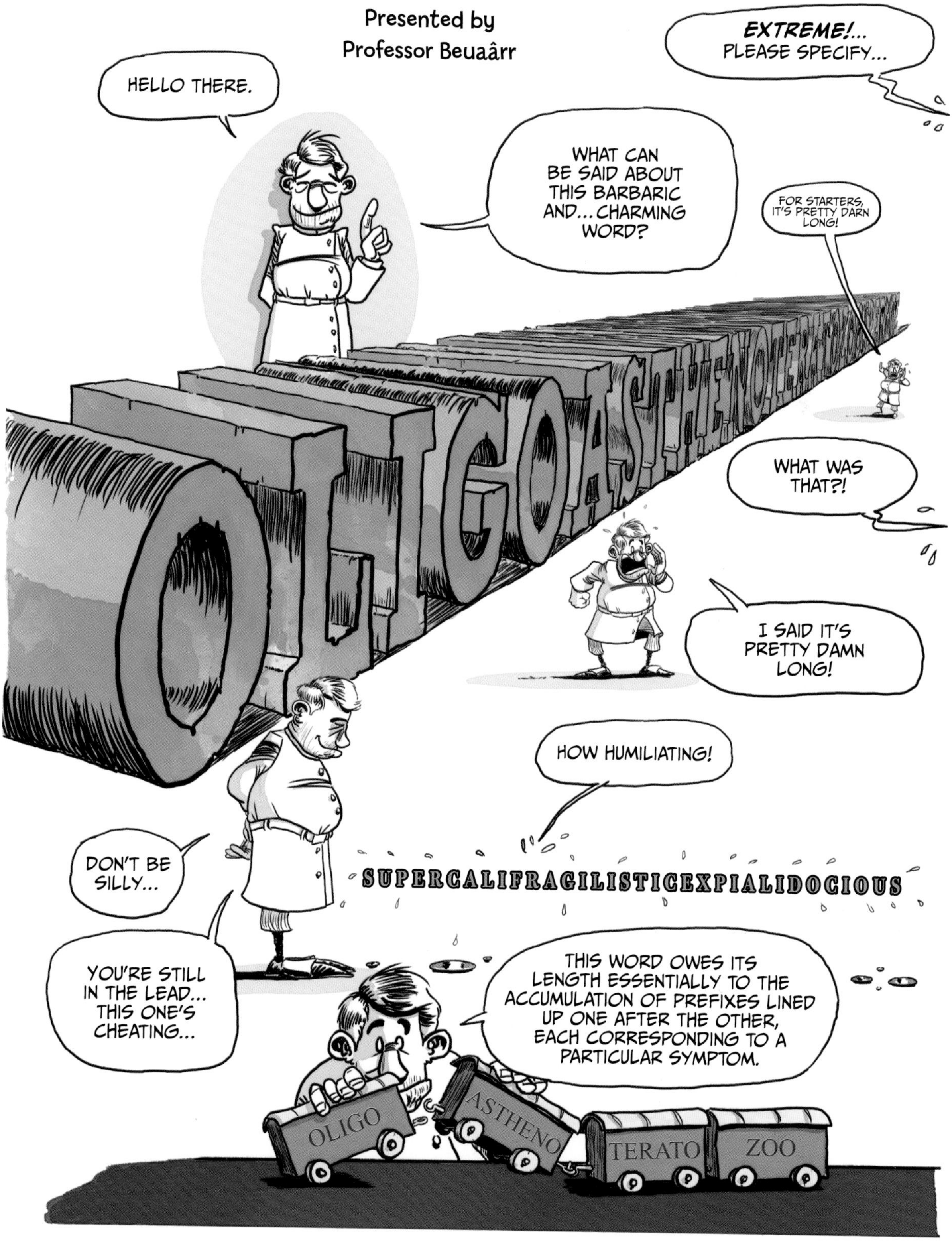

HELLO THERE.
WHAT CAN BE SAID ABOUT THIS BARBARIC AND... CHARMING WORD?
EXTREME!... PLEASE SPECIFY...
FOR STARTERS, IT'S PRETTY DARN LONG!
WHAT WAS THAT?!
I SAID IT'S PRETTY DAMN LONG!
HOW HUMILIATING!
SUPERCALIFRAGILISTICEXPIALIDOCIOUS
DON'T BE SILLY...
YOU'RE STILL IN THE LEAD... THIS ONE'S CHEATING...
THIS WORD OWES ITS LENGTH ESSENTIALLY TO THE ACCUMULATION OF PREFIXES LINED UP ONE AFTER THE OTHER, EACH CORRESPONDING TO A PARTICULAR SYMPTOM.
OLIGO
ASTHENO
TERATO
ZOO

THE ROOT OF THE WORD IS *SPERMIA*.

IT IS THEREFORE RELATED TO SEMEN AND SPERM.

IN ORDER TO UNDERSTAND THE DIFFERENT PREFIXES, LET'S ISOLATE A SPECIMEN!

IT IS CALLED ZOOSPERMIA BECAUSE THE STUDY FOCUSES ON THE LIVING ORGANISMS IN THE SAMPLE.

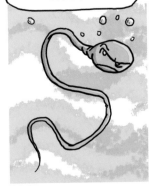

OLIGO: THERE ARE FEW INDIVIDUALS IN THE SAMPLE.

OH, HEY BRO.

SUP.

ASTHENO: THE FEW REMAINING ARE BARELY MOVING.

AND TERATO: MANY ARE MALFORMED AND DEGENERATE.

OLIGO-*YADA*-*YADA*, ALSO CALLED O.A.T., IS THEREFORE THE COMBINATION OF DIFFERENT ANOMALIES IN SPERMATOZOA...

IT CAN BE MODERATE, MAJOR OR SEVERE...

...OR IN THIS CASE, EXTREME... IN OTHER WORDS, THIS GENTLEMAN'S BALLS ARE HOUSING A REAL NAPOLEONIC BATTLEFIELD.

SERIOUSLY?

THE INTERNET CAN BE SO VULGAR!

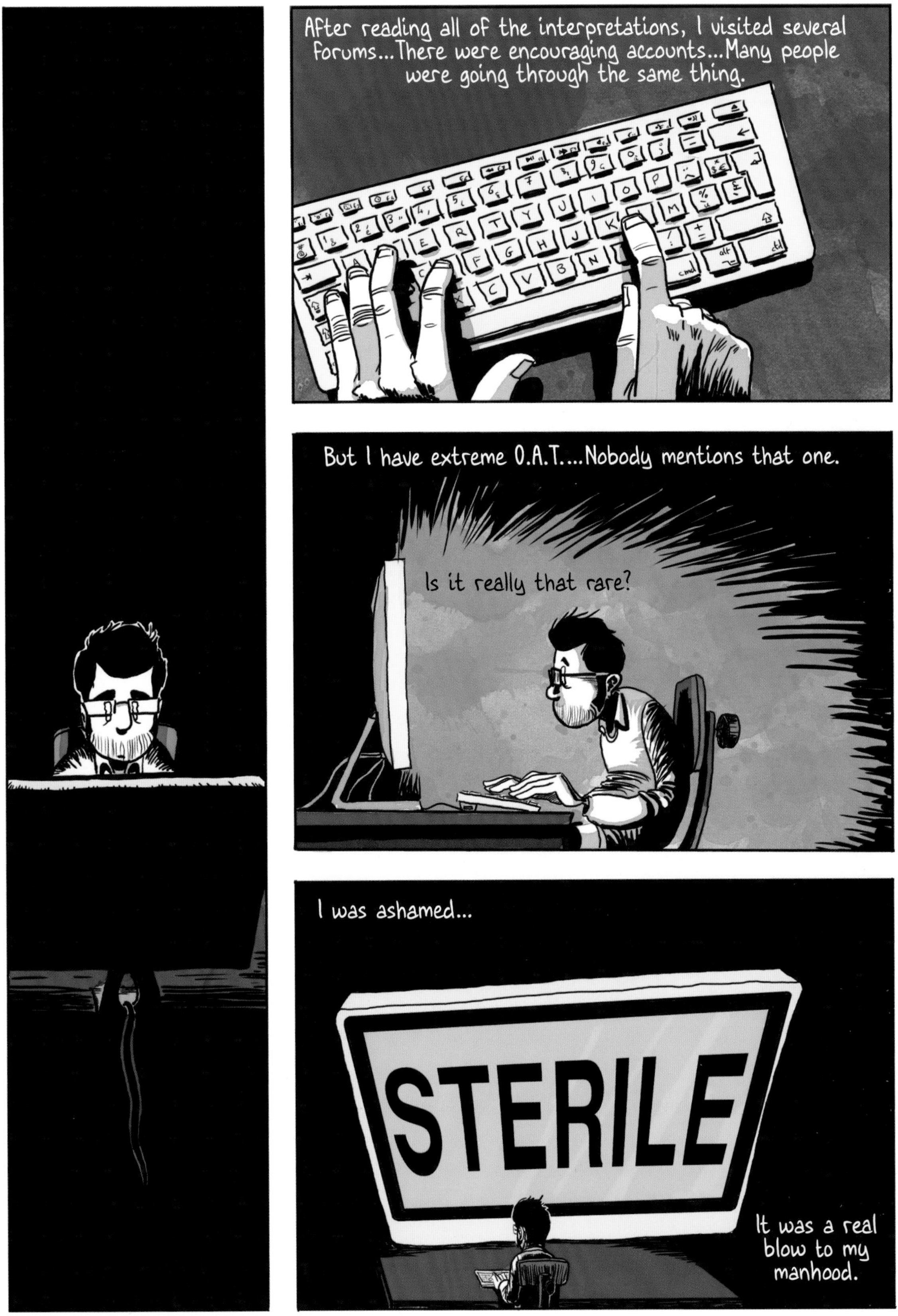
After reading all of the interpretations, I visited several forums...There were encouraging accounts...Many people were going through the same thing.
But I have extreme O.A.T....Nobody mentions that one.
Is it really that rare?
I was ashamed...
STERILE
It was a real blow to my manhood.

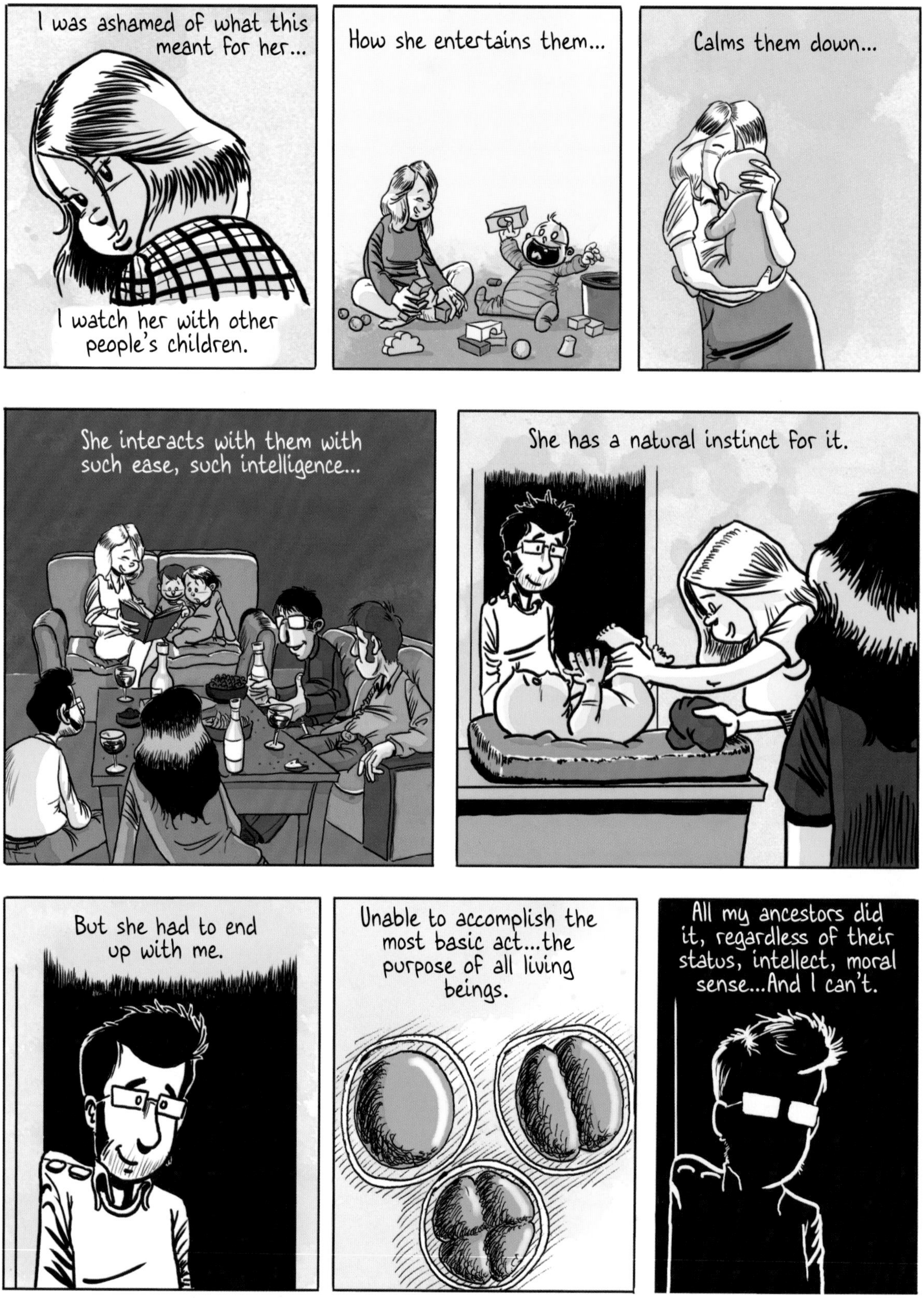
I was ashamed of what this meant for her...
I watch her with other people's children.
How she entertains them...
Calms them down...
She interacts with them with such ease, such intelligence...
She has a natural instinct for it.
But she had to end up with me.
Unable to accomplish the most basic act...the purpose of all living beings.
All my ancestors did it, regardless of their status, intellect, moral sense...And I can't.

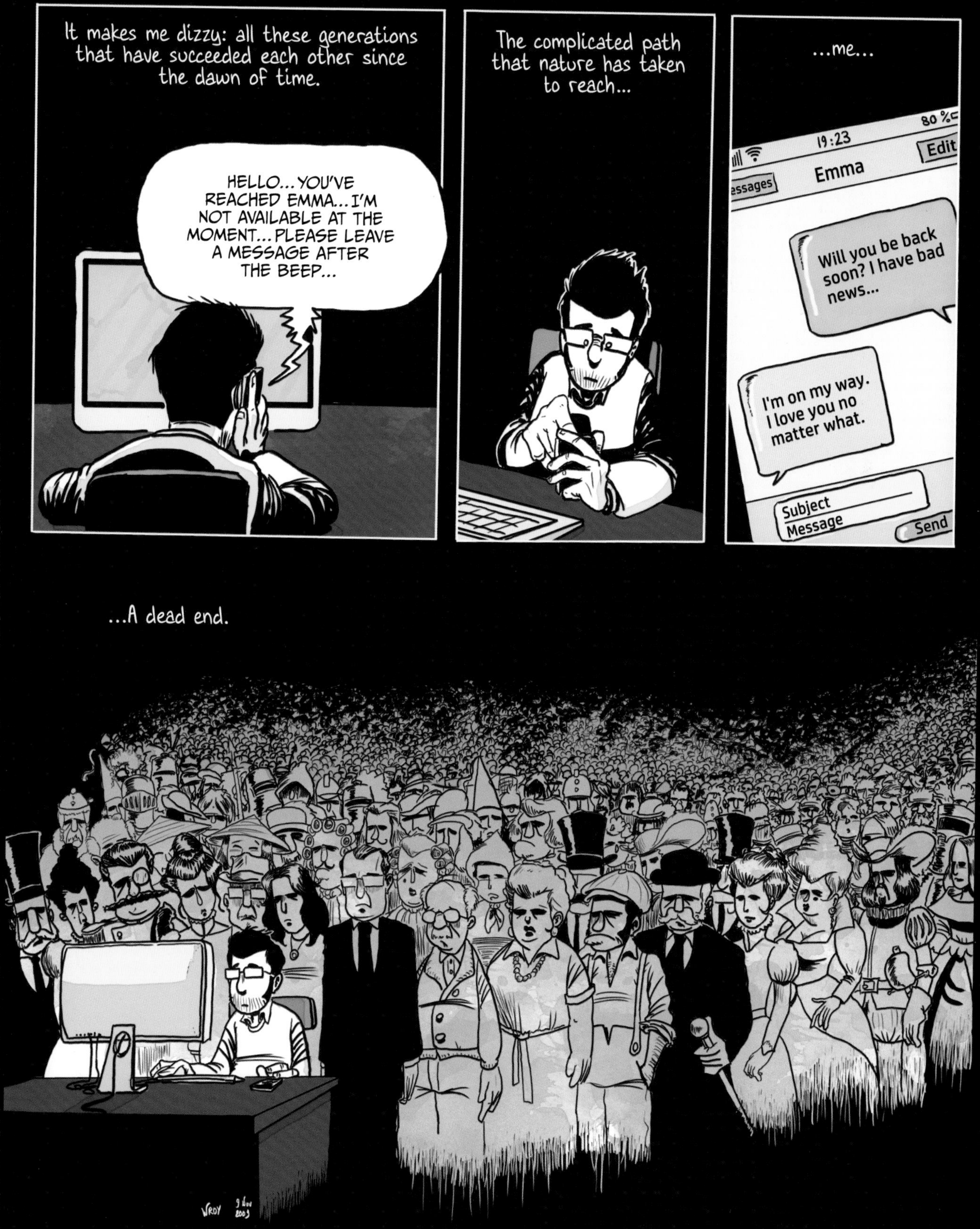
It makes me dizzy: all these generations that have succeeded each other since the dawn of time.
HELLO... YOU'VE REACHED EMMA... I'M NOT AVAILABLE AT THE MOMENT... PLEASE LEAVE A MESSAGE AFTER THE BEEP...
The complicated path that nature has taken to reach...
...me...
80 %
19:23
Edit
Emma
essages
Will you be back soon? I have bad news...
I'm on my way. I love you no matter what.
Subject
Message
Send
...A dead end.
VROY 9 Nov 2009

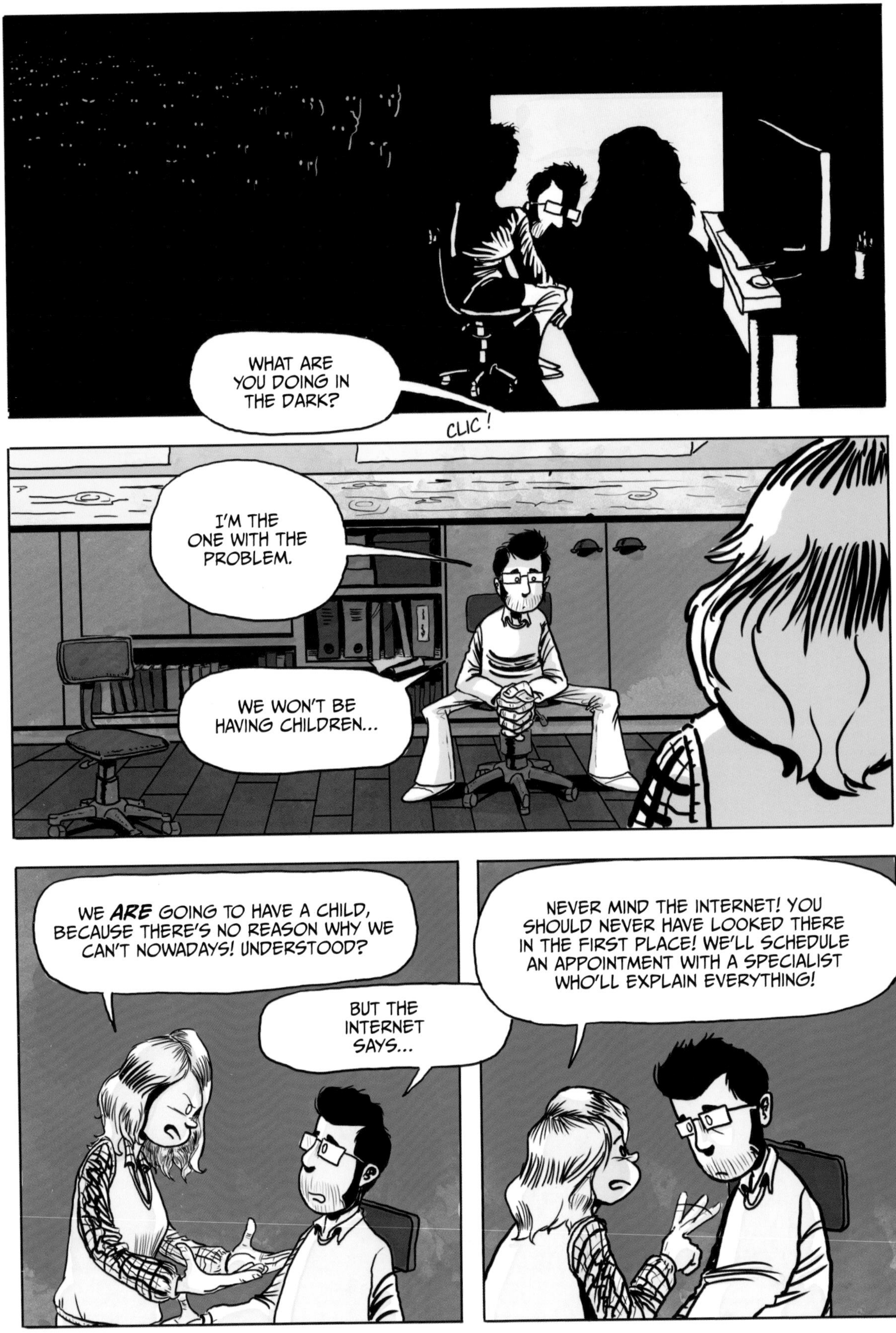
WHAT ARE YOU DOING IN THE DARK?
CLIC !
I'M THE ONE WITH THE PROBLEM.
WE WON'T BE HAVING CHILDREN...
WE **ARE** GOING TO HAVE A CHILD, BECAUSE THERE'S NO REASON WHY WE CAN'T NOWADAYS! UNDERSTOOD?
BUT THE INTERNET SAYS...
NEVER MIND THE INTERNET! YOU SHOULD NEVER HAVE LOOKED THERE IN THE FIRST PLACE! WE'LL SCHEDULE AN APPOINTMENT WITH A SPECIALIST WHO'LL EXPLAIN EVERYTHING!

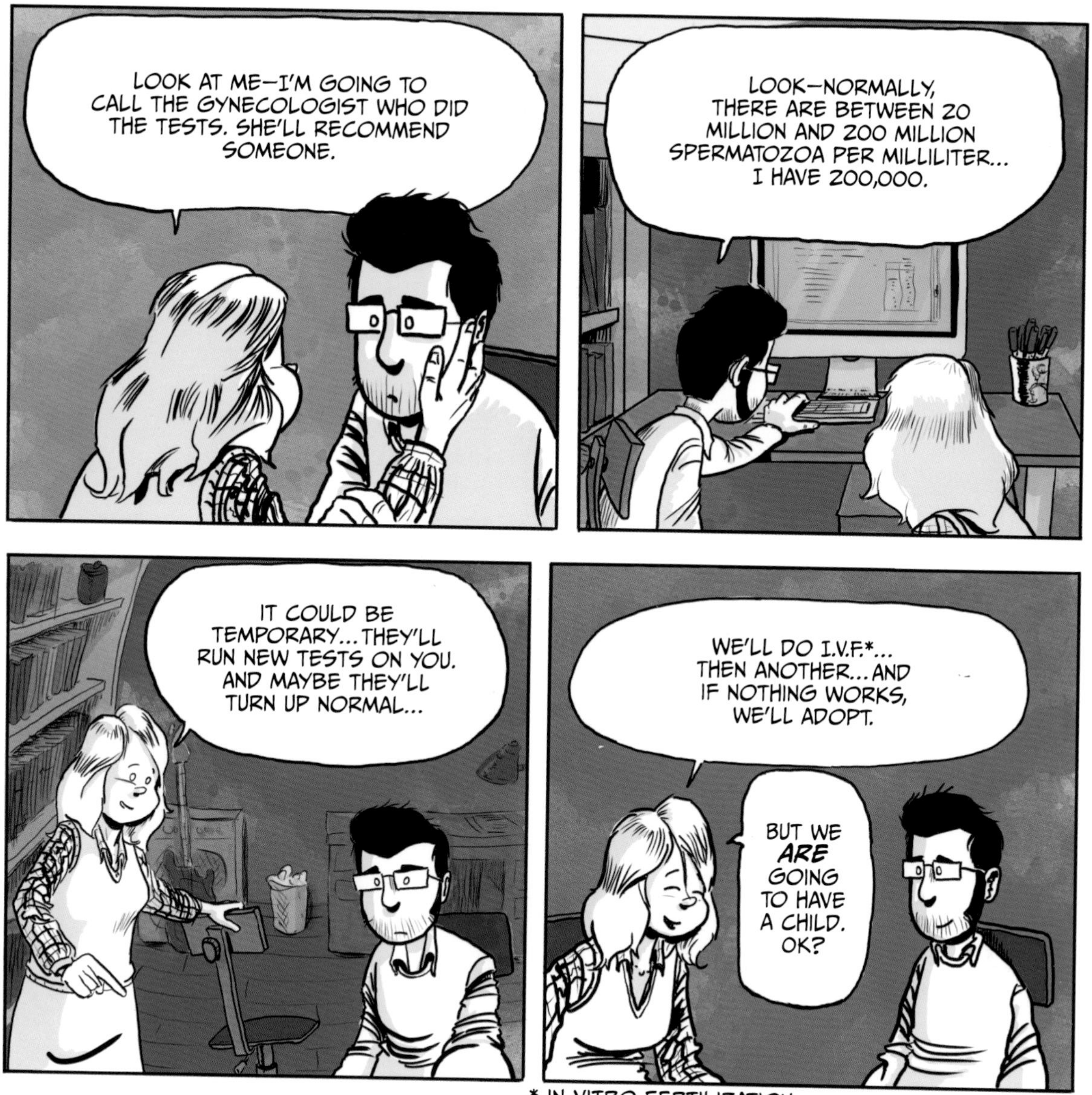
LOOK AT ME—I'M GOING TO CALL THE GYNECOLOGIST WHO DID THE TESTS. SHE'LL RECOMMEND SOMEONE.
LOOK—NORMALLY, THERE ARE BETWEEN 20 MILLION AND 200 MILLION SPERMATOZOA PER MILLILITER... I HAVE 200,000.
IT COULD BE TEMPORARY...THEY'LL RUN NEW TESTS ON YOU. AND MAYBE THEY'LL TURN UP NORMAL...
WE'LL DO I.V.F.*... THEN ANOTHER...AND IF NOTHING WORKS, WE'LL ADOPT.
BUT WE **ARE** GOING TO HAVE A CHILD. OK?

* IN VITRO FERTILIZATION

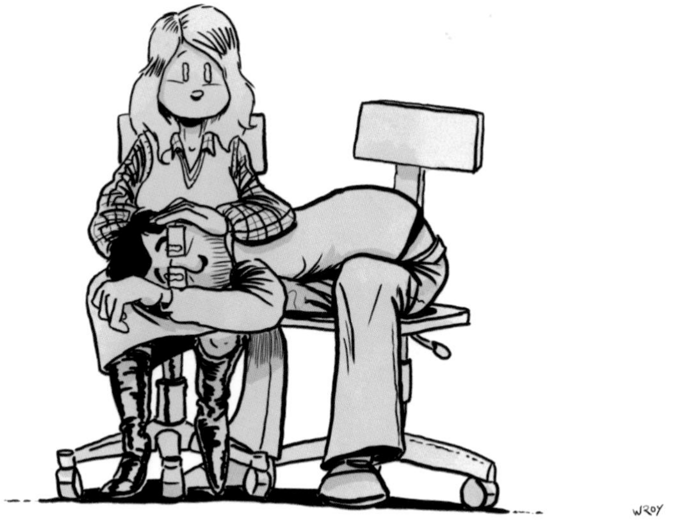

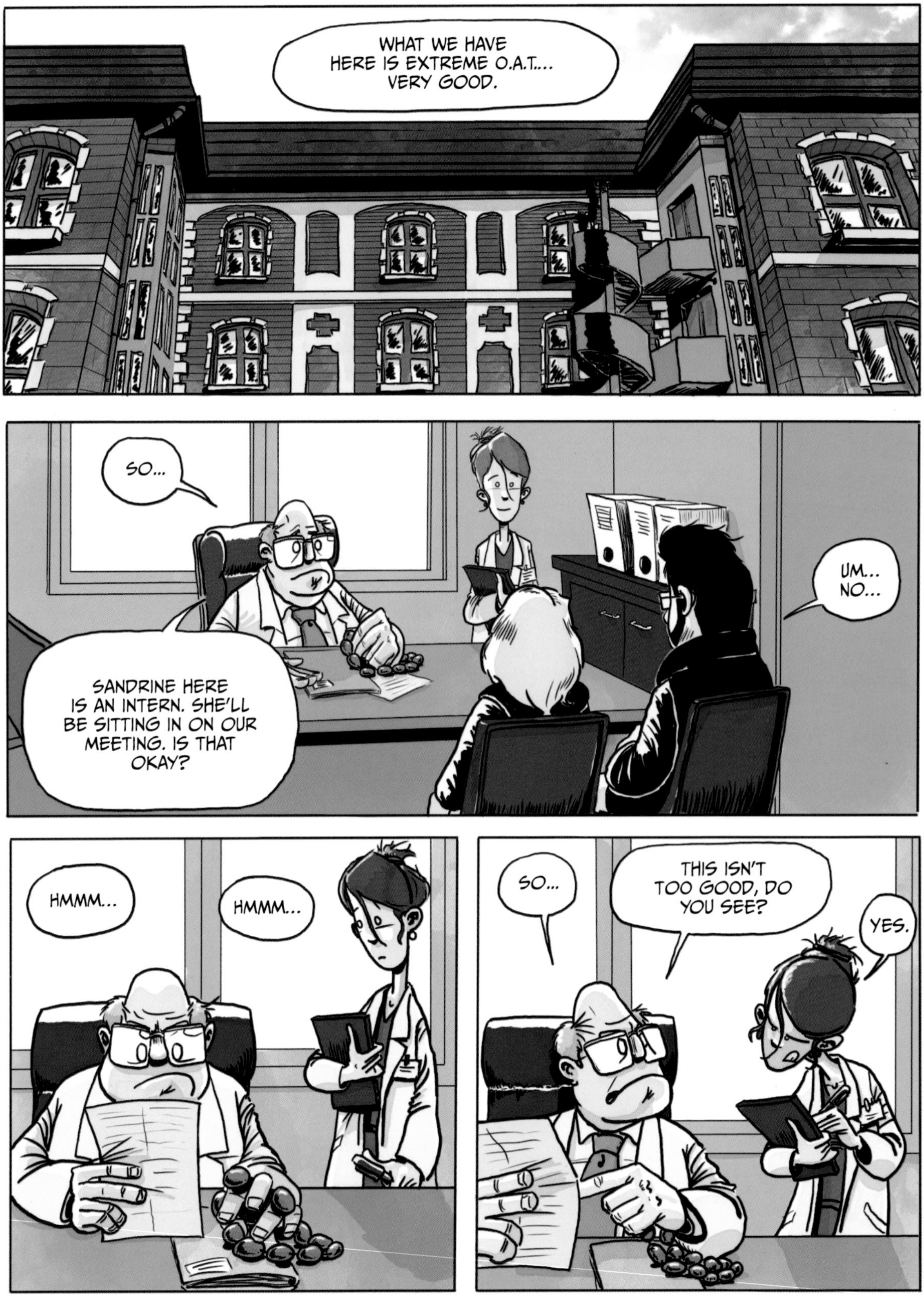
WHAT WE HAVE HERE IS EXTREME O.A.T.... VERY GOOD.
SO...
UM... NO...
SANDRINE HERE IS AN INTERN. SHE'LL BE SITTING IN ON OUR MEETING. IS THAT OKAY?
HMMM...
HMMM...
SO...
THIS ISN'T TOO GOOD, DO YOU SEE?
YES.

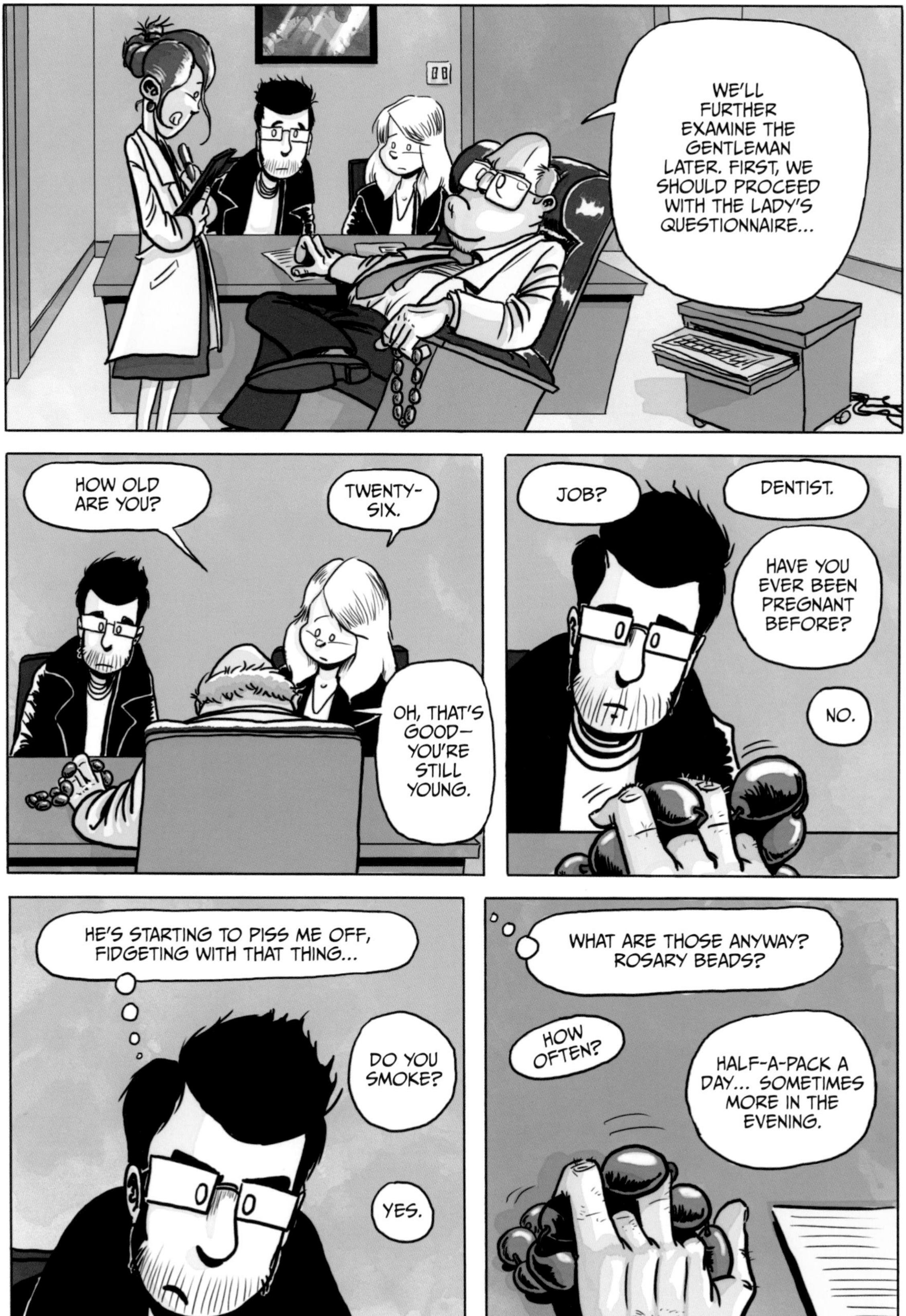
WE'LL FURTHER EXAMINE THE GENTLEMAN LATER. FIRST, WE SHOULD PROCEED WITH THE LADY'S QUESTIONNAIRE...
HOW OLD ARE YOU?
TWENTY-SIX.
OH, THAT'S GOOD— YOU'RE STILL YOUNG.
JOB?
DENTIST.
HAVE YOU EVER BEEN PREGNANT BEFORE?
NO.
HE'S STARTING TO PISS ME OFF, FIDGETING WITH THAT THING...
DO YOU SMOKE?
YES.
WHAT ARE THOSE ANYWAY? ROSARY BEADS?
HOW OFTEN?
HALF-A-PACK A DAY... SOMETIMES MORE IN THE EVENING.

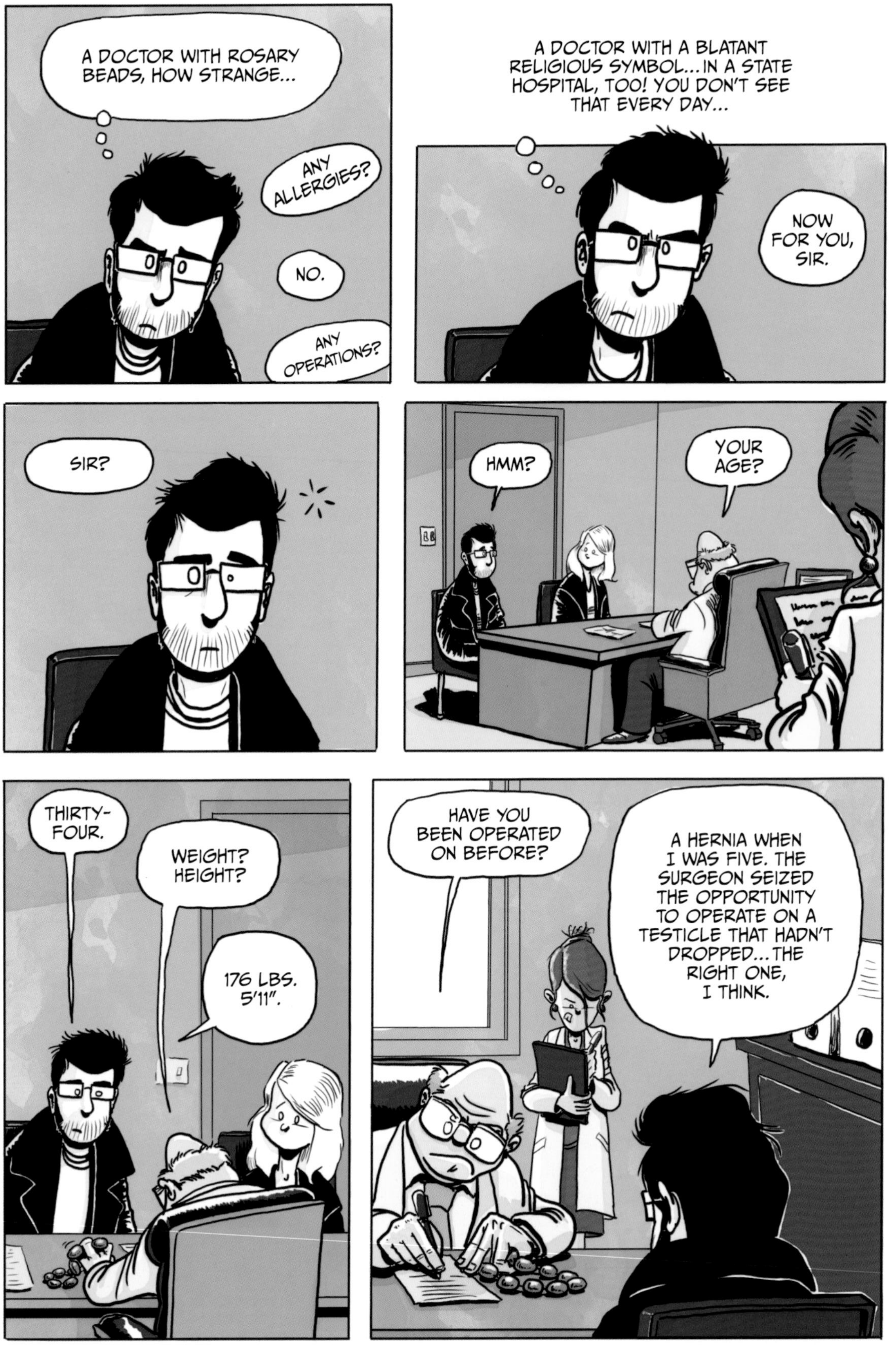
A DOCTOR WITH ROSARY BEADS, HOW STRANGE...
ANY ALLERGIES?
NO.
ANY OPERATIONS?
A DOCTOR WITH A BLATANT RELIGIOUS SYMBOL...IN A STATE HOSPITAL, TOO! YOU DON'T SEE THAT EVERY DAY...
NOW FOR YOU, SIR.
SIR?
HMM?
YOUR AGE?
THIRTY-FOUR.
WEIGHT? HEIGHT?
176 LBS. 5'11".
HAVE YOU BEEN OPERATED ON BEFORE?
A HERNIA WHEN I WAS FIVE. THE SURGEON SEIZED THE OPPORTUNITY TO OPERATE ON A TESTICLE THAT HADN'T DROPPED...THE RIGHT ONE, I THINK.

ORCHIOPEXY, THEN.
YES.
WE'RE GOING TO CHECK ALL THIS OUT...WOULD YOU FOLLOW ME INTO THE OTHER ROOM, PLEASE?
PLEASE REMOVE YOUR PANTS AND UNDERWEAR.
SO IN THIS CASE, SANDRINE,
THE PATIENT HAS REPORTED
HMM.
LET'S SEE...

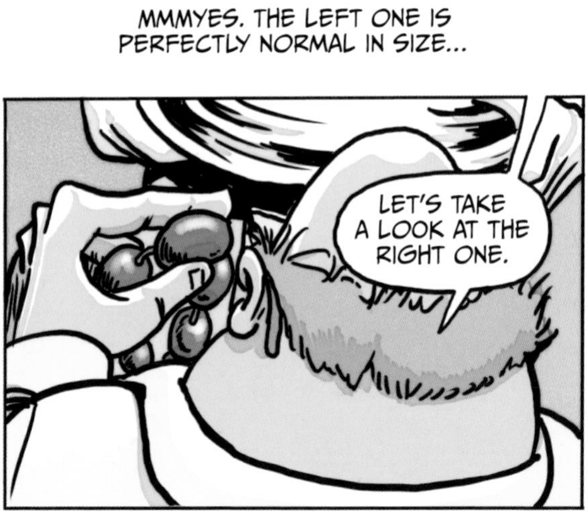
MMMYES. THE LEFT ONE IS PERFECTLY NORMAL IN SIZE...
LET'S TAKE A LOOK AT THE RIGHT ONE.

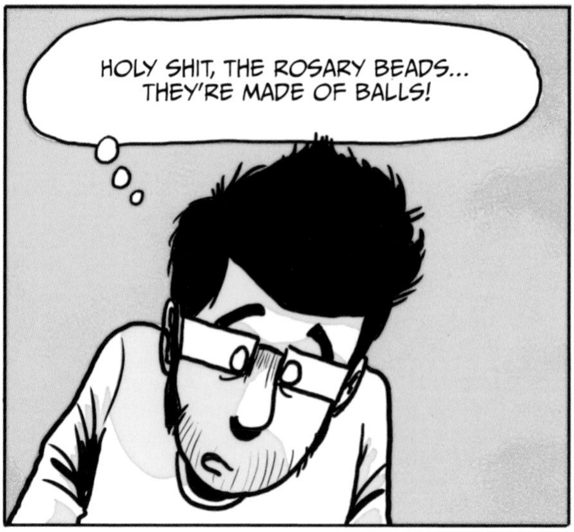
HOLY SHIT, THE ROSARY BEADS... THEY'RE MADE OF BALLS!

Today's lesson: **THE ORCHIDOMETER,**

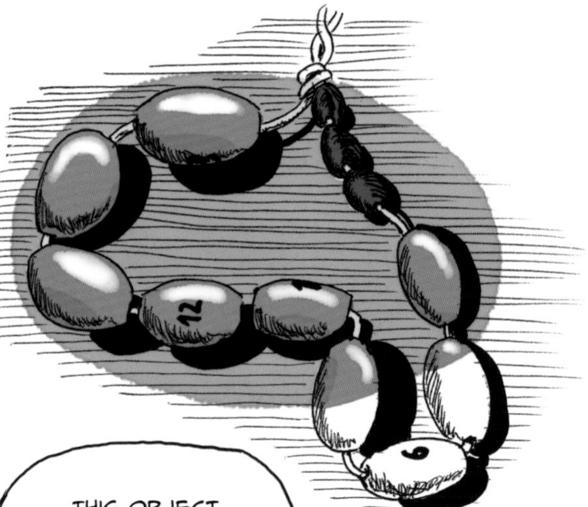

or more poetically, "Praders Balls" (named after its creator), is a medical device used to estimate the size of the testicles. Each orchidometer ball is identified by its volume in milliliters. It is used for certain gonadal disorders, or more generally to evaluate the proper growth of the bursa in adolescents during puberty...

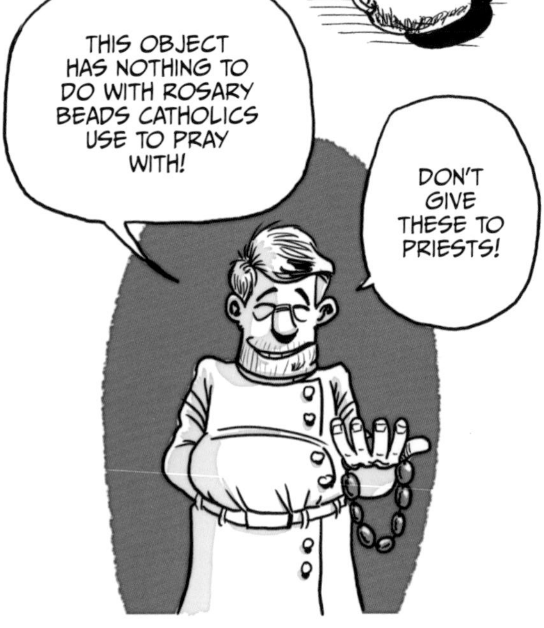
THIS OBJECT HAS NOTHING TO DO WITH ROSARY BEADS CATHOLICS USE TO PRAY WITH!
DON'T GIVE THESE TO PRIESTS!

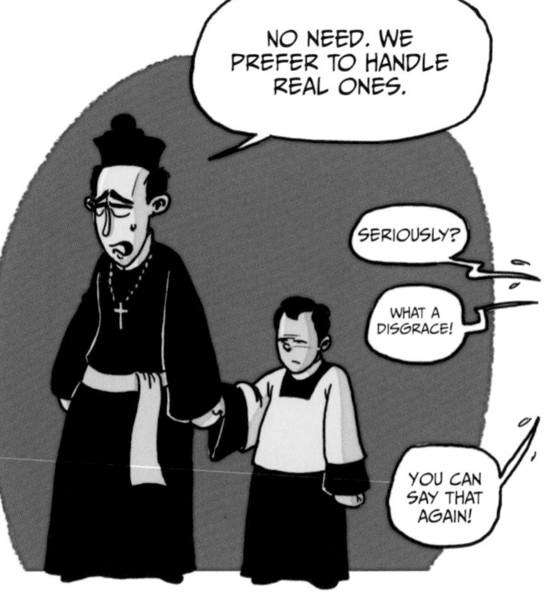
NO NEED. WE PREFER TO HANDLE REAL ONES.
SERIOUSLY?
WHAT A DISGRACE!
YOU CAN SAY THAT AGAIN!

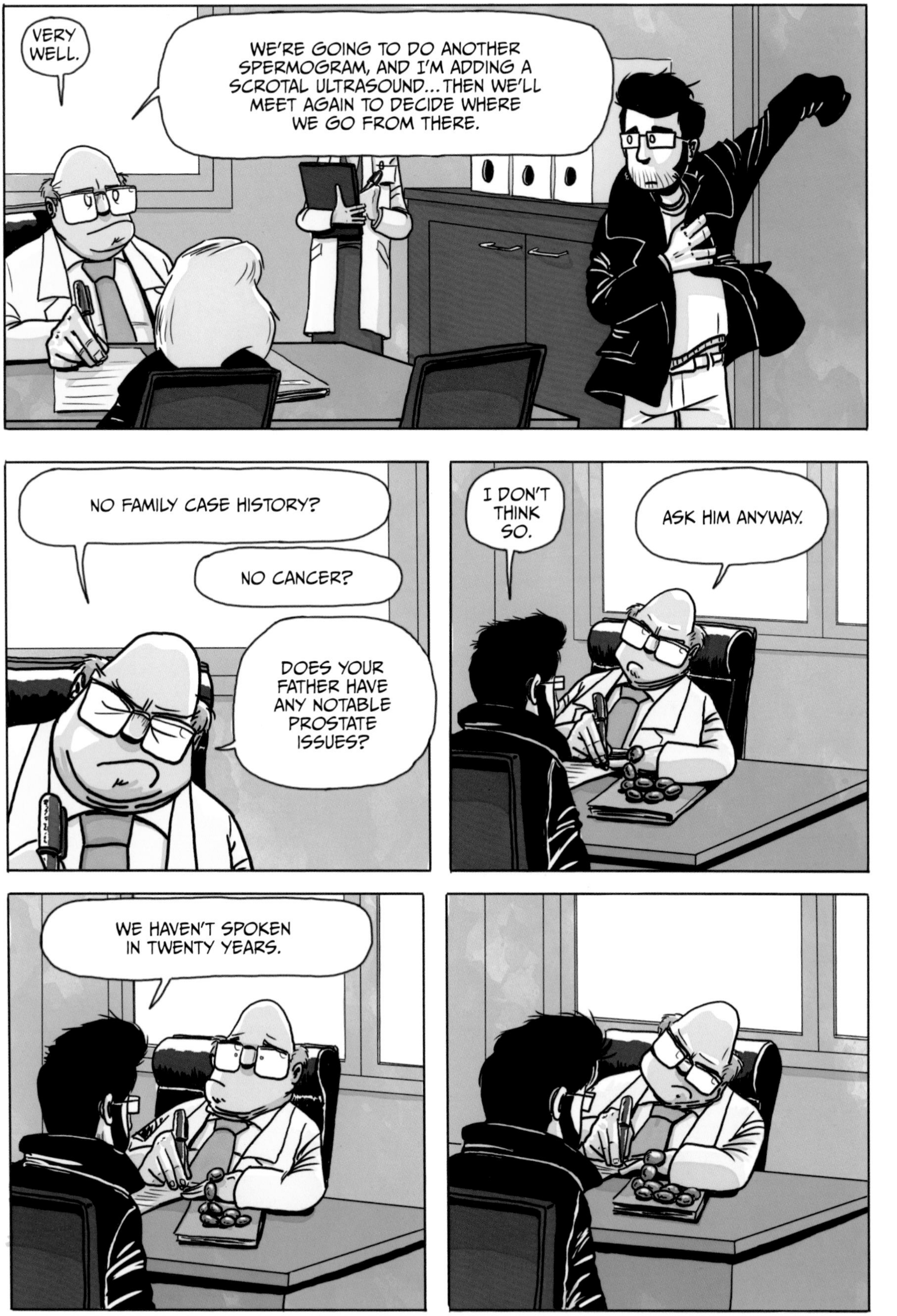
VERY WELL.
WE'RE GOING TO DO ANOTHER SPERMOGRAM, AND I'M ADDING A SCROTAL ULTRASOUND... THEN WE'LL MEET AGAIN TO DECIDE WHERE WE GO FROM THERE.
NO FAMILY CASE HISTORY?
NO CANCER?
DOES YOUR FATHER HAVE ANY NOTABLE PROSTATE ISSUES?
I DON'T THINK SO.
ASK HIM ANYWAY.
WE HAVEN'T SPOKEN IN TWENTY YEARS.

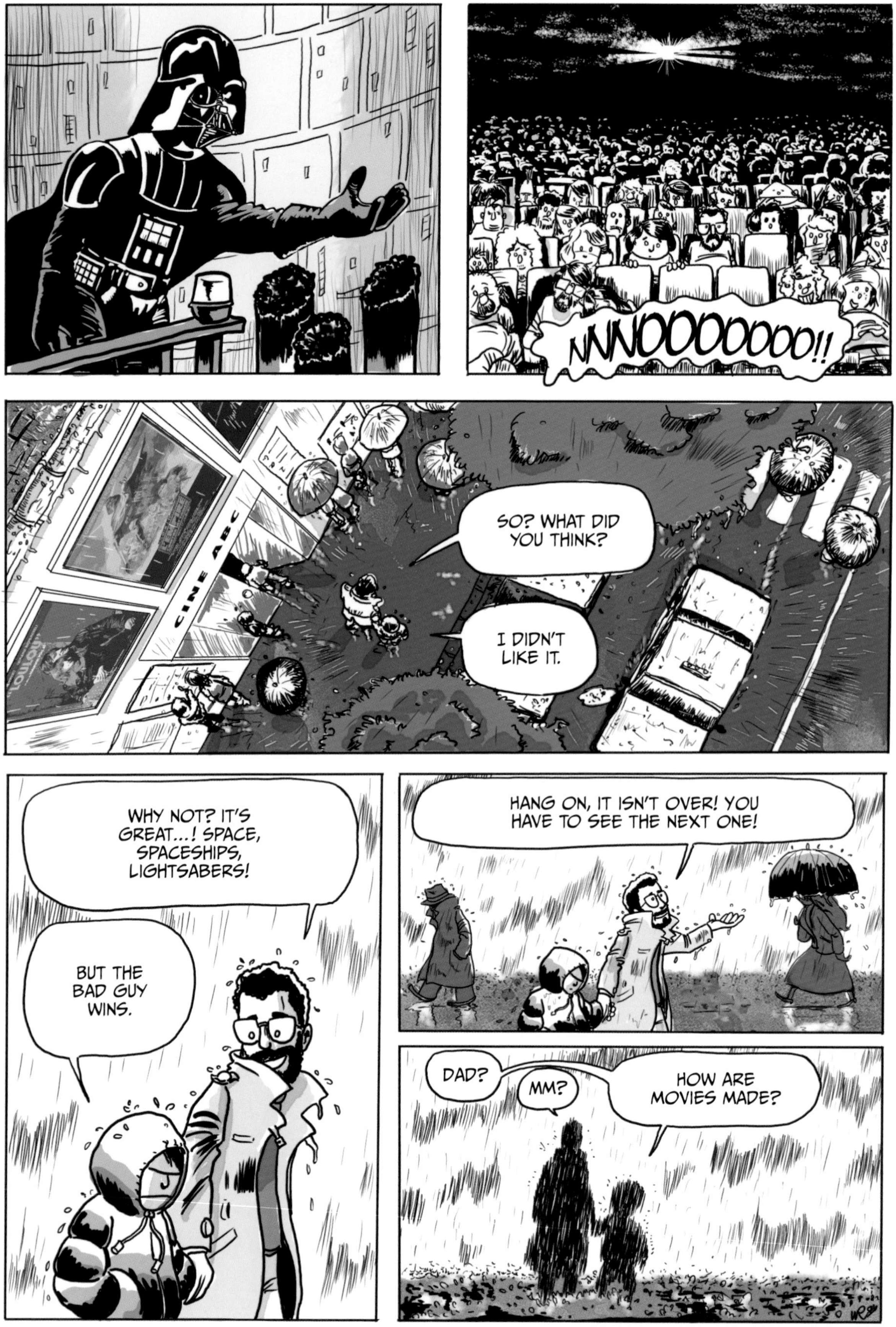
NNNOOOOOOO!!
CINE ABC
LOULOU
SO? WHAT DID YOU THINK?
I DIDN'T LIKE IT.
WHY NOT? IT'S GREAT...! SPACE, SPACESHIPS, LIGHTSABERS!
BUT THE BAD GUY WINS.
HANG ON, IT ISN'T OVER! YOU HAVE TO SEE THE NEXT ONE!
DAD?
MM?
HOW ARE MOVIES MADE?

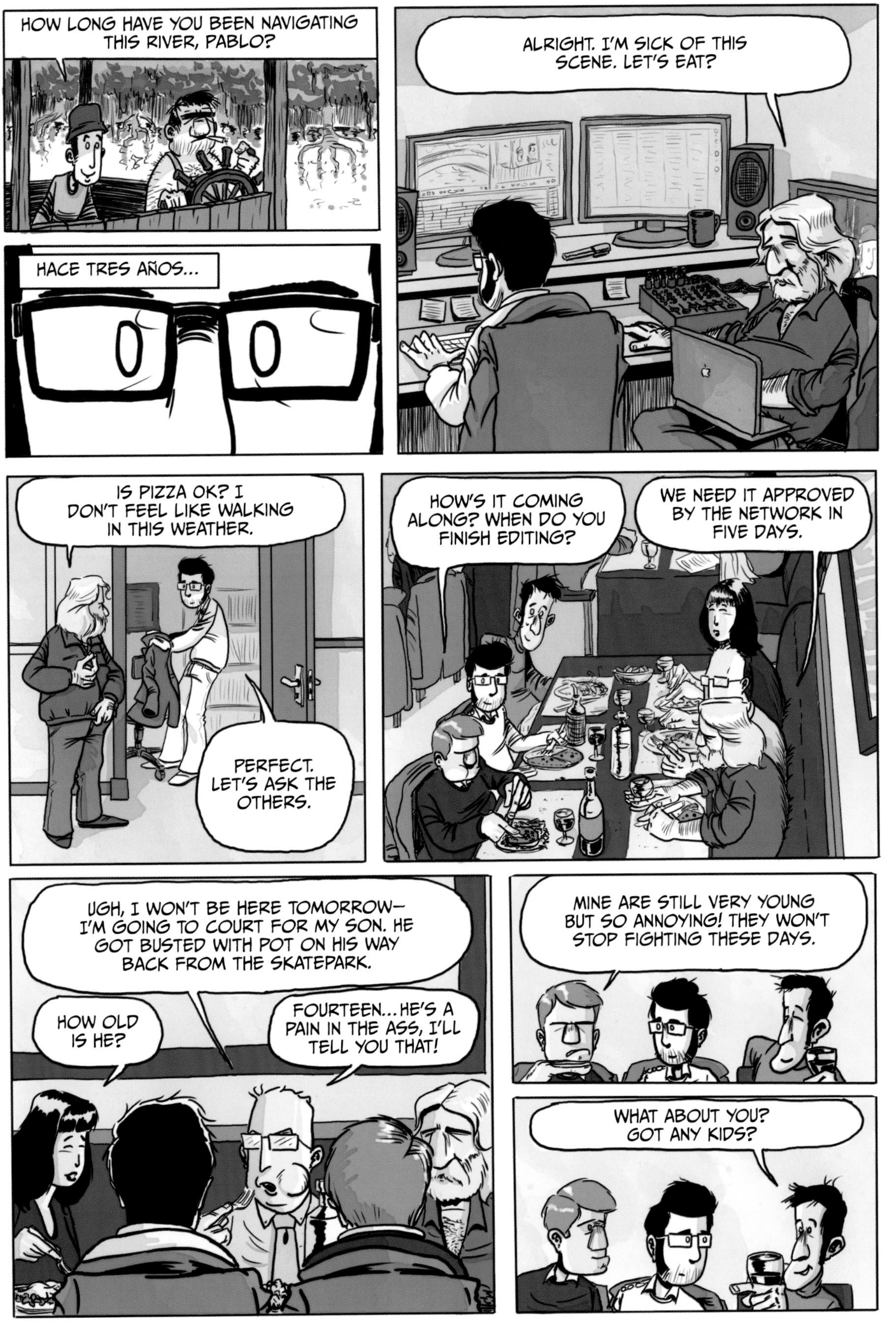

HOW LONG HAVE YOU BEEN NAVIGATING THIS RIVER, PABLO?
HACE TRES AÑOS...
ALRIGHT. I'M SICK OF THIS SCENE. LET'S EAT?
IS PIZZA OK? I DON'T FEEL LIKE WALKING IN THIS WEATHER.
PERFECT. LET'S ASK THE OTHERS.
HOW'S IT COMING ALONG? WHEN DO YOU FINISH EDITING?
WE NEED IT APPROVED BY THE NETWORK IN FIVE DAYS.
UGH, I WON'T BE HERE TOMORROW— I'M GOING TO COURT FOR MY SON. HE GOT BUSTED WITH POT ON HIS WAY BACK FROM THE SKATEPARK.
HOW OLD IS HE?
FOURTEEN... HE'S A PAIN IN THE ASS, I'LL TELL YOU THAT!
MINE ARE STILL VERY YOUNG BUT SO ANNOYING! THEY WON'T STOP FIGHTING THESE DAYS.
WHAT ABOUT YOU? GOT ANY KIDS?

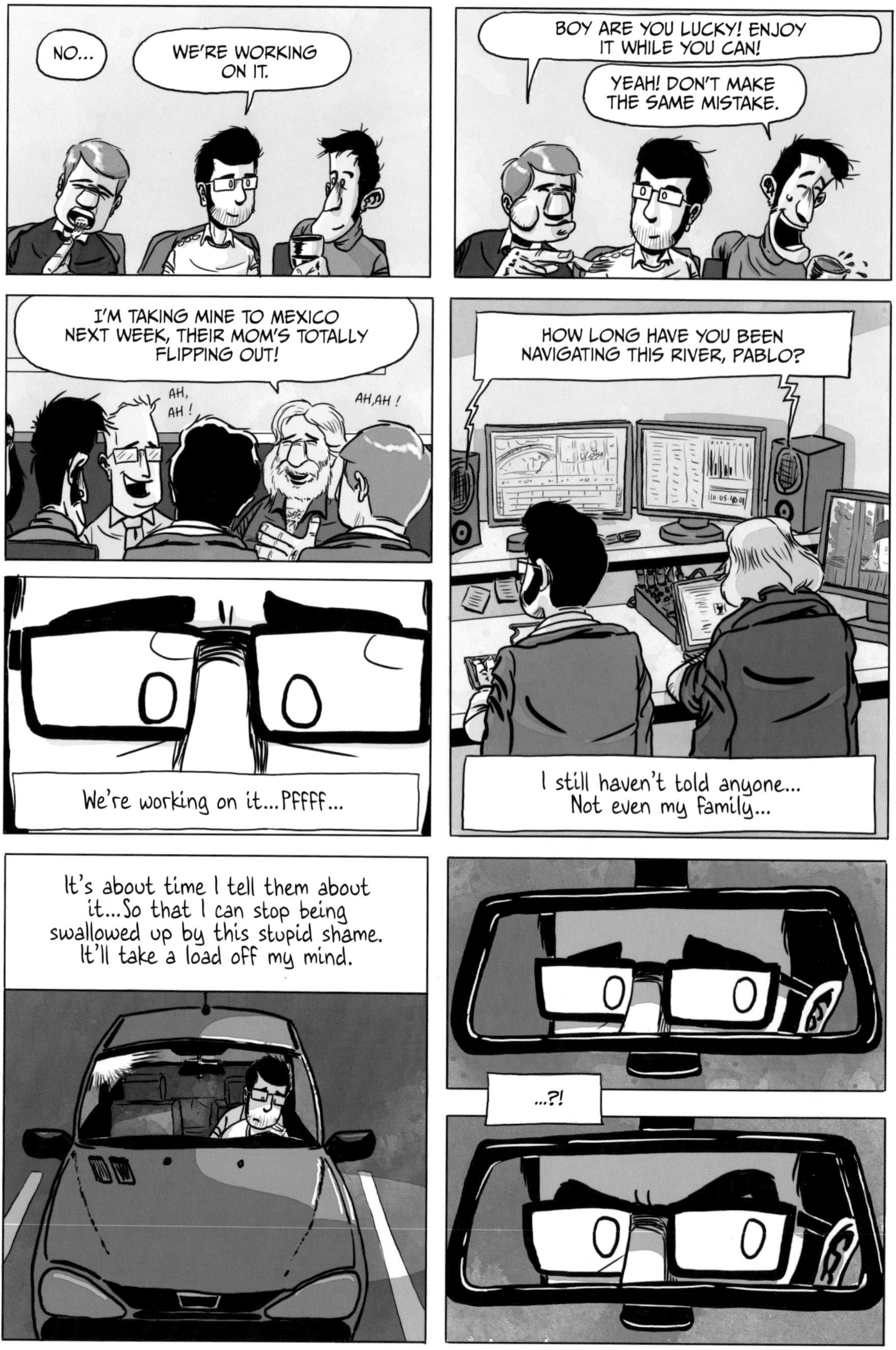
NO...
WE'RE WORKING ON IT.
BOY ARE YOU LUCKY! ENJOY IT WHILE YOU CAN!
YEAH! DON'T MAKE THE SAME MISTAKE.
I'M TAKING MINE TO MEXICO NEXT WEEK, THEIR MOM'S TOTALLY FLIPPING OUT!
AH, AH!
AH, AH!
HOW LONG HAVE YOU BEEN NAVIGATING THIS RIVER, PABLO?
We're working on it... PFFFF...
I still haven't told anyone... Not even my family...
It's about time I tell them about it... So that I can stop being swallowed up by this stupid shame. It'll take a load off my mind.
...?!

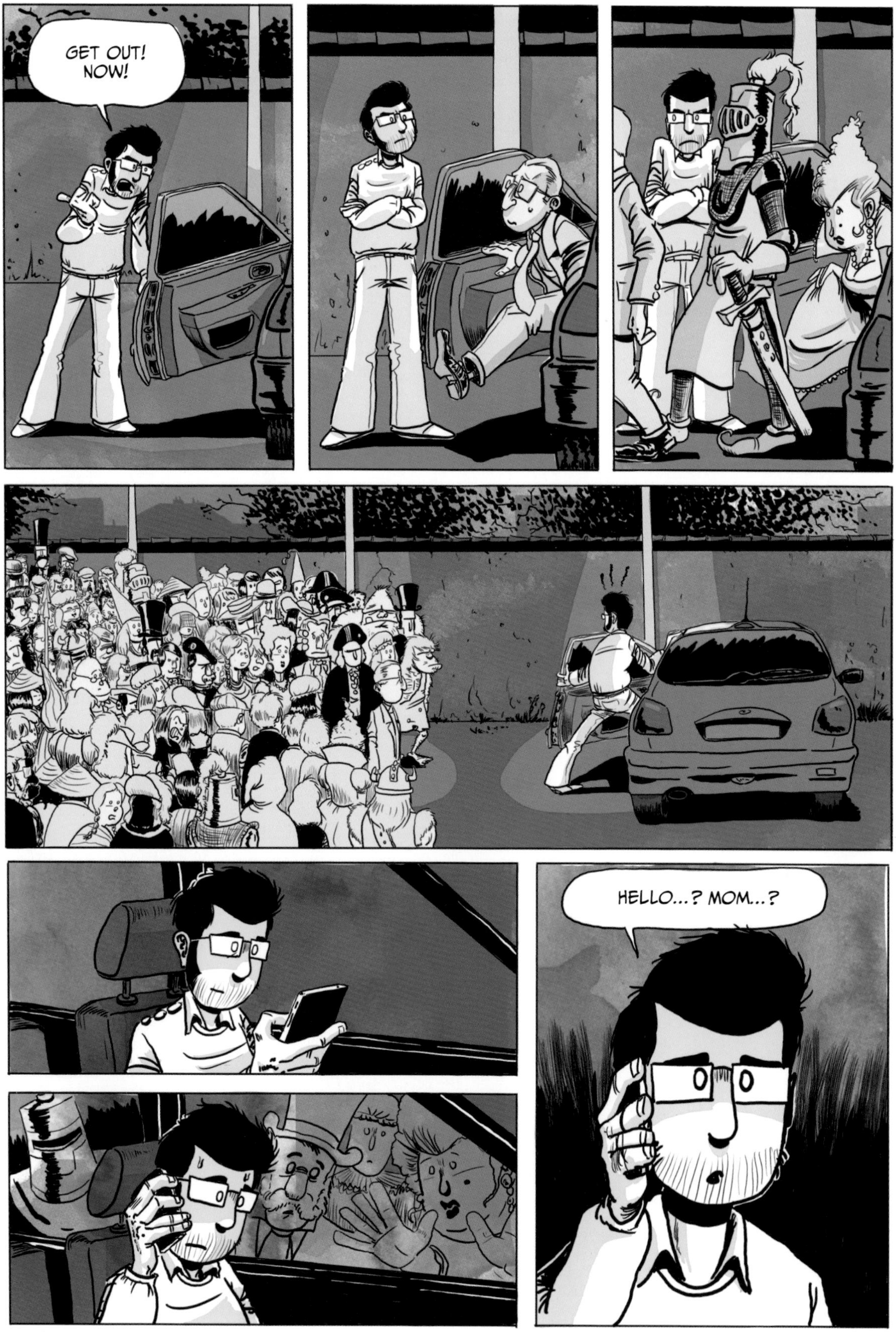
GET OUT! NOW!
HELLO...? MOM...?

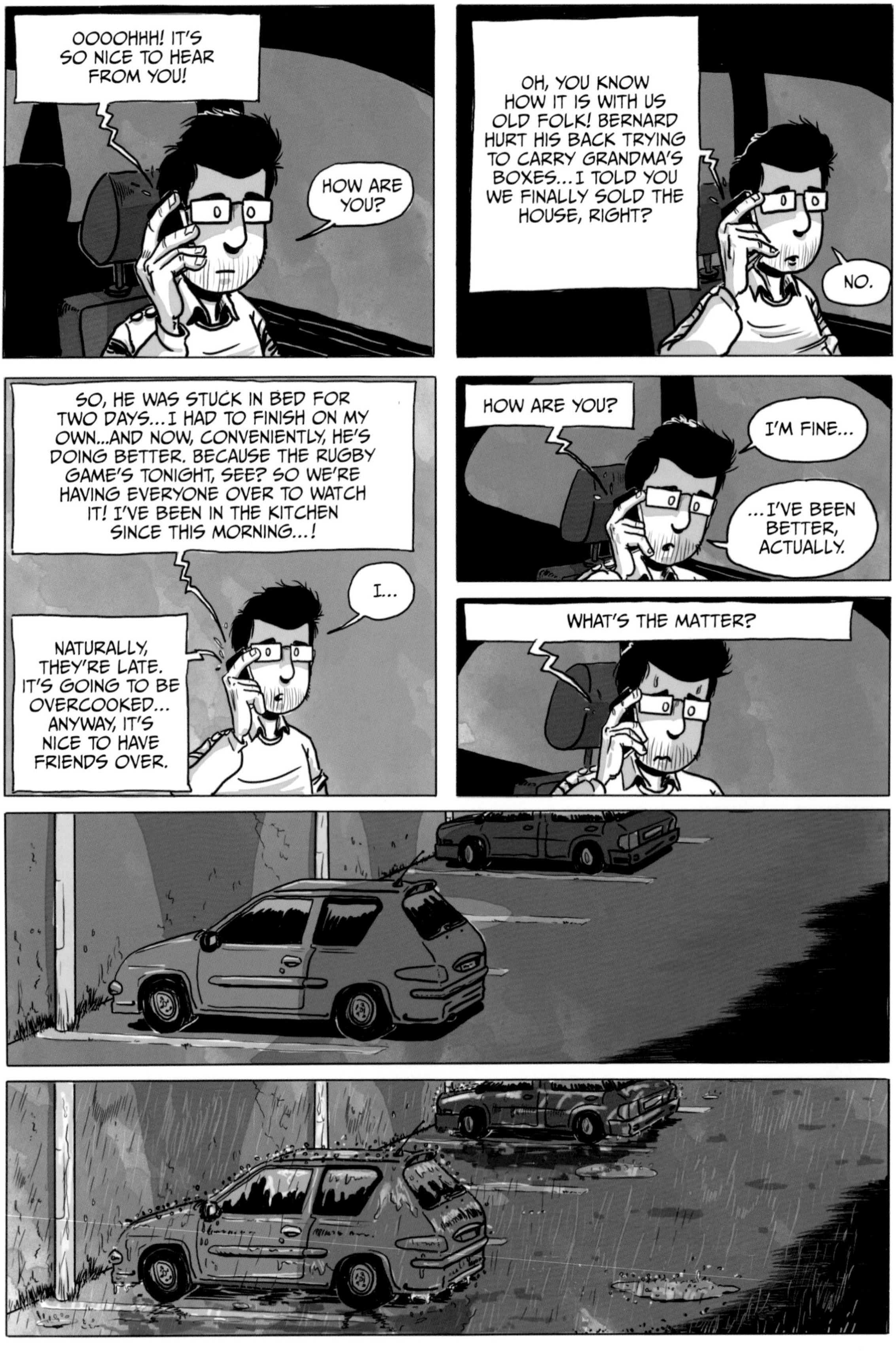
OOOOHHH! IT'S SO NICE TO HEAR FROM YOU!
HOW ARE YOU?
OH, YOU KNOW HOW IT IS WITH US OLD FOLK! BERNARD HURT HIS BACK TRYING TO CARRY GRANDMA'S BOXES... I TOLD YOU WE FINALLY SOLD THE HOUSE, RIGHT?
NO.
SO, HE WAS STUCK IN BED FOR TWO DAYS... I HAD TO FINISH ON MY OWN...AND NOW, CONVENIENTLY, HE'S DOING BETTER. BECAUSE THE RUGBY GAME'S TONIGHT, SEE? SO WE'RE HAVING EVERYONE OVER TO WATCH IT! I'VE BEEN IN THE KITCHEN SINCE THIS MORNING...!
I...
NATURALLY, THEY'RE LATE. IT'S GOING TO BE OVERCOOKED... ANYWAY, IT'S NICE TO HAVE FRIENDS OVER.
HOW ARE YOU?
I'M FINE...
...I'VE BEEN BETTER, ACTUALLY.
WHAT'S THE MATTER?

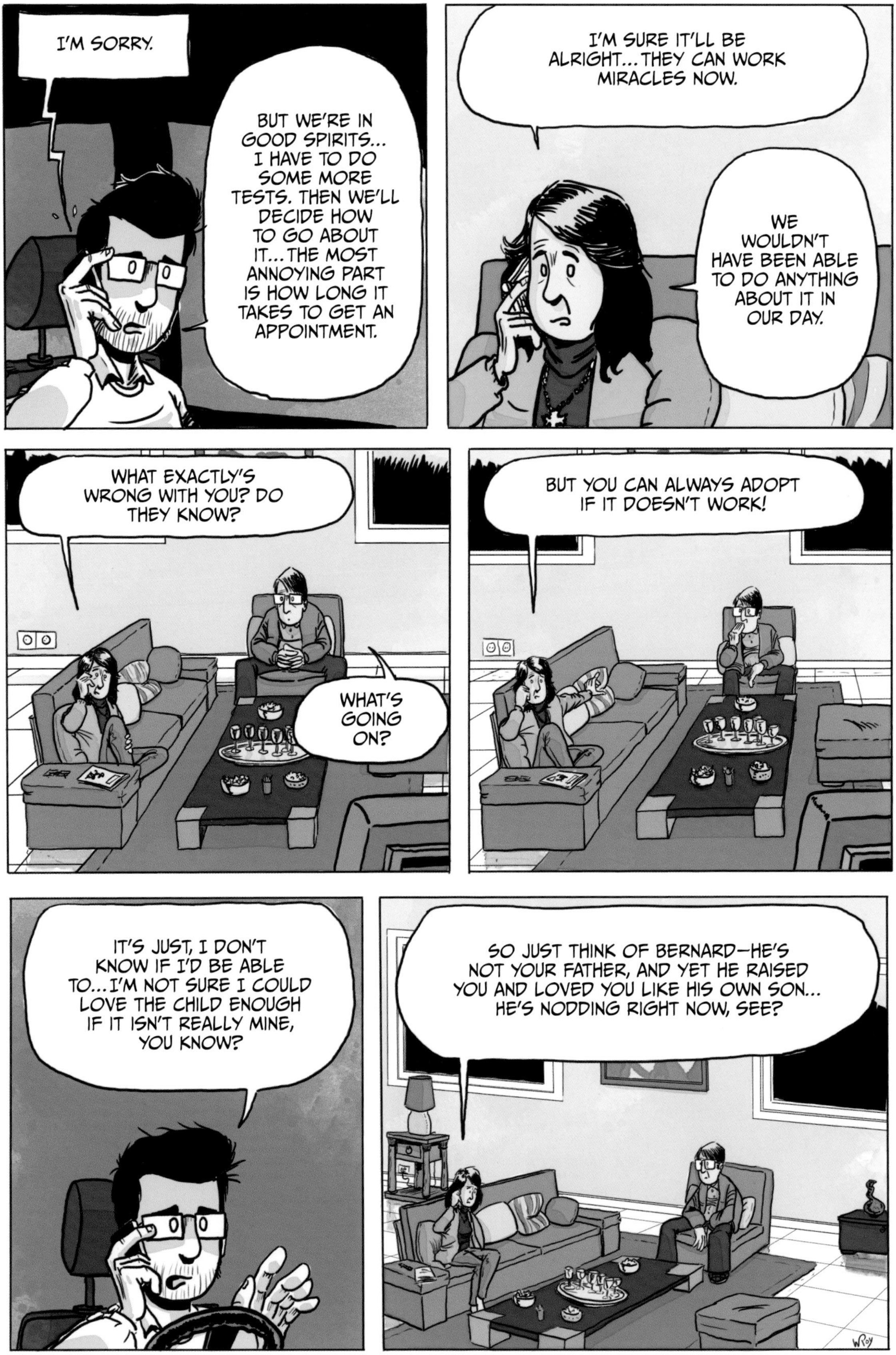
I'M SORRY.
BUT WE'RE IN GOOD SPIRITS... I HAVE TO DO SOME MORE TESTS. THEN WE'LL DECIDE HOW TO GO ABOUT IT... THE MOST ANNOYING PART IS HOW LONG IT TAKES TO GET AN APPOINTMENT.
I'M SURE IT'LL BE ALRIGHT... THEY CAN WORK MIRACLES NOW.
WE WOULDN'T HAVE BEEN ABLE TO DO ANYTHING ABOUT IT IN OUR DAY.
WHAT EXACTLY'S WRONG WITH YOU? DO THEY KNOW?
WHAT'S GOING ON?
BUT YOU CAN ALWAYS ADOPT IF IT DOESN'T WORK!
IT'S JUST, I DON'T KNOW IF I'D BE ABLE TO... I'M NOT SURE I COULD LOVE THE CHILD ENOUGH IF IT ISN'T REALLY MINE, YOU KNOW?
SO JUST THINK OF BERNARD—HE'S NOT YOUR FATHER, AND YET HE RAISED YOU AND LOVED YOU LIKE HIS OWN SON... HE'S NODDING RIGHT NOW, SEE?
WRoy

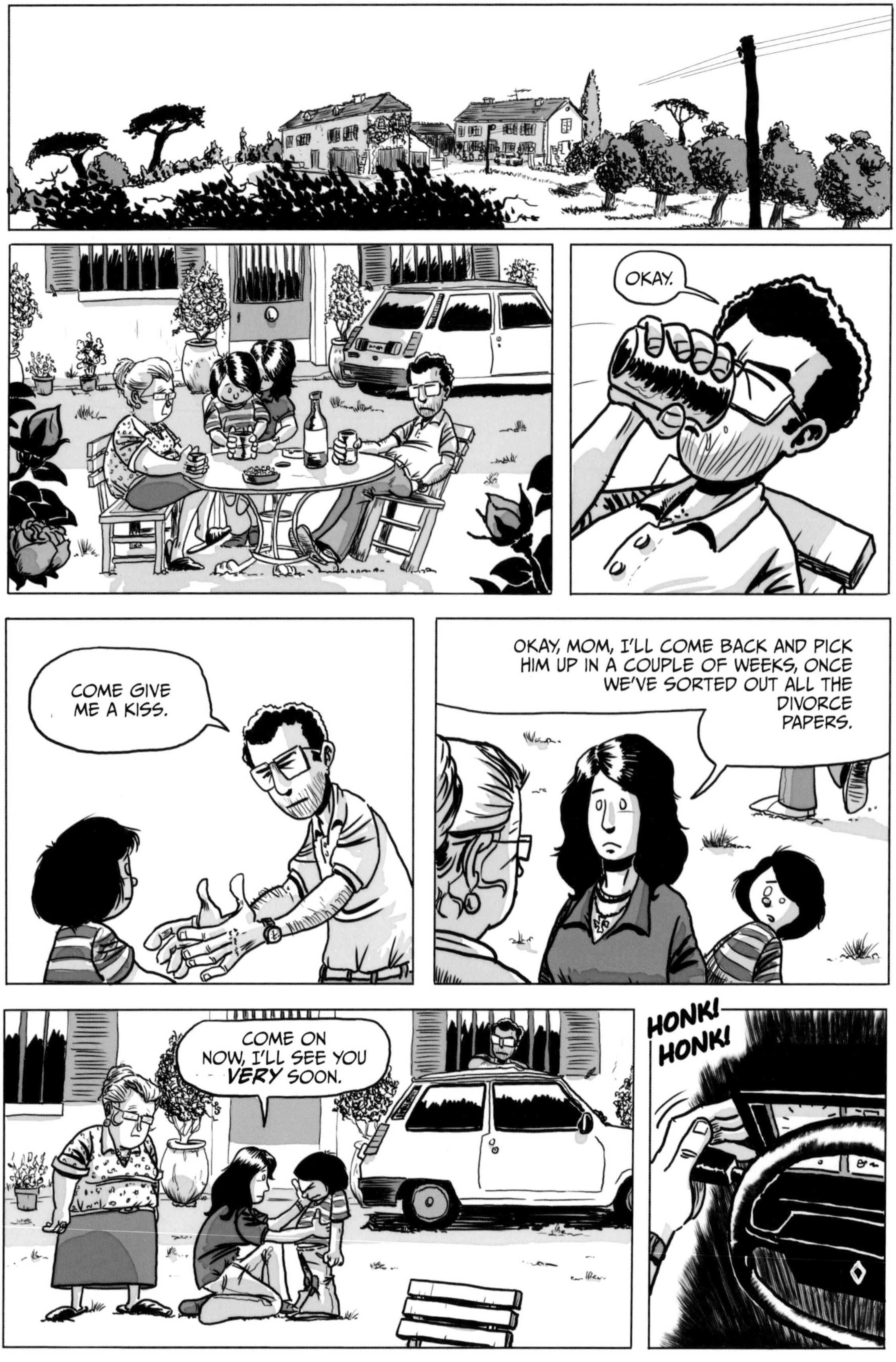
OKAY.
COME GIVE ME A KISS.
OKAY, MOM, I'LL COME BACK AND PICK HIM UP IN A COUPLE OF WEEKS, ONCE WE'VE SORTED OUT ALL THE DIVORCE PAPERS.
COME ON NOW, I'LL SEE YOU *VERY* SOON.
HONK! HONK!

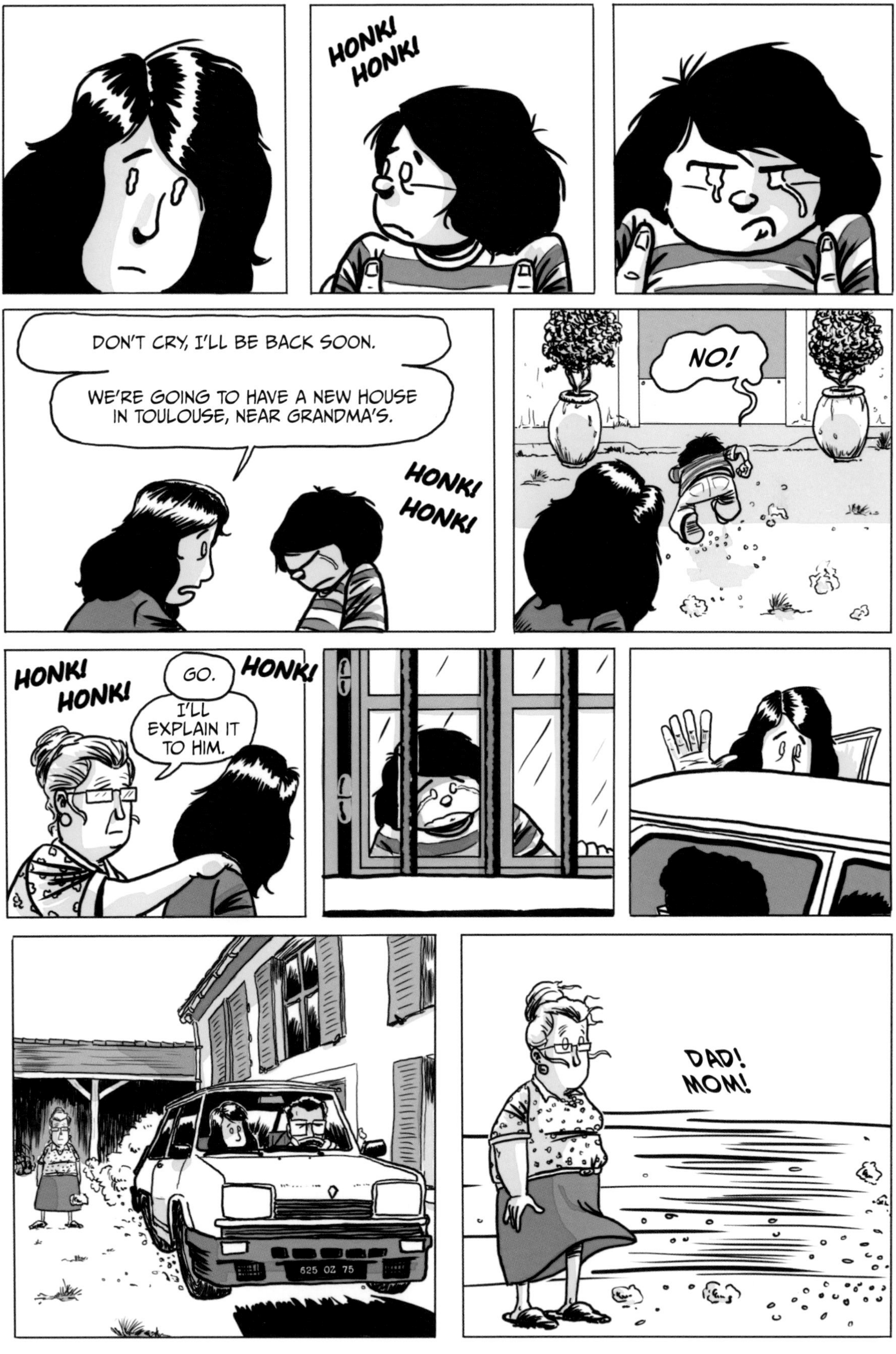
HONK! HONK!
DON'T CRY, I'LL BE BACK SOON.
WE'RE GOING TO HAVE A NEW HOUSE IN TOULOUSE, NEAR GRANDMA'S.
HONK! HONK!
NO!
HONK! HONK!
GO.
I'LL EXPLAIN IT TO HIM.
HONK!
625 OZ 75
DAD! MOM!

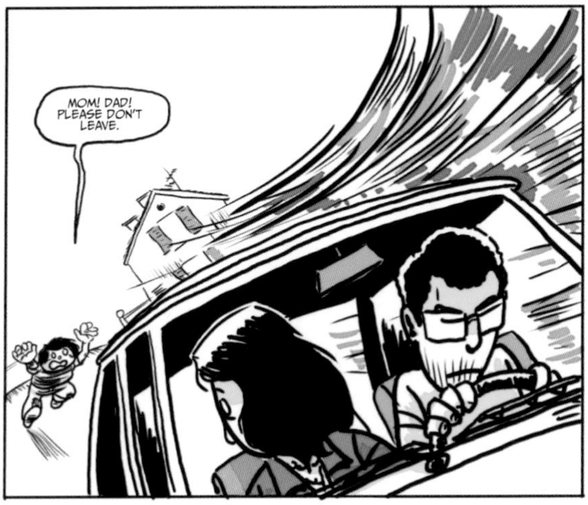
MOM! DAD! PLEASE DON'T LEAVE.

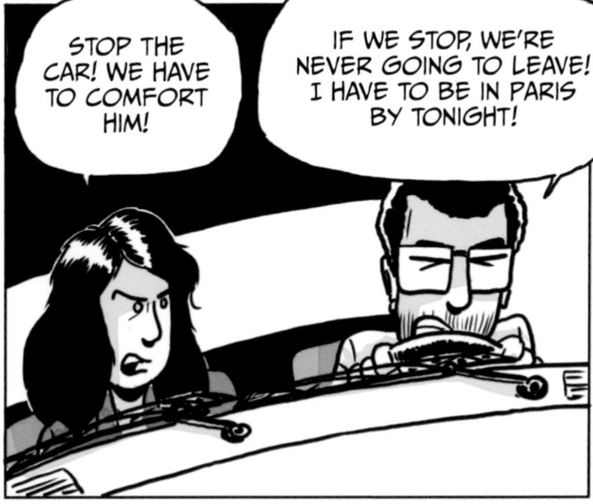
STOP THE CAR! WE HAVE TO COMFORT HIM!
IF WE STOP, WE'RE NEVER GOING TO LEAVE! I HAVE TO BE IN PARIS BY TONIGHT!

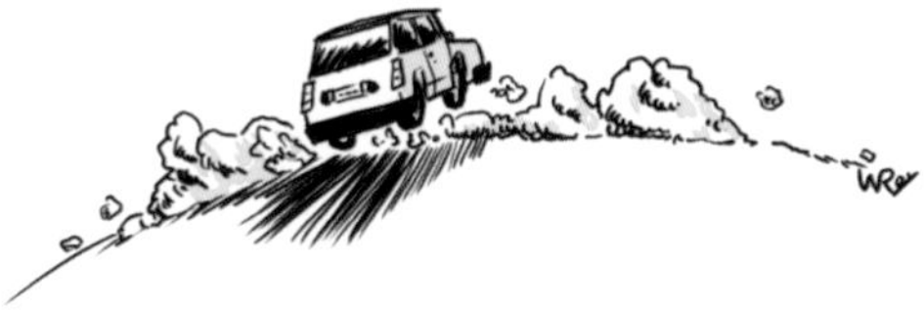

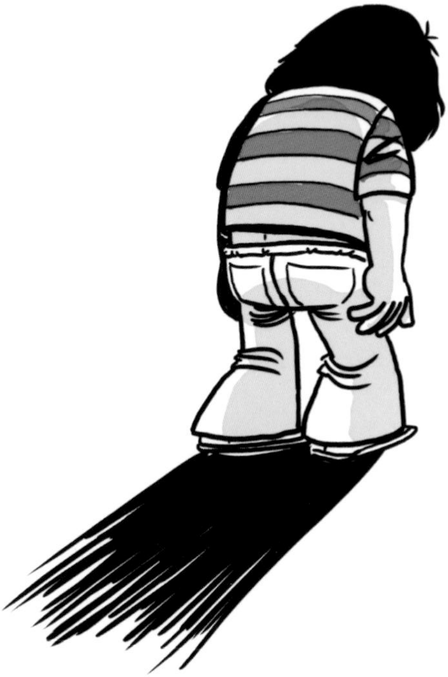

THE SPERMOGRAM...

WHAT IS IT?

Professor Beuaârr
Specialist

A SPERM ANALYSIS, BASED ON PH, VISCOSITY... MOBILITY, QUANTITY AND VITALITY OF THE SPERMATOZOA.

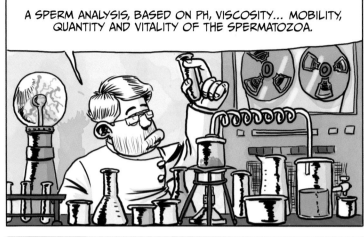

THE TEST IS CONDUCTED AFTER THREE TO FIVE DAYS OF ABSTINENCE. THE ANALYZED SAMPLE IS COLLECTED BY MASTURBATION.

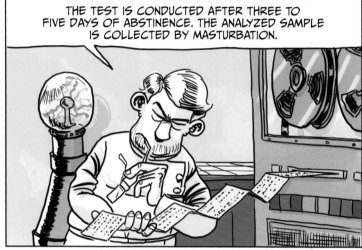

THIS IS OBVIOUSLY PAINLESS, BUT SOME FIND THE PROCEDURE TO BE SOMEWHAT TRAUMATIC DUE TO THE DISCOMFORT THAT THE COLLECTION PROCESS CAN CAUSE.

YEAH, RIGHT!

BS!

I'LL BET THEY'RE HAPPY STROKING AWAY AT ALL THAT FREE PORN!

PERVERTS!

NOT AGAIN!

WHAT ARE THIS GUY'S QUALIFICATIONS, ANYWAY?

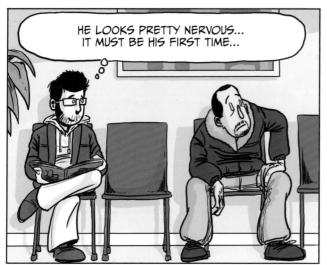

HE LOOKS PRETTY NERVOUS...
IT MUST BE HIS FIRST TIME...

I STILL REMEMBER MY
FIRST TIME...I WAS SO
UNCOMFORTABLE...

The regulars had seemed very strange to me...

CLONK

CLONK

CLONK

CLONK

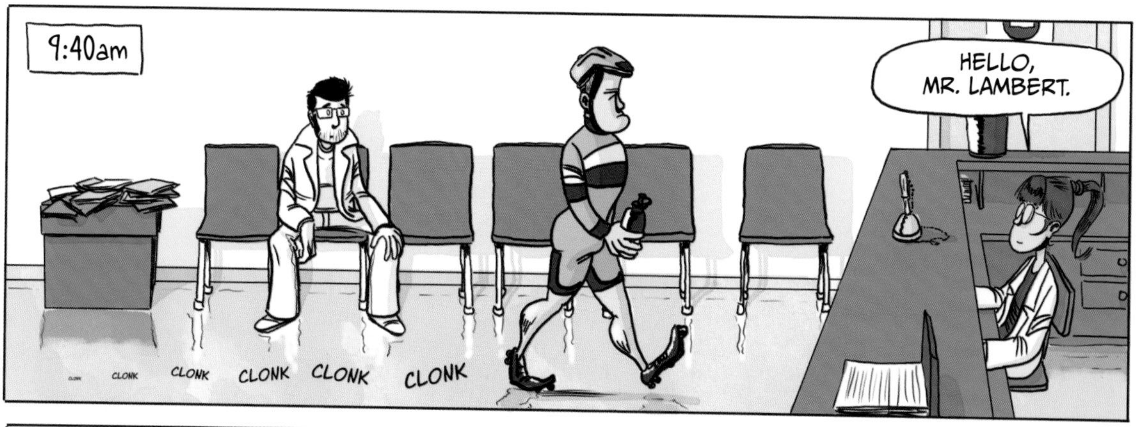
9:40am
HELLO, MR. LAMBERT.
CLONK CLONK CLONK CLONK CLONK CLONK

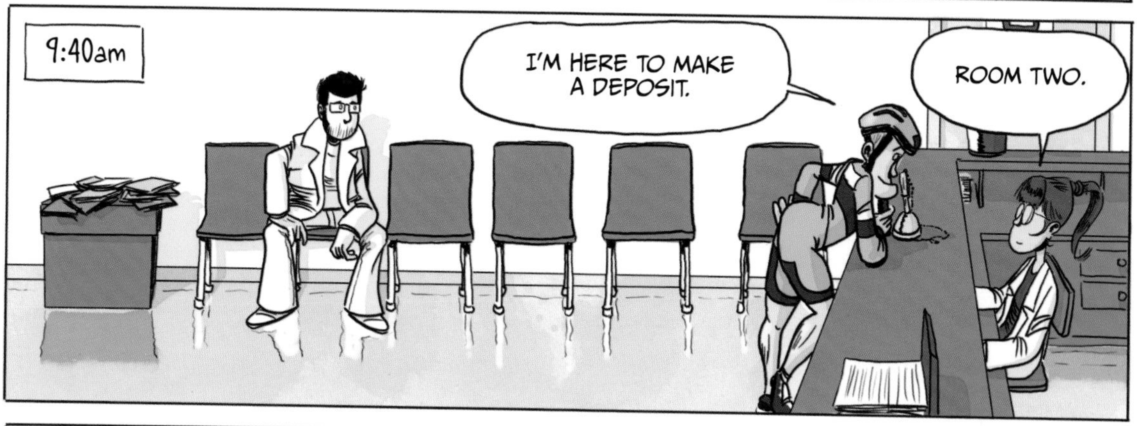
9:40am
I'M HERE TO MAKE A DEPOSIT.
ROOM TWO.

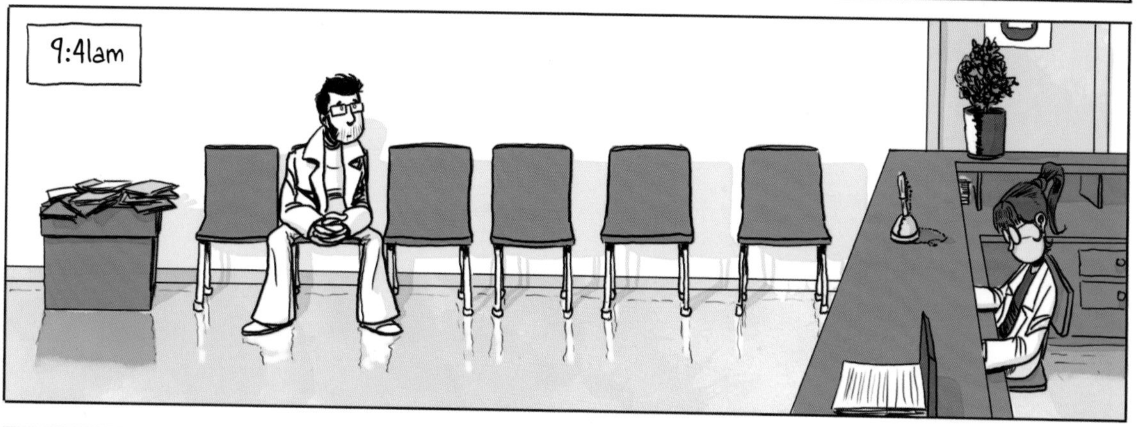
9:41am

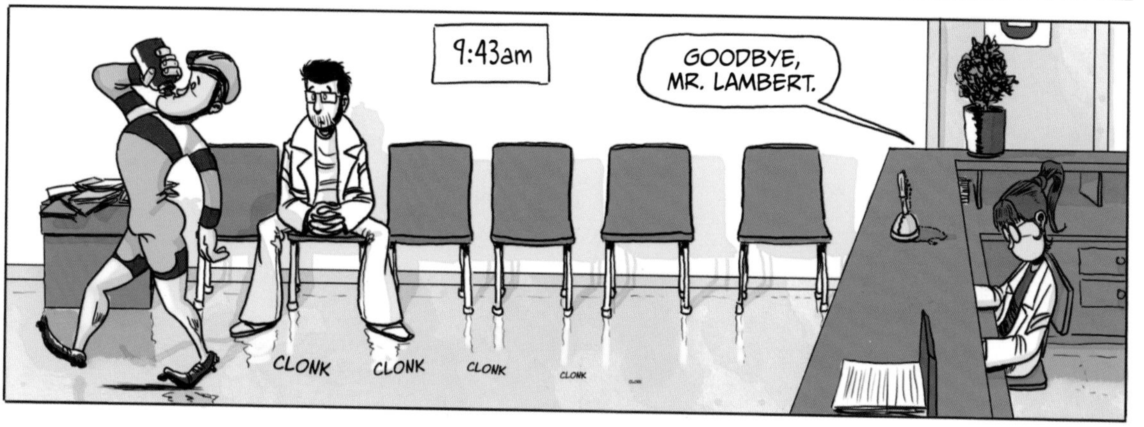
9:43am
GOODBYE, MR. LAMBERT.
CLONK CLONK CLONK CLONK

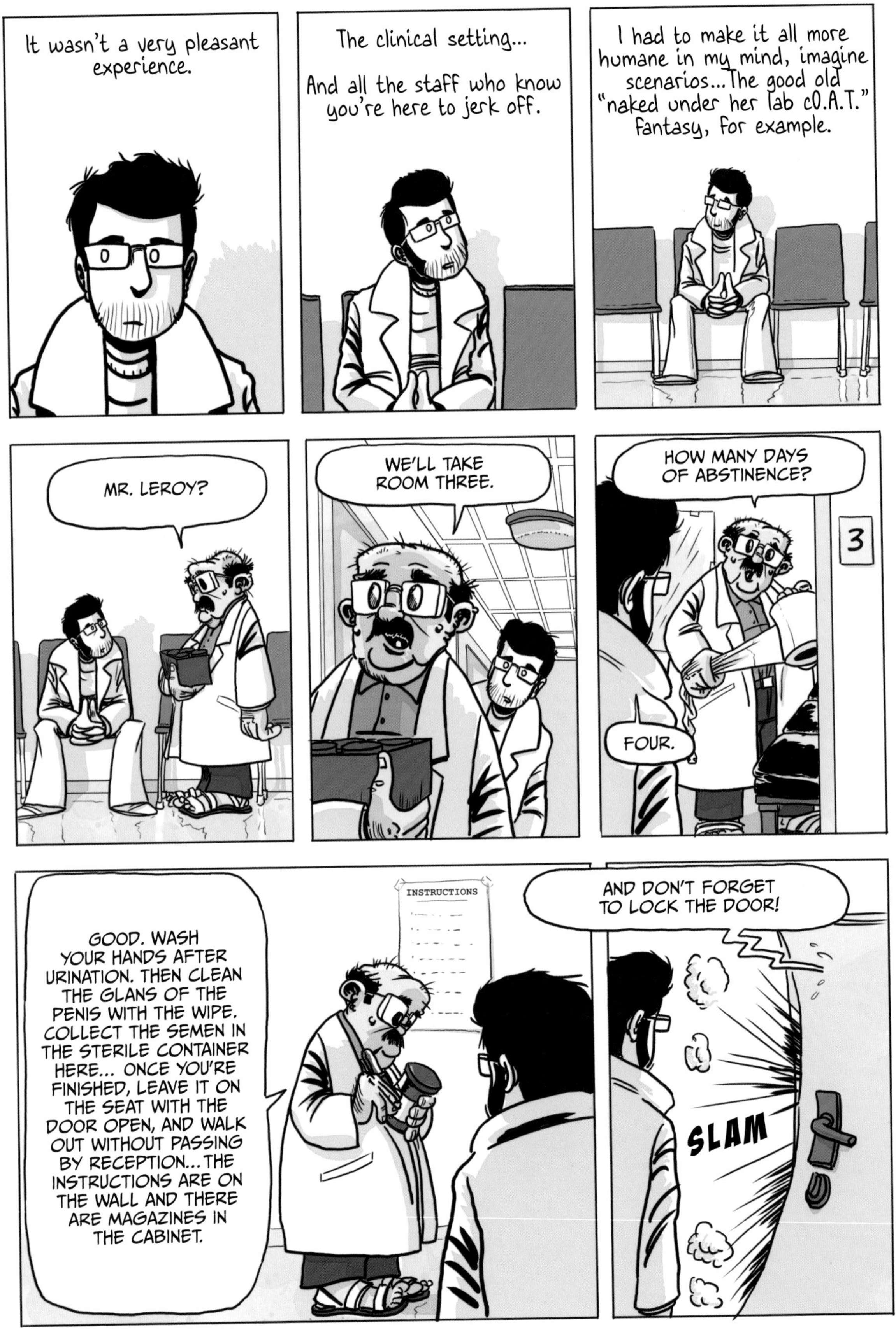

It wasn't a very pleasant experience.
The clinical setting...
And all the staff who know you're here to jerk off.
I had to make it all more humane in my mind, imagine scenarios...The good old "naked under her lab c0.A.T." fantasy, for example.
MR. LEROY?
WE'LL TAKE ROOM THREE.
HOW MANY DAYS OF ABSTINENCE?
3
FOUR.
GOOD. WASH YOUR HANDS AFTER URINATION. THEN CLEAN THE GLANS OF THE PENIS WITH THE WIPE. COLLECT THE SEMEN IN THE STERILE CONTAINER HERE... ONCE YOU'RE FINISHED, LEAVE IT ON THE SEAT WITH THE DOOR OPEN, AND WALK OUT WITHOUT PASSING BY RECEPTION...THE INSTRUCTIONS ARE ON THE WALL AND THERE ARE MAGAZINES IN THE CABINET.
INSTRUCTIONS
AND DON'T FORGET TO LOCK THE DOOR!
SLAM

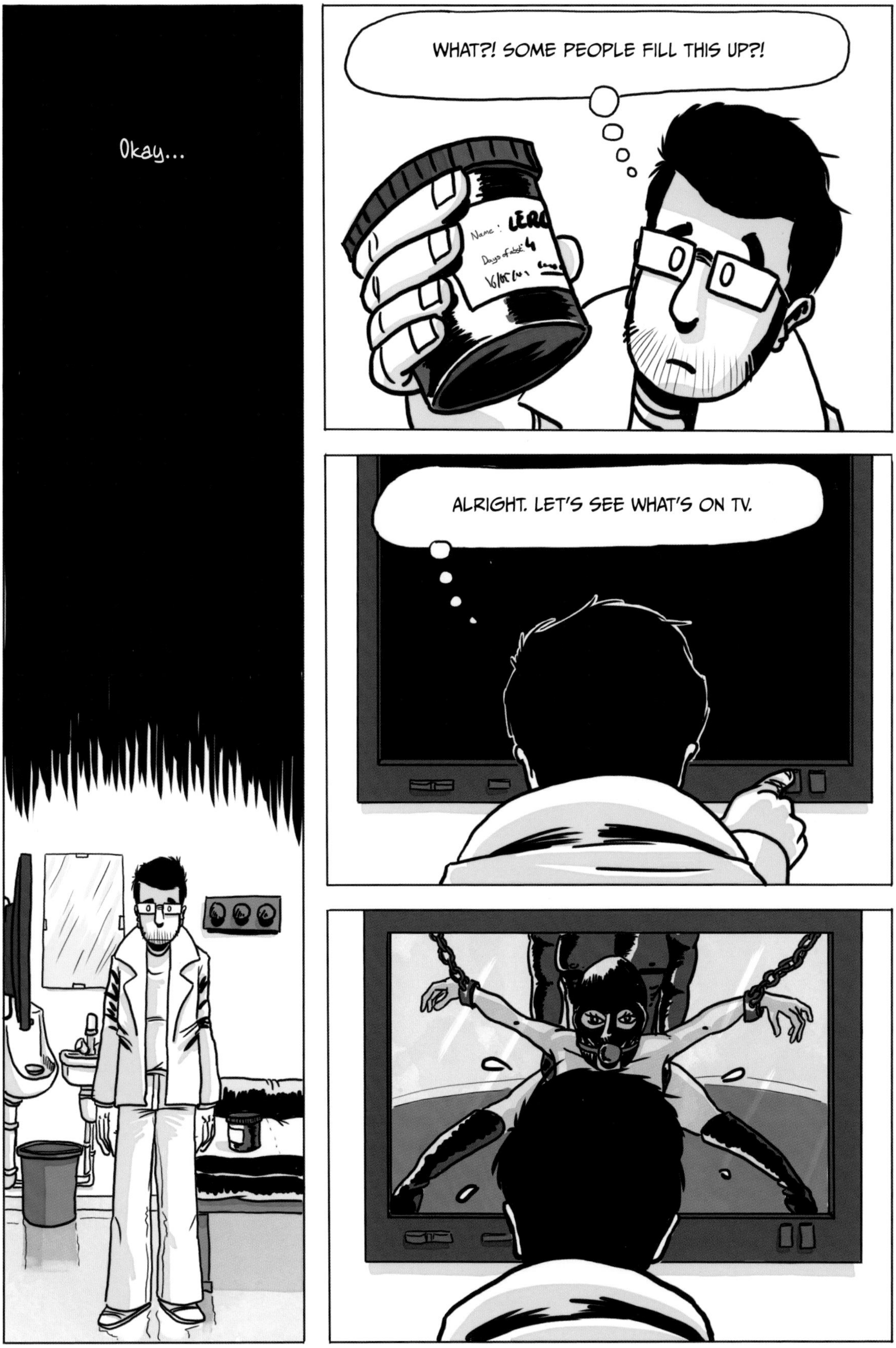
Okay...
WHAT?! SOME PEOPLE FILL THIS UP?!
ALRIGHT. LET'S SEE WHAT'S ON TV.

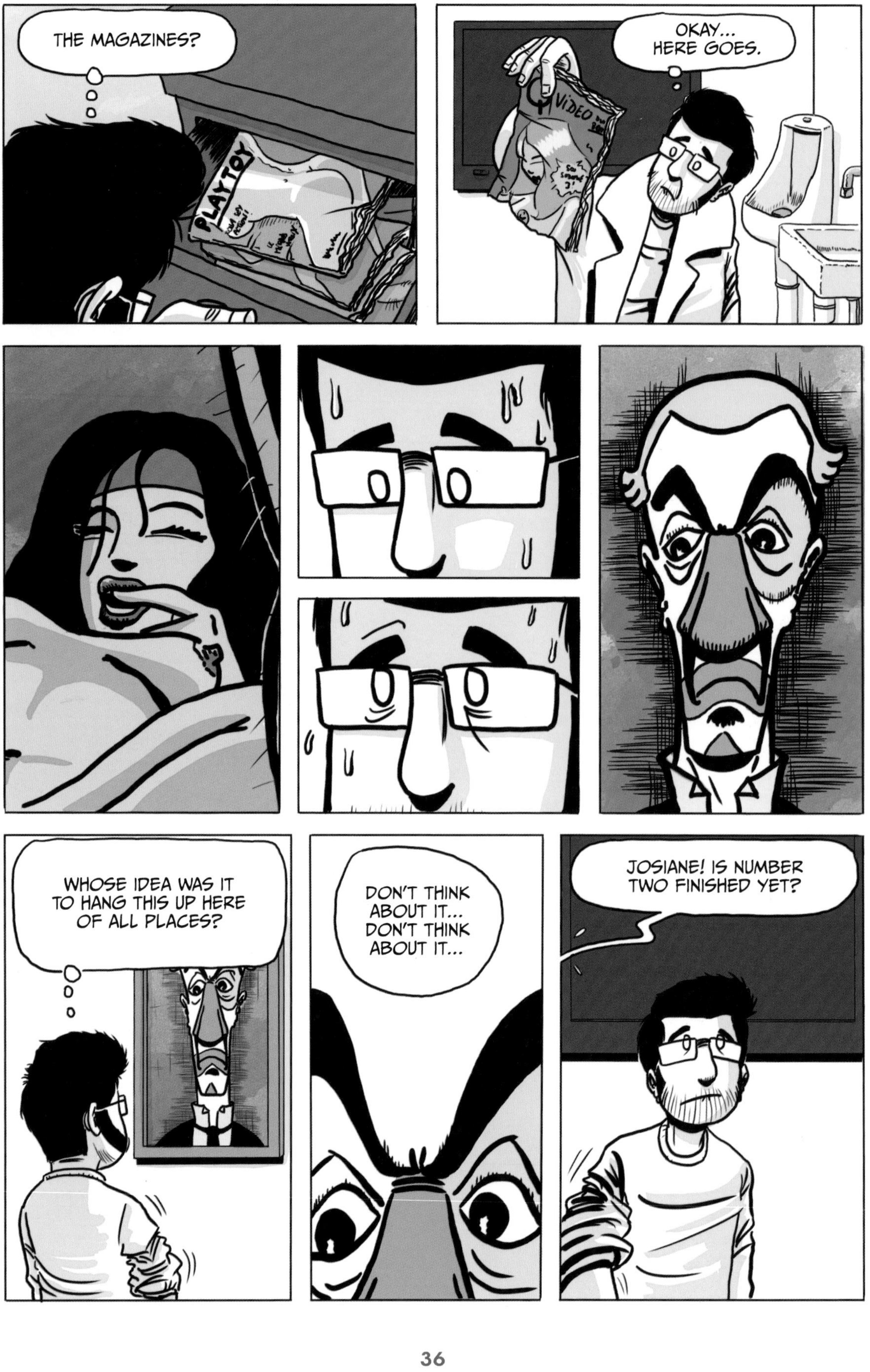
THE MAGAZINES?
PLAYTOY
OKAY... HERE GOES.
VIDEO
WHOSE IDEA WAS IT TO HANG THIS UP HERE OF ALL PLACES?
DON'T THINK ABOUT IT... DON'T THINK ABOUT IT...
JOSIANE! IS NUMBER TWO FINISHED YET?

MR. LEROY?

ARE YOU FAMILIAR WITH THE PROCEDURE?

YES.

URINATE, WASH YOUR HANDS AND GLANS WITH THE WIPE...

HOW MANY DAYS OF ABSTINENCE?

FIVE.

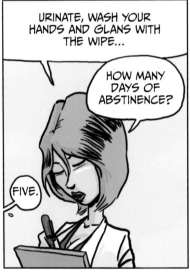

COLLECT THE SEMEN IN THIS TUBE.

AH, THEY HAVE DECENT-SIZED CONTAINERS HERE.

FILL IT UP TO THE FIRST MARKER. OTHERWISE, YOU'LL HAVE TO START OVER.

COME TO THINK OF IT...

ONCE YOU'RE DONE, LEAVE THE TUBE ON THIS SHELF BESIDE THE DOOR.

AND YOU CAN GO.

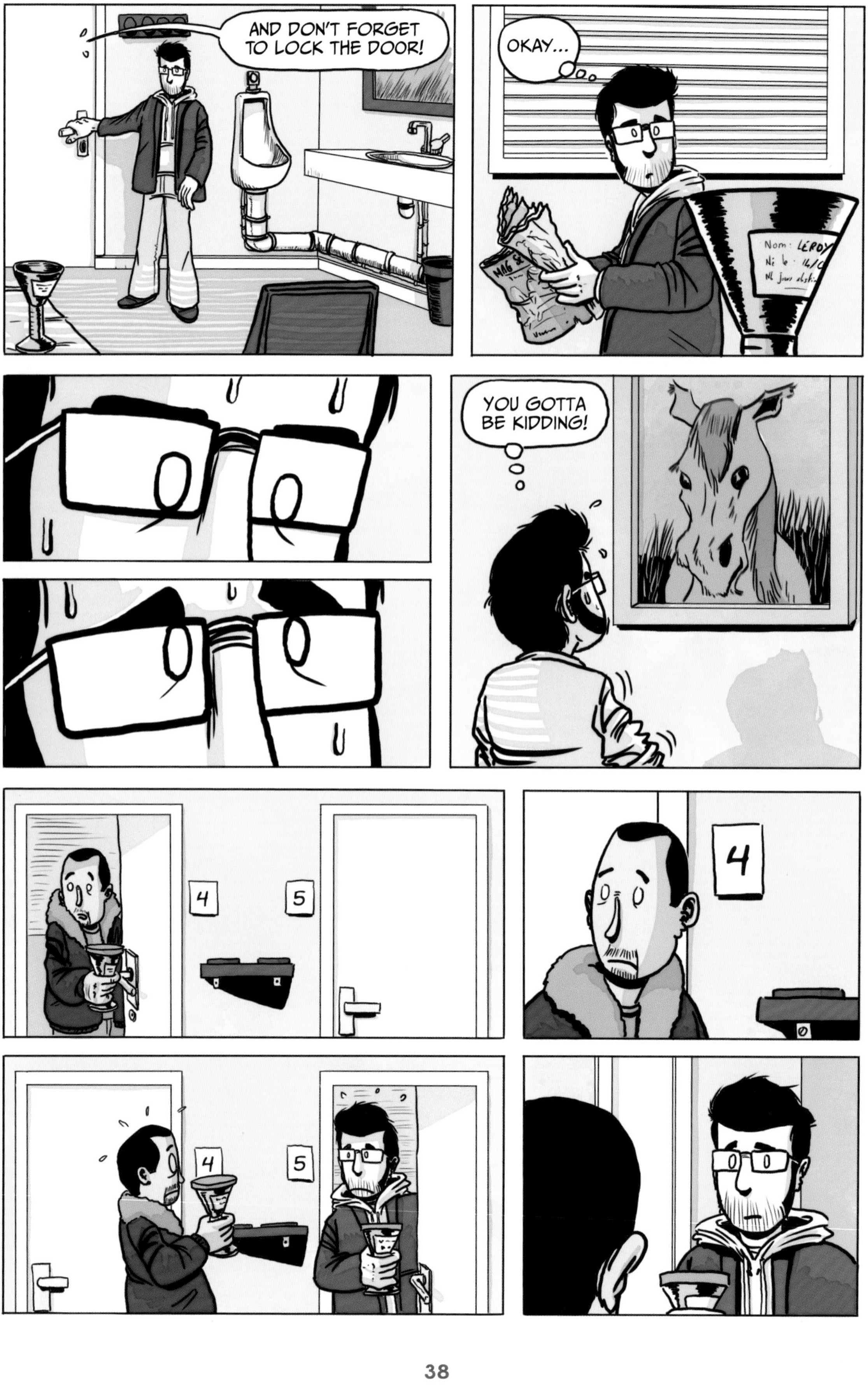
AND DON'T FORGET TO LOCK THE DOOR!
OKAY...
YOU GOTTA BE KIDDING!

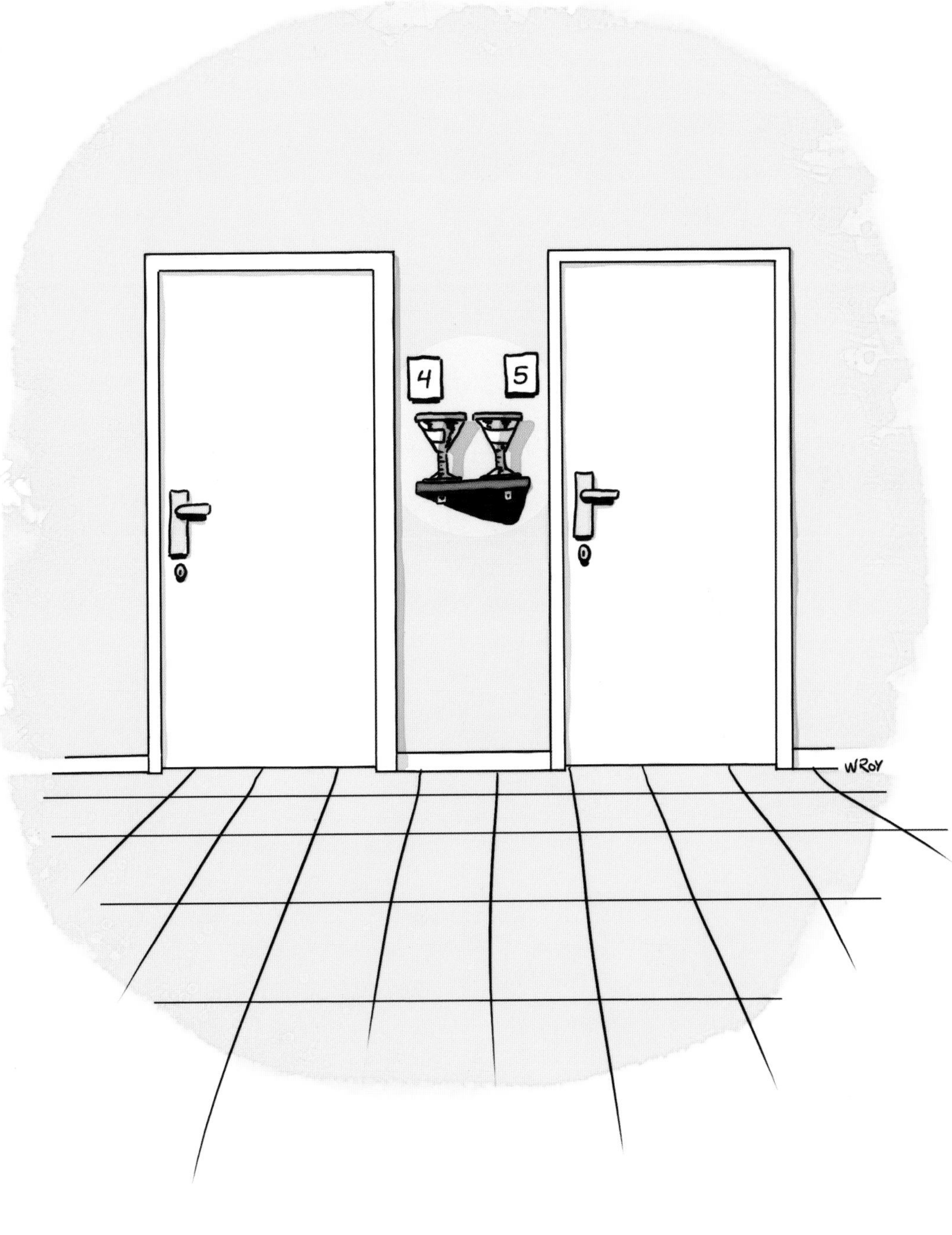
4
5
WRoy

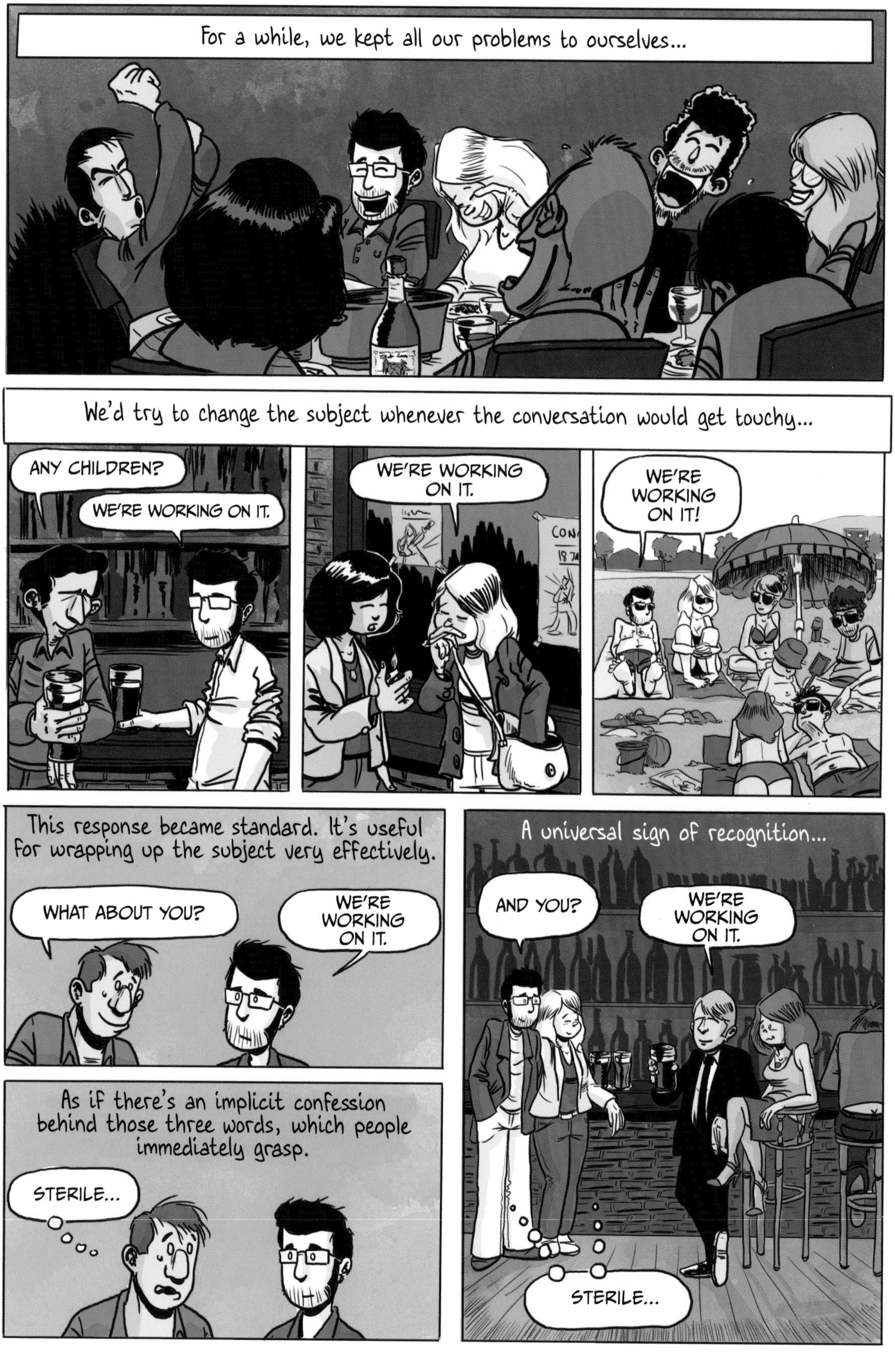
For a while, we kept all our problems to ourselves...
We'd try to change the subject whenever the conversation would get touchy...
ANY CHILDREN?
WE'RE WORKING ON IT.
WE'RE WORKING ON IT.
WE'RE WORKING ON IT!
This response became standard. It's useful for wrapping up the subject very effectively.
WHAT ABOUT YOU?
WE'RE WORKING ON IT.
As if there's an implicit confession behind those three words, which people immediately grasp.
STERILE...
A universal sign of recognition...
AND YOU?
WE'RE WORKING ON IT.
STERILE...

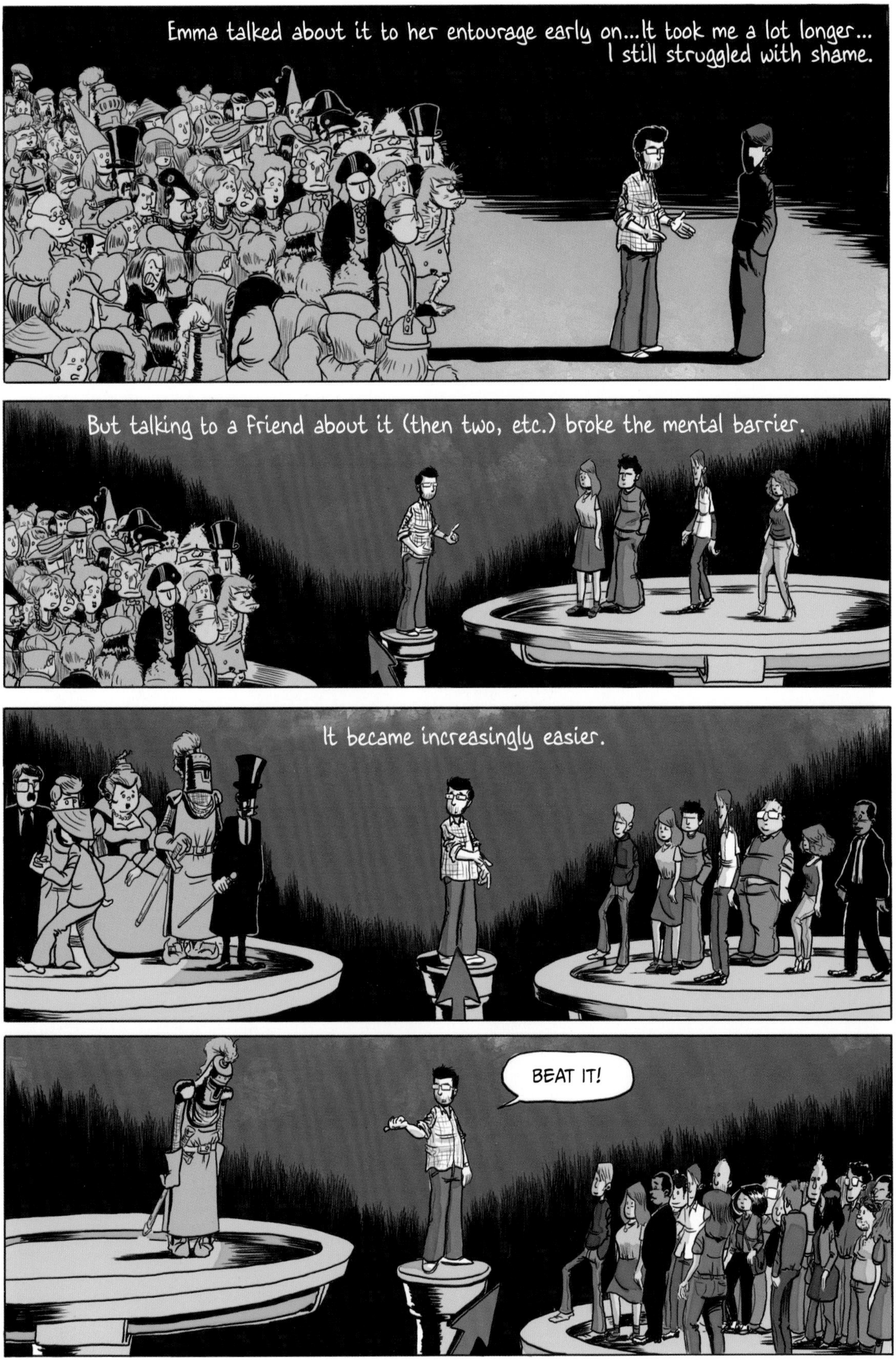
Emma talked about it to her entourage early on...It took me a lot longer... I still struggled with shame.
But talking to a friend about it (then two, etc.) broke the mental barrier.
It became increasingly easier.
BEAT IT!

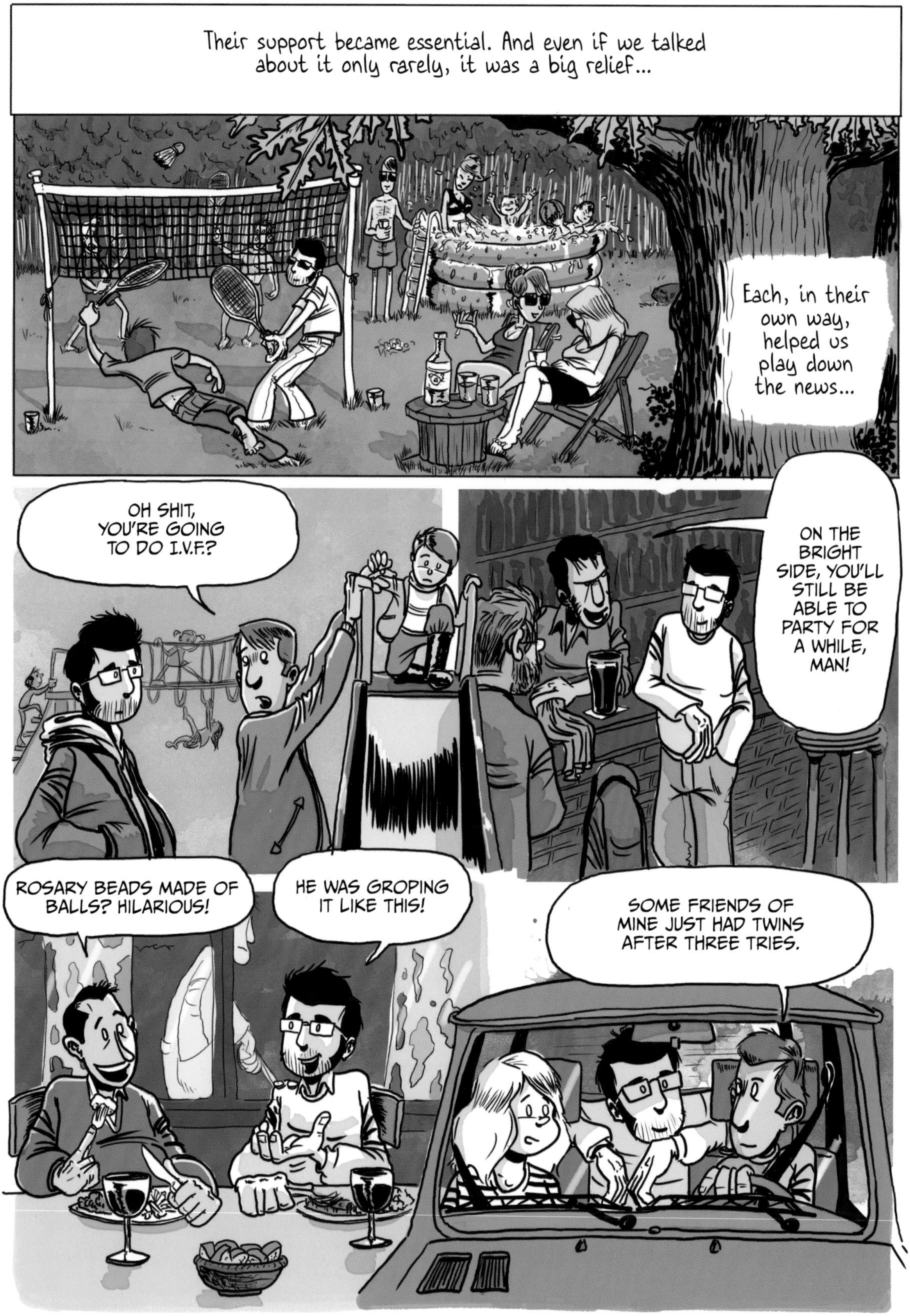
Their support became essential. And even if we talked about it only rarely, it was a big relief...
Each, in their own way, helped us play down the news...
OH SHIT, YOU'RE GOING TO DO I.V.F.?
ON THE BRIGHT SIDE, YOU'LL STILL BE ABLE TO PARTY FOR A WHILE, MAN!
ROSARY BEADS MADE OF BALLS? HILARIOUS!
HE WAS GROPING IT LIKE THIS!
SOME FRIENDS OF MINE JUST HAD TWINS AFTER THREE TRIES.

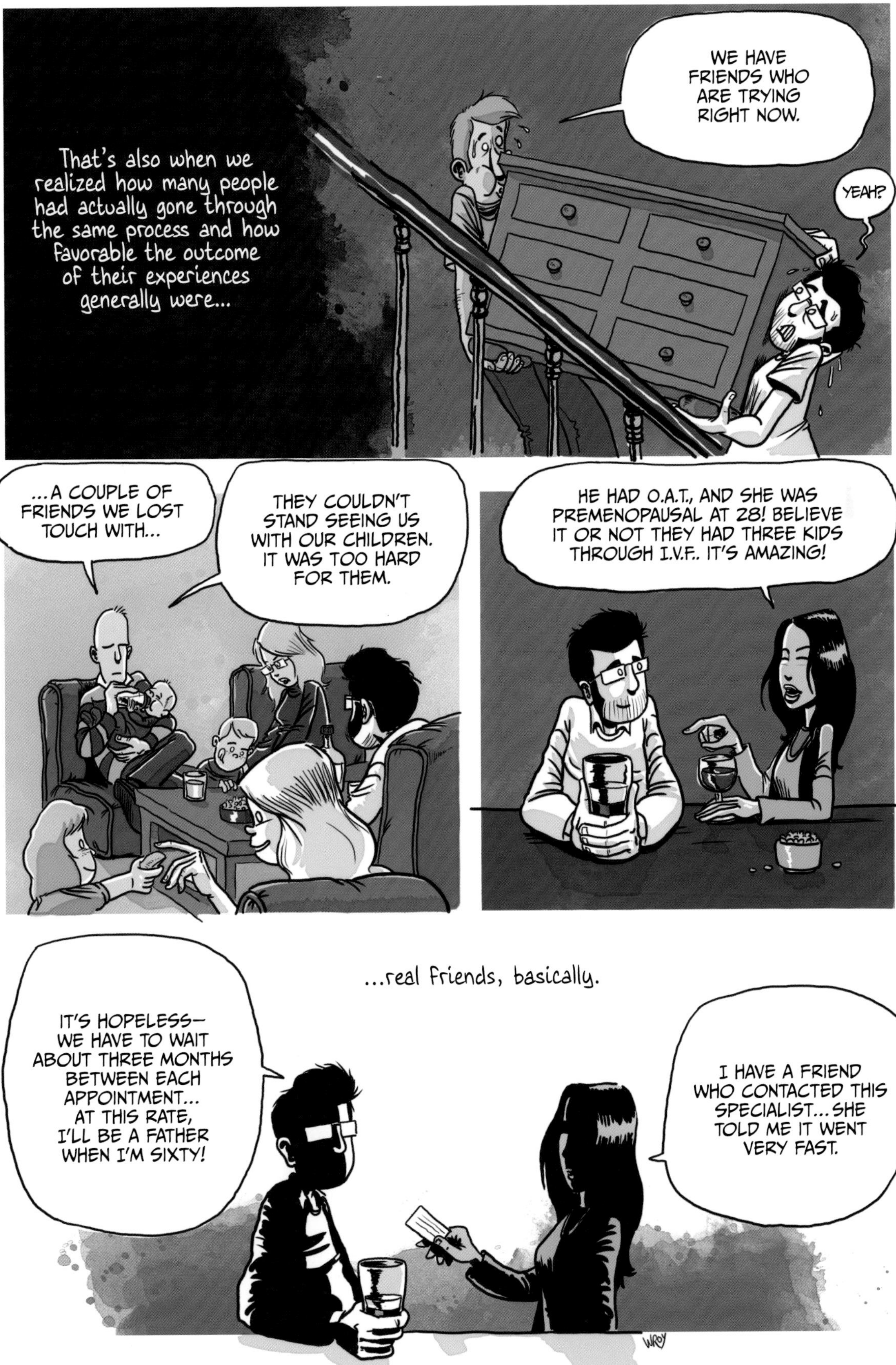
That's also when we realized how many people had actually gone through the same process and how favorable the outcome of their experiences generally were...
WE HAVE FRIENDS WHO ARE TRYING RIGHT NOW.
YEAH?
...A COUPLE OF FRIENDS WE LOST TOUCH WITH...
THEY COULDN'T STAND SEEING US WITH OUR CHILDREN. IT WAS TOO HARD FOR THEM.
HE HAD O.A.T., AND SHE WAS PREMENOPAUSAL AT 28! BELIEVE IT OR NOT THEY HAD THREE KIDS THROUGH I.V.F.. IT'S AMAZING!
...real friends, basically.
IT'S HOPELESS— WE HAVE TO WAIT ABOUT THREE MONTHS BETWEEN EACH APPOINTMENT... AT THIS RATE, I'LL BE A FATHER WHEN I'M SIXTY!
I HAVE A FRIEND WHO CONTACTED THIS SPECIALIST... SHE TOLD ME IT WENT VERY FAST.

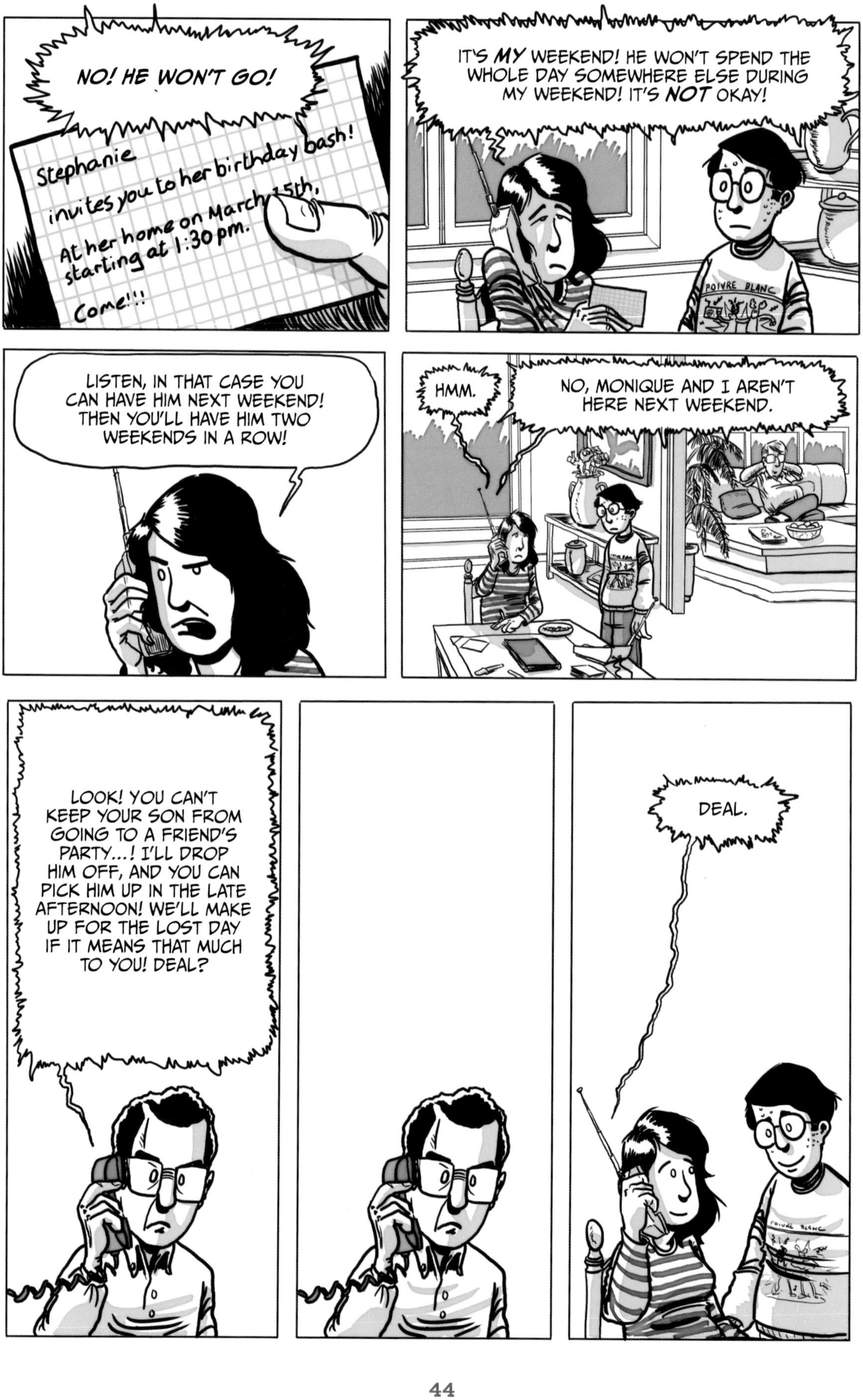
NO! HE WON'T GO!
Stephanie
invites you to her birthday bash!
At her home on March 15th,
starting at 1:30 pm.
Come!!!
IT'S MY WEEKEND! HE WON'T SPEND THE WHOLE DAY SOMEWHERE ELSE DURING MY WEEKEND! IT'S NOT OKAY!
POIVRE BLANC
LISTEN, IN THAT CASE YOU CAN HAVE HIM NEXT WEEKEND! THEN YOU'LL HAVE HIM TWO WEEKENDS IN A ROW!
HMM.
NO, MONIQUE AND I AREN'T HERE NEXT WEEKEND.
LOOK! YOU CAN'T KEEP YOUR SON FROM GOING TO A FRIEND'S PARTY...! I'LL DROP HIM OFF, AND YOU CAN PICK HIM UP IN THE LATE AFTERNOON! WE'LL MAKE UP FOR THE LOST DAY IF IT MEANS THAT MUCH TO YOU! DEAL?
DEAL.
POIVRE BLANC

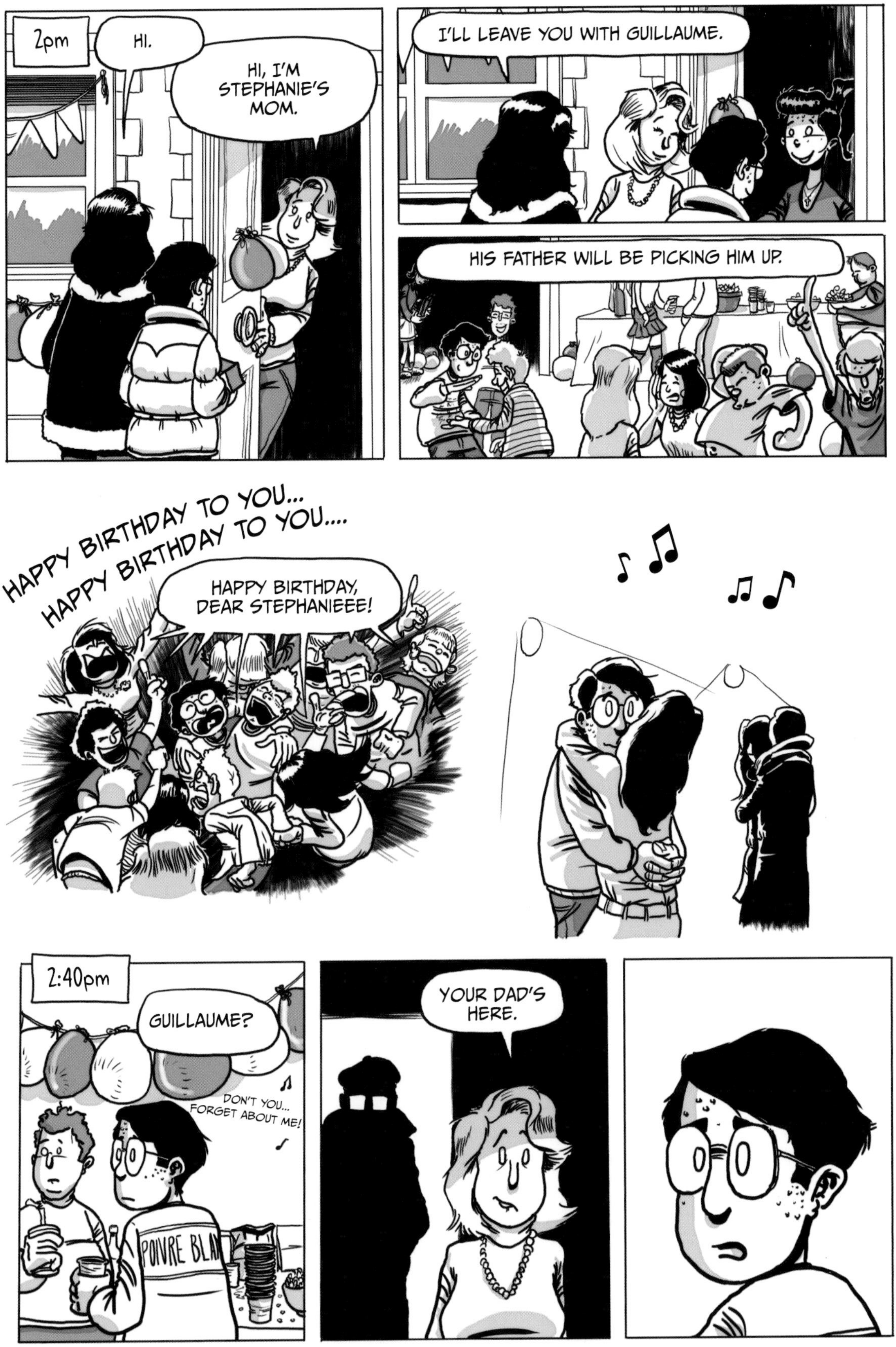

2pm
HI.
HI, I'M STEPHANIE'S MOM.
I'LL LEAVE YOU WITH GUILLAUME.
HIS FATHER WILL BE PICKING HIM UP.
HAPPY BIRTHDAY TO YOU...
HAPPY BIRTHDAY TO YOU....
HAPPY BIRTHDAY, DEAR STEPHANIEEE!
2:40pm
GUILLAUME?
DON'T YOU... FORGET ABOUT ME!
POIVRE BLA
YOUR DAD'S HERE.

BUT I JUST GOT HERE! I'M NOT GOING TO LEAVE *NOW!*

GET IN THE CAR THIS INSTANT. MONIQUE'S WAITING FOR US...

IT'S SUCH A SHAME HE CAN'T STAY LONGER. IT WAS VERY SHORT... NOT EVERYONE'S HERE YET.

I'M AFRAID WE HAVE PLANS.

COME ON, SAY BYE AND GET IN THE CAR.

BYE.

GOODBYE, GUILLAUME.

IT'S NOT FAIR!

YOU TELL THAT TO YOUR MOTHER...WHAT'S NOT FAIR IS YOU GOING SOMEWHERE ELSE DURING *MY* WEEKEND. YOU COME TO SEE ME, NOT TO SPEND YOUR DAY WITH FRIENDS YOU SEE EVERY DAY...! AND IT ALSO HAPPENS WE HAVE TICKETS FOR A HORSE SHOW AT 4:00.

IT'S NOT FAIR!

YOUR HORSES MAKE ME SICK!

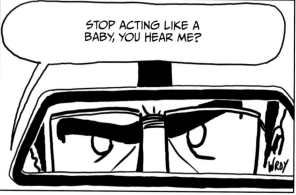

STOP ACTING LIKE A BABY, YOU HEAR ME?

46

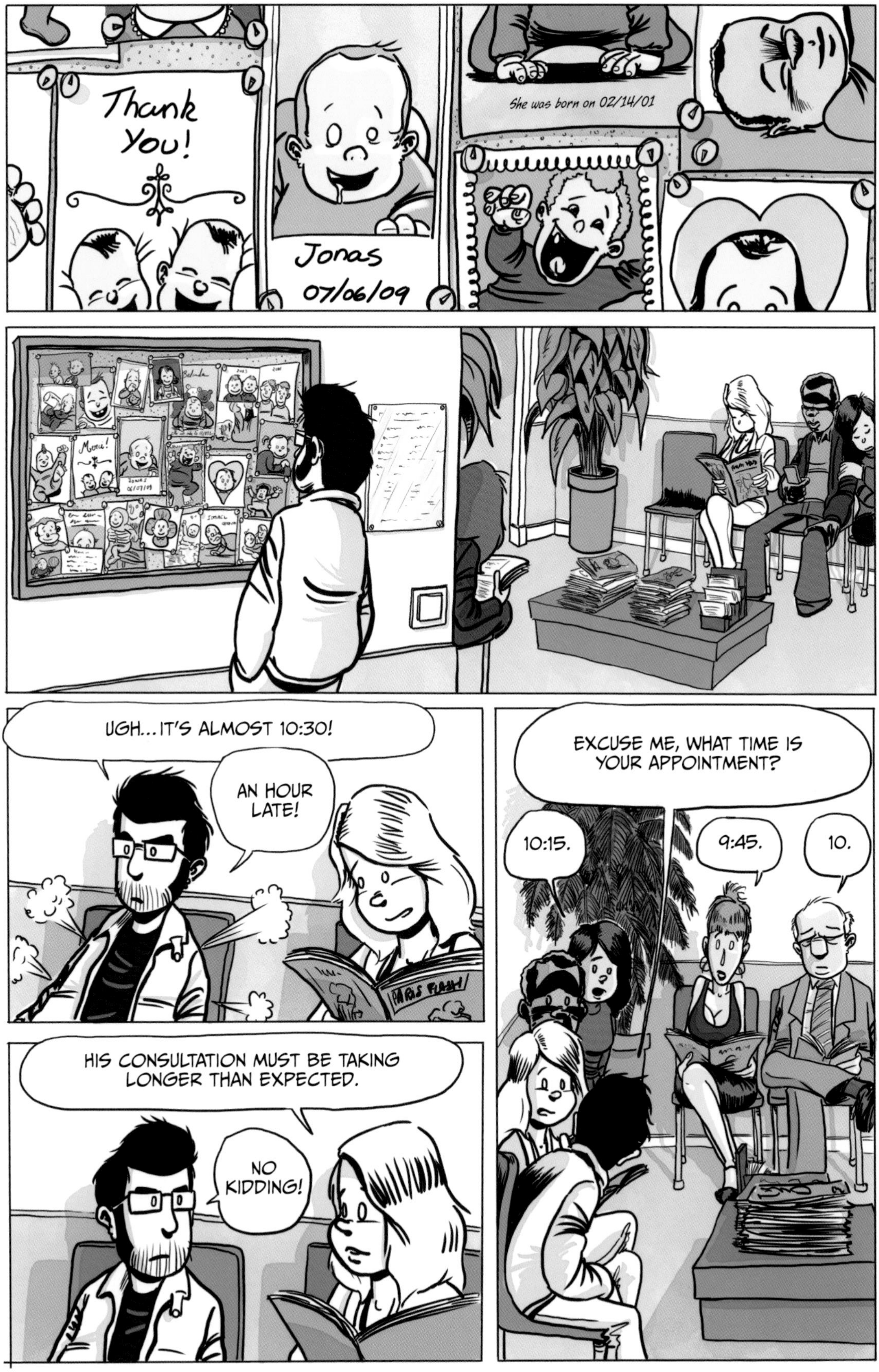

Thank You!
Jonas 07/06/09
She was born on 02/14/01
UGH... IT'S ALMOST 10:30!
AN HOUR LATE!
PARIS FLASH
HIS CONSULTATION MUST BE TAKING LONGER THAN EXPECTED.
NO KIDDING!
EXCUSE ME, WHAT TIME IS YOUR APPOINTMENT?
10:15.
9:45.
10.

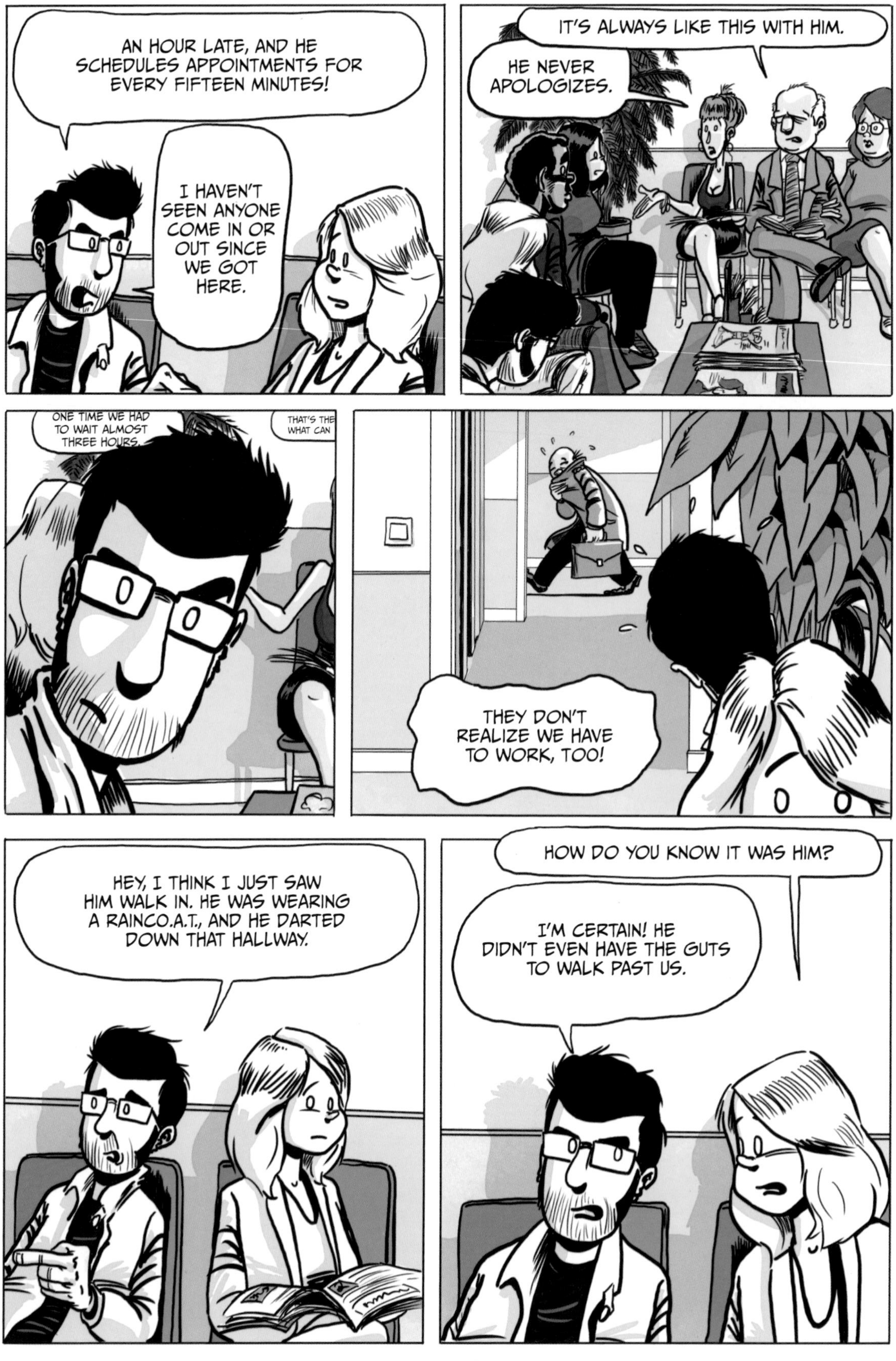
AN HOUR LATE, AND HE SCHEDULES APPOINTMENTS FOR EVERY FIFTEEN MINUTES!
I HAVEN'T SEEN ANYONE COME IN OR OUT SINCE WE GOT HERE.
IT'S ALWAYS LIKE THIS WITH HIM.
HE NEVER APOLOGIZES.
ONE TIME WE HAD TO WAIT ALMOST THREE HOURS.
THAT'S THE
WHAT CAN
THEY DON'T REALIZE WE HAVE TO WORK, TOO!
HEY, I THINK I JUST SAW HIM WALK IN. HE WAS WEARING A RAINCO.A.T., AND HE DARTED DOWN THAT HALLWAY.
HOW DO YOU KNOW IT WAS HIM?
I'M CERTAIN! HE DIDN'T EVEN HAVE THE GUTS TO WALK PAST US.

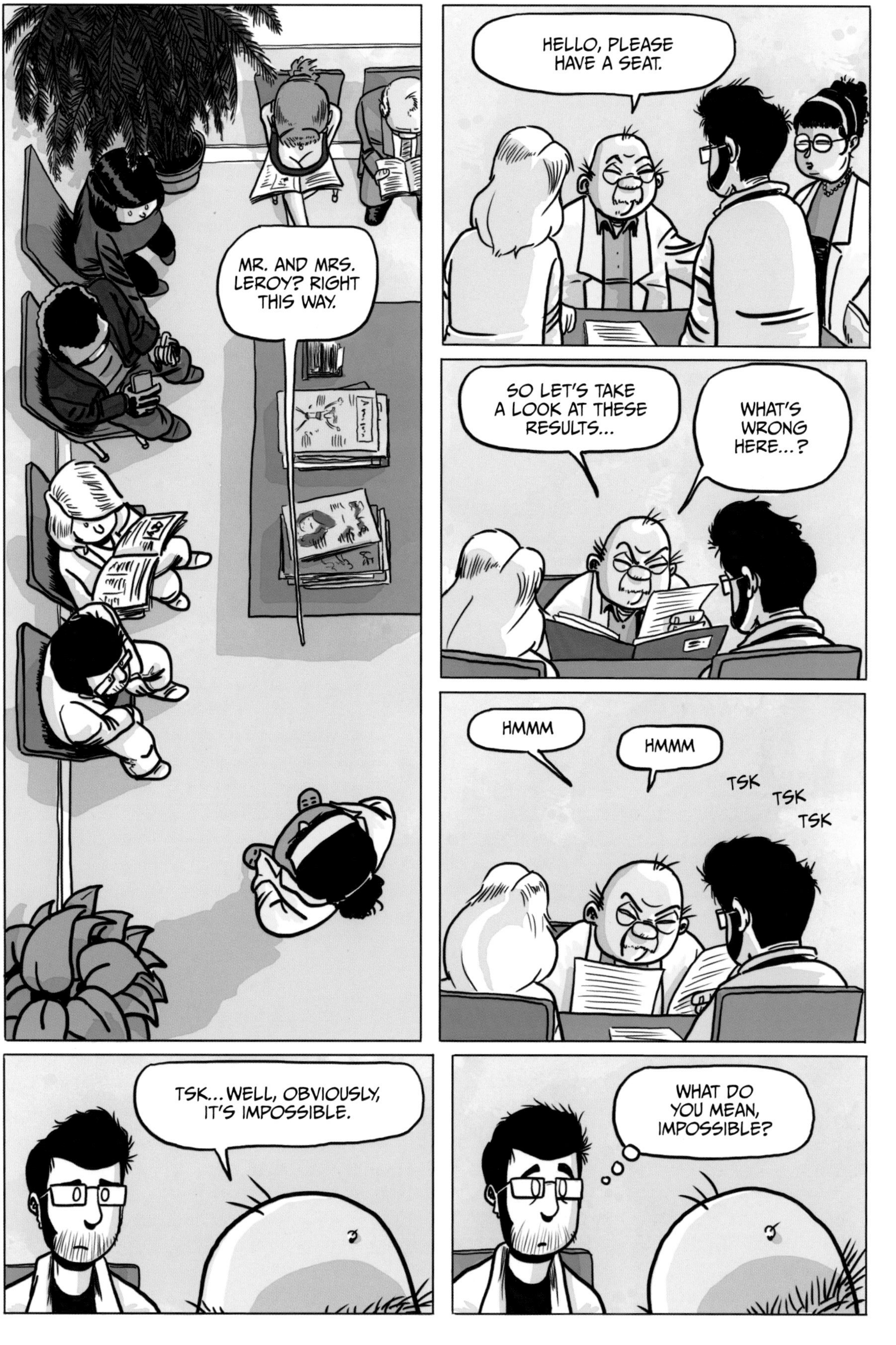
MR. AND MRS. LEROY? RIGHT THIS WAY.
HELLO, PLEASE HAVE A SEAT.
SO LET'S TAKE A LOOK AT THESE RESULTS...
WHAT'S WRONG HERE...?
HMMM
HMMM
TSK
TSK
TSK
TSK...WELL, OBVIOUSLY, IT'S IMPOSSIBLE.
WHAT DO YOU MEAN, IMPOSSIBLE?

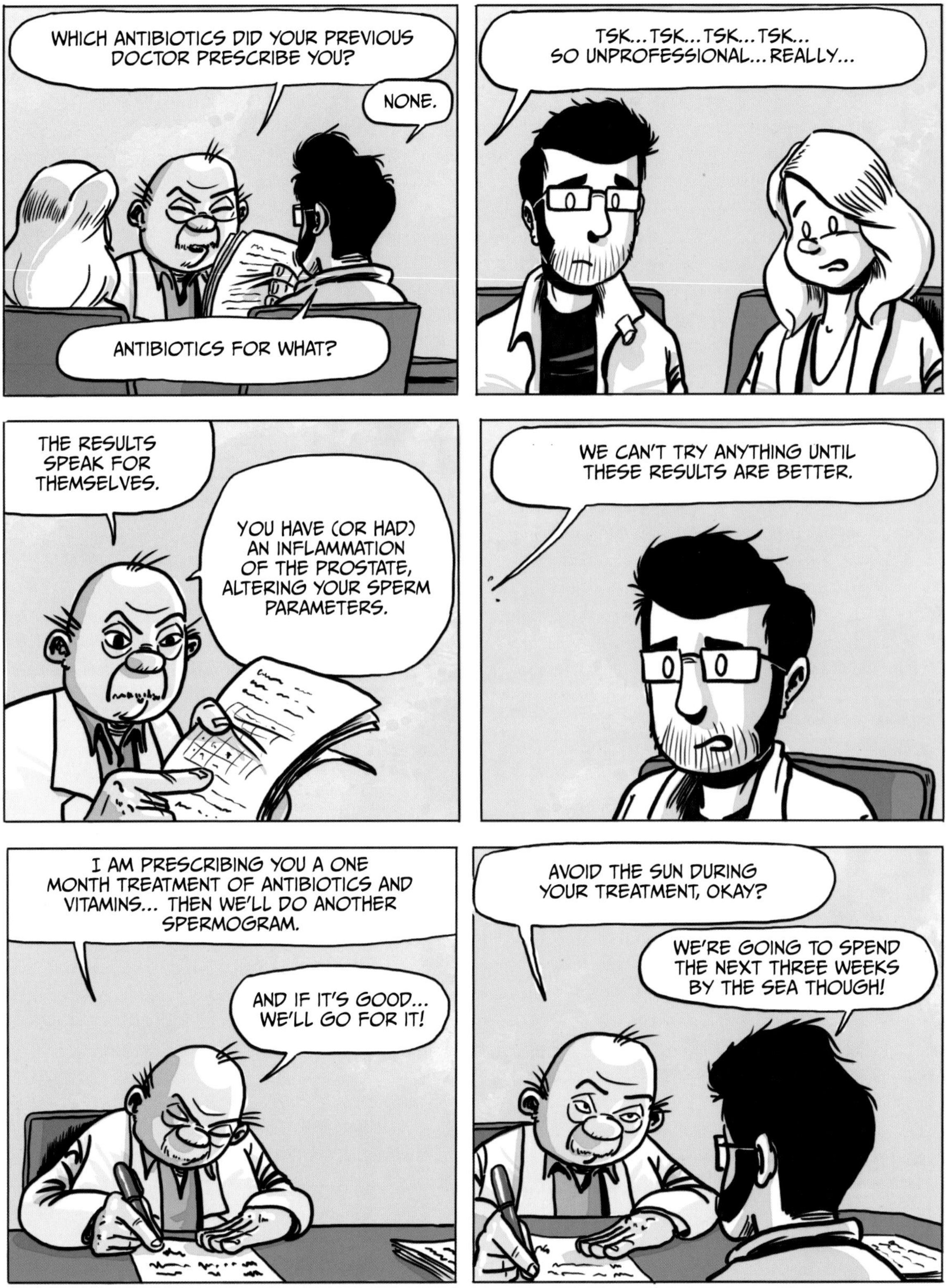
WHICH ANTIBIOTICS DID YOUR PREVIOUS DOCTOR PRESCRIBE YOU?
NONE.
ANTIBIOTICS FOR WHAT?
TSK... TSK... TSK... TSK... SO UNPROFESSIONAL... REALLY...
THE RESULTS SPEAK FOR THEMSELVES.
YOU HAVE (OR HAD) AN INFLAMMATION OF THE PROSTATE, ALTERING YOUR SPERM PARAMETERS.
WE CAN'T TRY ANYTHING UNTIL THESE RESULTS ARE BETTER.
I AM PRESCRIBING YOU A ONE MONTH TREATMENT OF ANTIBIOTICS AND VITAMINS... THEN WE'LL DO ANOTHER SPERMOGRAM.
AND IF IT'S GOOD... WE'LL GO FOR IT!
AVOID THE SUN DURING YOUR TREATMENT, OKAY?
WE'RE GOING TO SPEND THE NEXT THREE WEEKS BY THE SEA THOUGH!

MOST IMPORTANTLY, WE HAVE TO PROCEED AS SOON AS THE RESULTS ARE CONFIRMED!

AND WHAT'S THE PROCEDURE?

WE'RE GOING TO DO IN VITRO FERTILIZATION.

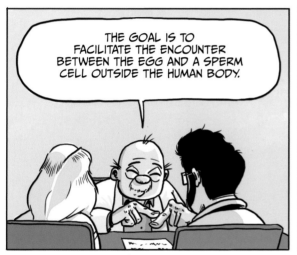

THE GOAL IS TO FACILITATE THE ENCOUNTER BETWEEN THE EGG AND A SPERM CELL OUTSIDE THE HUMAN BODY.

AN OVUM IS EXTRACTED FROM THE LADY WITH A NEEDLE AND PLACED IN A TEST TUBE IN THE PRESENCE OF THE GENTLEMAN'S SPERMATOZOA...

THERE ARE SEVERAL METHODS.

WE CHOOSE THE BEST SUITED...

...TO EACH CASE...

WITH CLASSIC I.V.F....

...WE WAIT FOR A SPERM CELL TO PENETRATE THE EGG IN VITRO...

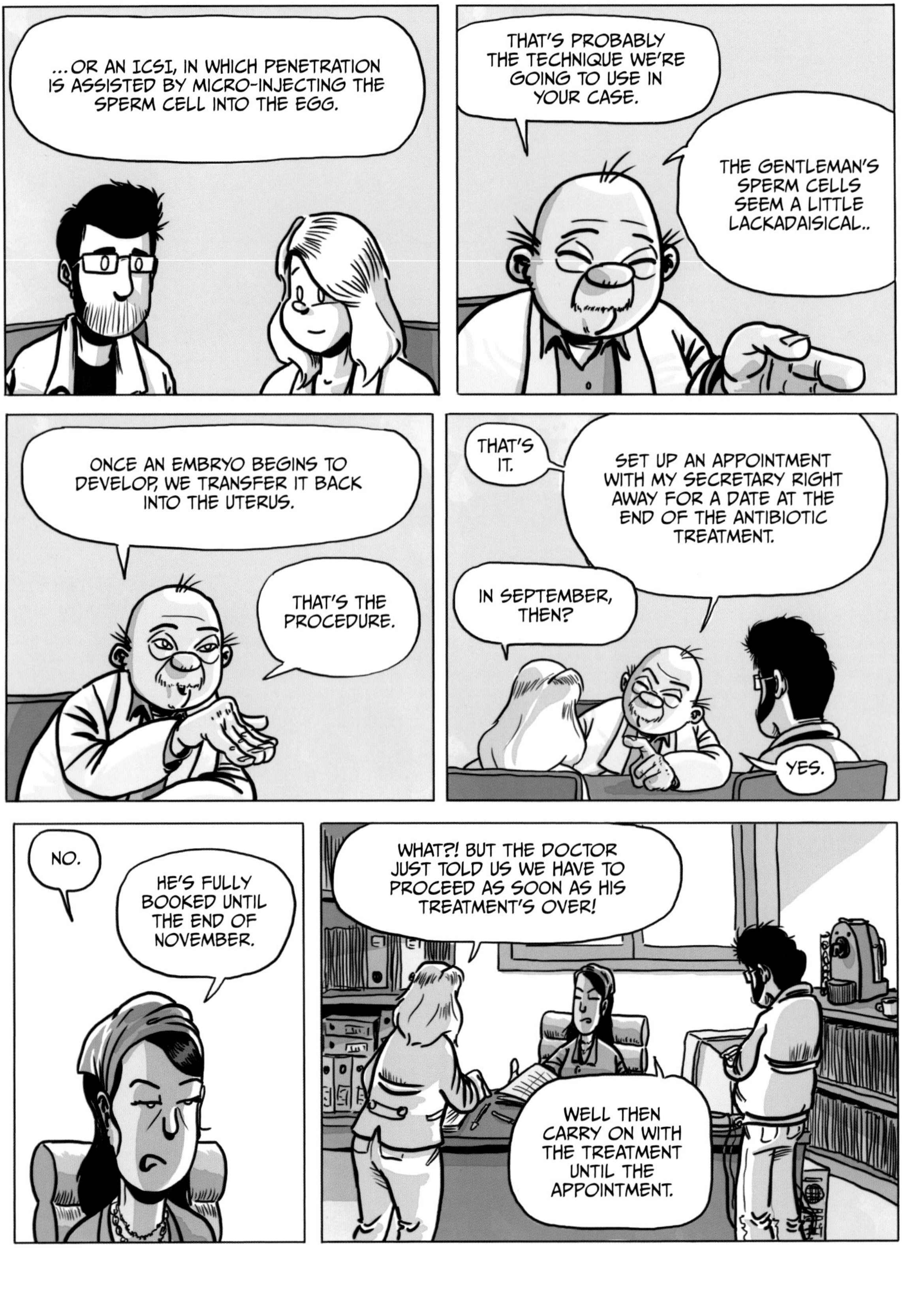
...OR AN ICSI, IN WHICH PENETRATION IS ASSISTED BY MICRO-INJECTING THE SPERM CELL INTO THE EGG.
THAT'S PROBABLY THE TECHNIQUE WE'RE GOING TO USE IN YOUR CASE.
THE GENTLEMAN'S SPERM CELLS SEEM A LITTLE LACKADAISICAL..
ONCE AN EMBRYO BEGINS TO DEVELOP, WE TRANSFER IT BACK INTO THE UTERUS.
THAT'S THE PROCEDURE.
THAT'S IT.
SET UP AN APPOINTMENT WITH MY SECRETARY RIGHT AWAY FOR A DATE AT THE END OF THE ANTIBIOTIC TREATMENT.
IN SEPTEMBER, THEN?
YES.
NO.
HE'S FULLY BOOKED UNTIL THE END OF NOVEMBER.
WHAT?! BUT THE DOCTOR JUST TOLD US WE HAVE TO PROCEED AS SOON AS HIS TREATMENT'S OVER!
WELL THEN CARRY ON WITH THE TREATMENT UNTIL THE APPOINTMENT.

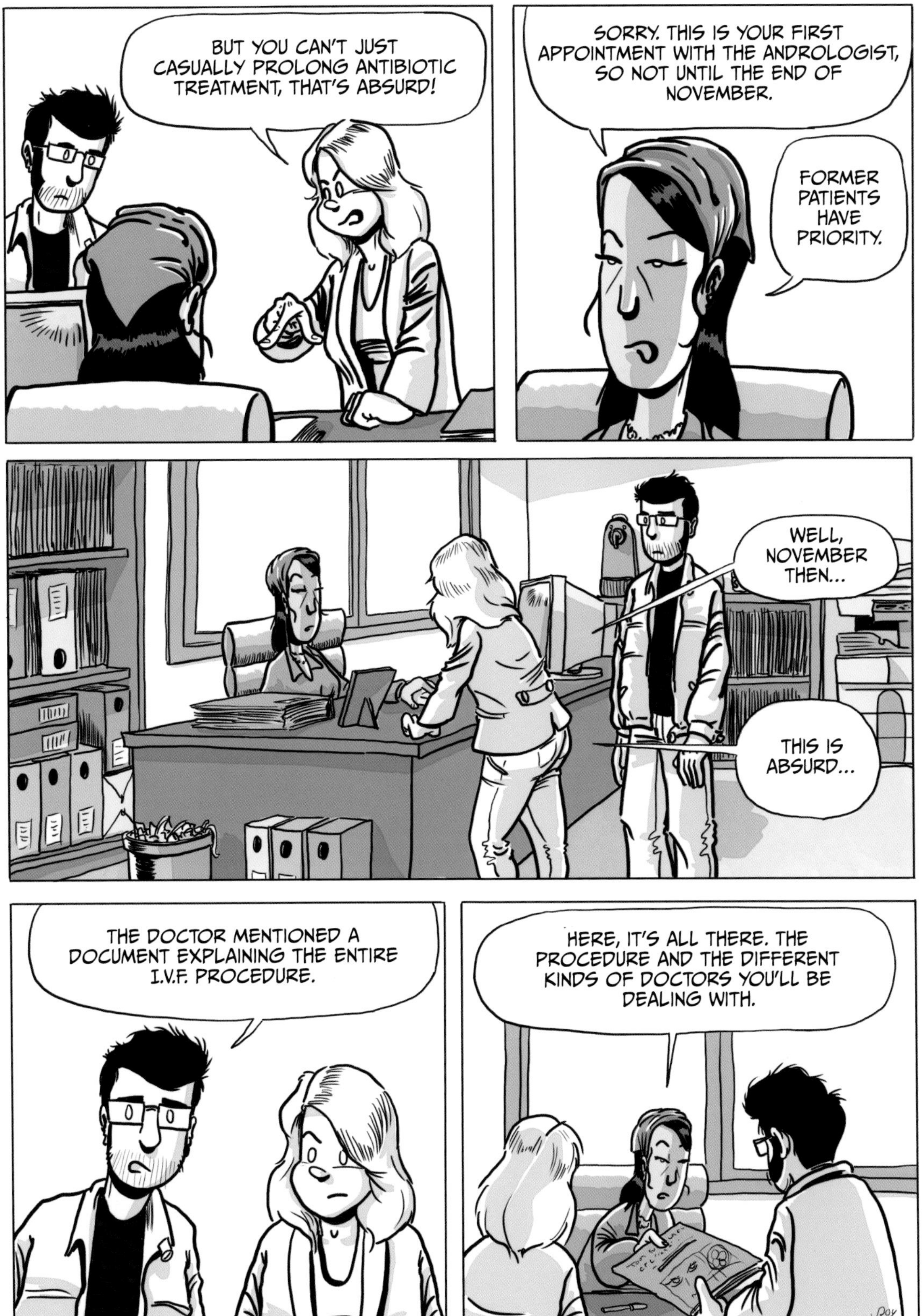
BUT YOU CAN'T JUST CASUALLY PROLONG ANTIBIOTIC TREATMENT, THAT'S ABSURD!
SORRY. THIS IS YOUR FIRST APPOINTMENT WITH THE ANDROLOGIST, SO NOT UNTIL THE END OF NOVEMBER.
FORMER PATIENTS HAVE PRIORITY.
WELL, NOVEMBER THEN...
THIS IS ABSURD...
THE DOCTOR MENTIONED A DOCUMENT EXPLAINING THE ENTIRE I.V.F. PROCEDURE.
HERE, IT'S ALL THERE. THE PROCEDURE AND THE DIFFERENT KINDS OF DOCTORS YOU'LL BE DEALING WITH.

"I HAVE A BAD FEELING ABOUT THIS DOCTOR..."

"WELL, LET'S TRUST HIM. YOU KNOW HOW THEY ARE, IT
DOESN'T MEAN ANYTHING."

HELLO, DEAR FRIENDS. NOW THAT THE ANTIBIOTIC TREATMENT IS OVER, AND THAT WE'VE CONDUCTED A NEW SPERMOGRAM, WE ARE ABLE TO IDENTIFY MR. LEROY'S PATHOLOGY.

Professor Beuaârr
Specialist

WHAT WE HAVE HERE IS AN OBSTRUCTED EPIDIDYMAL CANAL.

LET'S HAVE A CLOSER LOOK.

THE EPIDIDYMIS IS A KIND OF VERY LONG TUBE (SEVERAL FEET) WRAPPED AROUND ITSELF, LOCATED BEHIND THE BALLS.

IT CHANNELS SPERM CELLS AS THEY LEAVE THE TESTICLE.

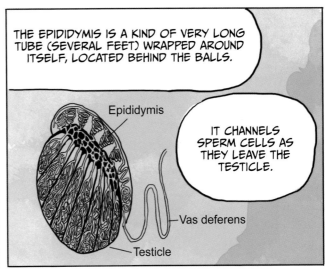

Epididymis

Vas deferens

Testicle

IN THIS CASE, THE VAS DEFERENS IS OBSTRUCTED IN ONE OR MORE PLACES.

LIKE A KNOTTED ROPE.

THE SPERM CELLS PASS THROUGH DURING EJACULATION, BUT IN LIMITED NUMBERS... AND SINCE THE ROUTE IS ROUGHER THAN USUAL, THEY DON'T MAKE IT OUT TOO FRESH.

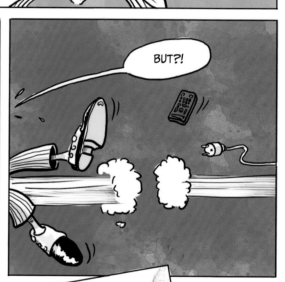

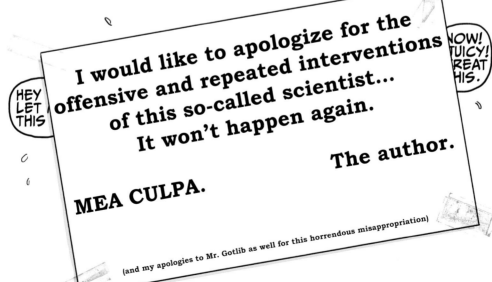

I.V.F.

Assisted Reproductive Technology
The ICSI procedure

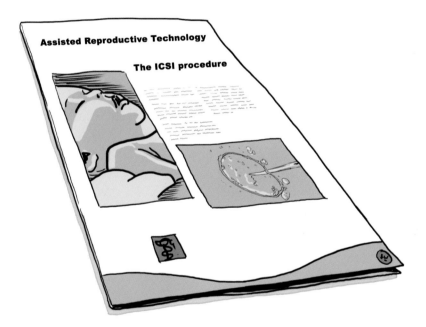

AT LAST

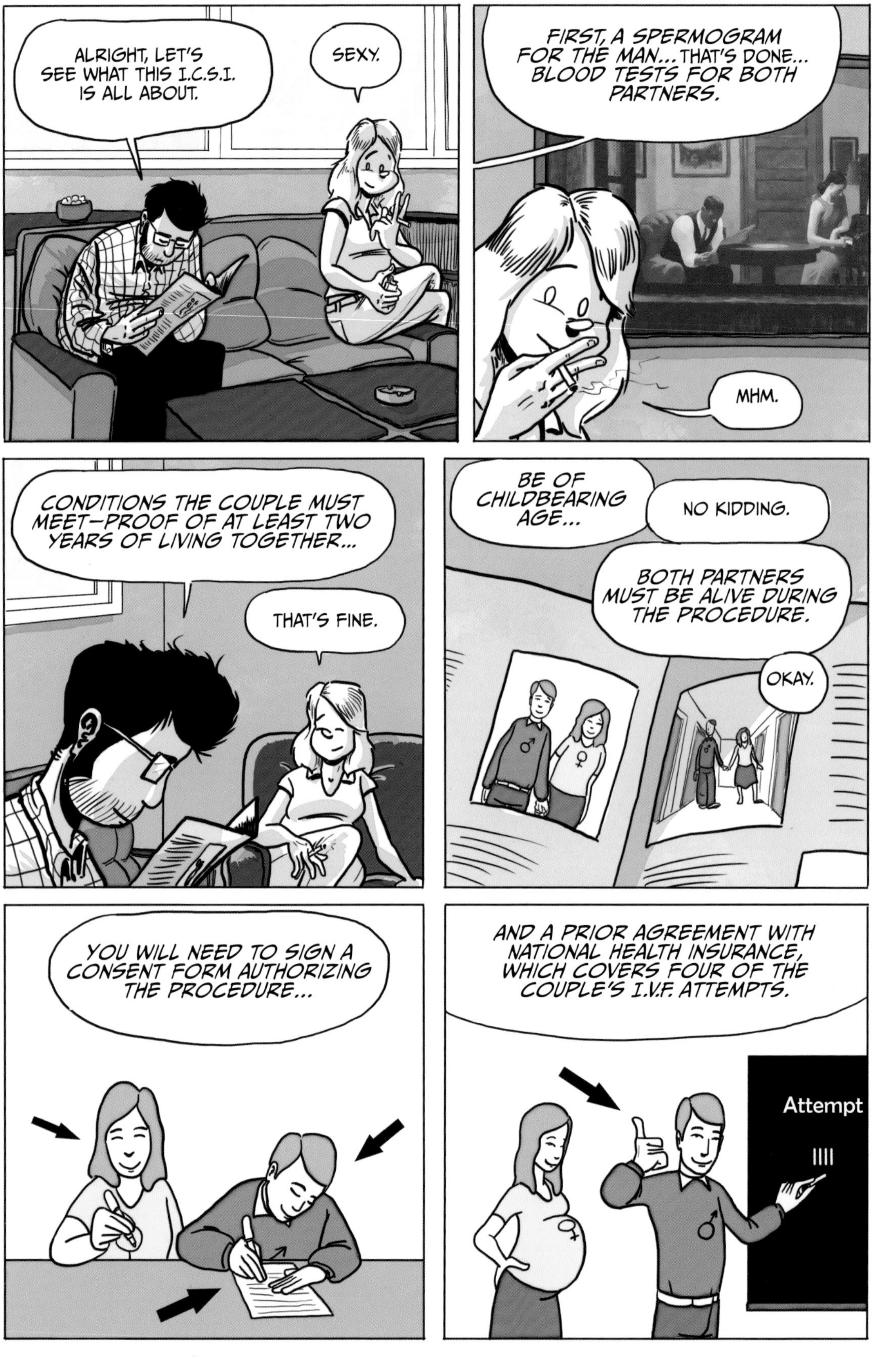
ALRIGHT, LET'S SEE WHAT THIS I.C.S.I. IS ALL ABOUT.
SEXY.
FIRST, A SPERMOGRAM FOR THE MAN... THAT'S DONE... BLOOD TESTS FOR BOTH PARTNERS.
MHM.
CONDITIONS THE COUPLE MUST MEET—PROOF OF AT LEAST TWO YEARS OF LIVING TOGETHER...
THAT'S FINE.
BE OF CHILDBEARING AGE...
NO KIDDING.
BOTH PARTNERS MUST BE ALIVE DURING THE PROCEDURE.
OKAY.
YOU WILL NEED TO SIGN A CONSENT FORM AUTHORIZING THE PROCEDURE...
AND A PRIOR AGREEMENT WITH NATIONAL HEALTH INSURANCE, WHICH COVERS FOUR OF THE COUPLE'S I.V.F. ATTEMPTS.
Attempt
IIII

YOU WILL ENCOUNTER DIFFERENT DOCTORS THROUGHOUT THE PROCEDURE.

1. THE BIOLOGIST: RESPONSIBLE FOR THE BIOLOGICAL STAGES OF I.V.F....

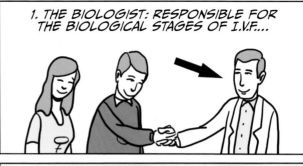

...AND THE RESULTING EMBRYOS.

HAVE A SEAT.

NOW.

I'M GOING TO TALK YOU THROUGH AN ICSI PROCEDURE.

ON DAY ZERO, WE RETRIEVE FOLLICLES FROM THE WOMAN'S OVARIES.

Follicular Puncture

MEANWHILE, THE MAN COLLECTS A SPERM SAMPLE.

AFTER VARIOUS STAGES OF PREPARATION, WE INJECT A SPERM CELL INTO EACH OOCYTE OBTAINED BY PUNCTURING THE FOLLICLES.

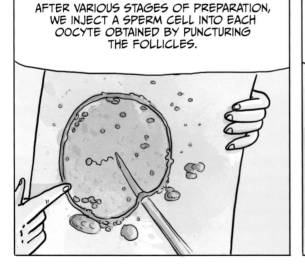

THE OOCYTES ARE PAMPERED AND MONITORED FOR THE FOLLOWING TWO DAYS. SOME WILL END UP DEVELOPING INTO EMBRYOS.

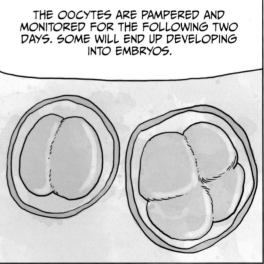

WE SELECT THE BEST LOOKING ONES FOR TRANSFER...WE CAN ALSO FREEZE SOME OF THEM.

IF THERE IS ANY DOUBT ABOUT THEIR QUALITY, THE CULTURE CAN BE EXTENDED TO FIVE DAYS UP TO THE BLASTOCYST STAGE. THIS COULD IMPROVE YOUR CHANCES.

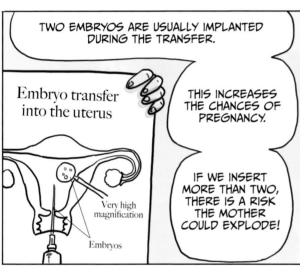

TWO EMBRYOS ARE USUALLY IMPLANTED DURING THE TRANSFER.

Embryo transfer into the uterus

Very high magnification

Embryos

THIS INCREASES THE CHANCES OF PREGNANCY.

IF WE INSERT MORE THAN TWO, THERE IS A RISK THE MOTHER COULD EXPLODE!

IT SHOULD BE NOTED THAT THE PROBABILITY OF HAVING TWINS IS ABOUT TWENTY PERCENT.

THAT'S TWENTY TIMES MORE THAN A NATURAL PREGNANCY.

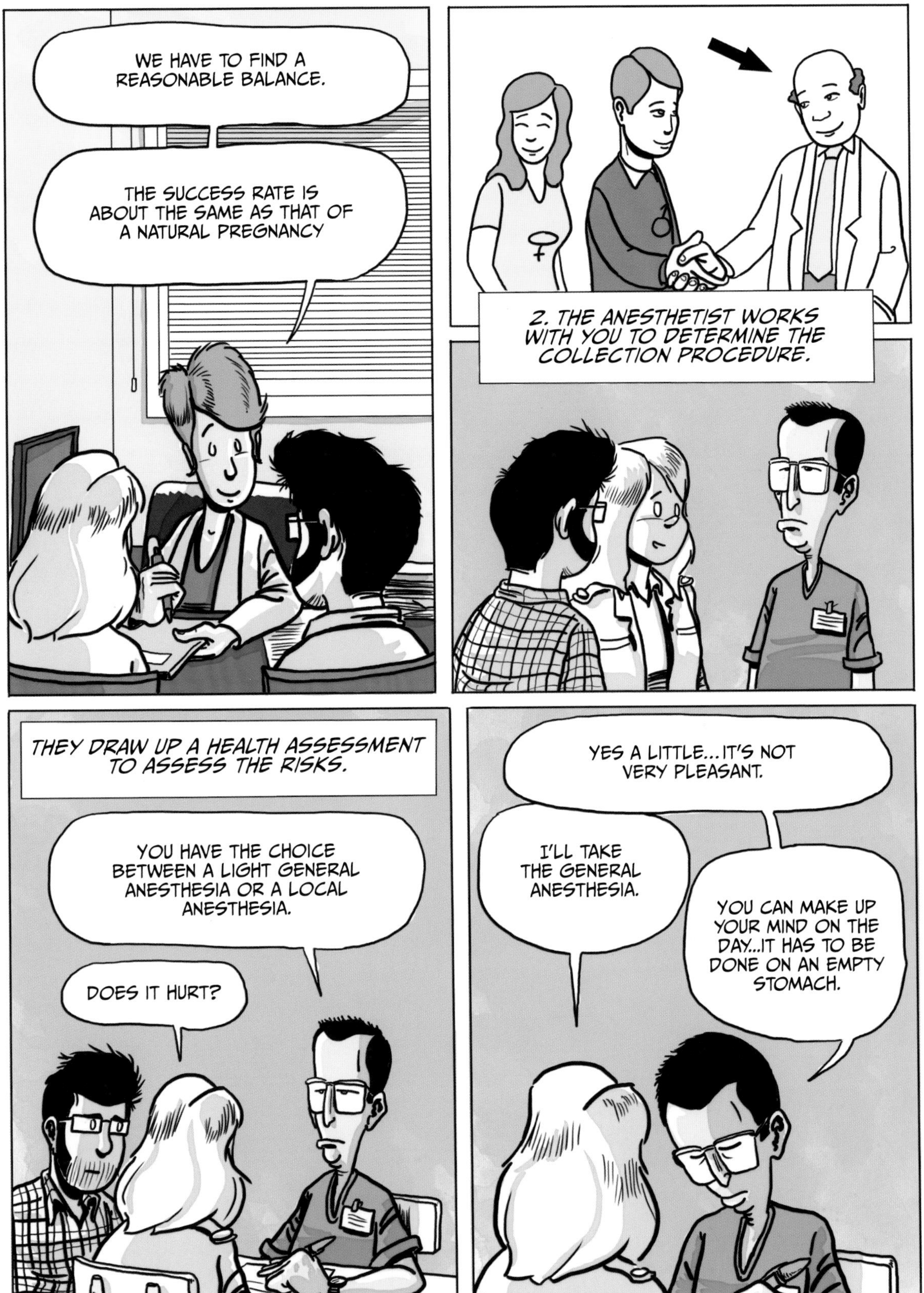
WE HAVE TO FIND A REASONABLE BALANCE.
THE SUCCESS RATE IS ABOUT THE SAME AS THAT OF A NATURAL PREGNANCY
2. THE ANESTHETIST WORKS WITH YOU TO DETERMINE THE COLLECTION PROCEDURE.
THEY DRAW UP A HEALTH ASSESSMENT TO ASSESS THE RISKS.
YOU HAVE THE CHOICE BETWEEN A LIGHT GENERAL ANESTHESIA OR A LOCAL ANESTHESIA.
DOES IT HURT?
YES A LITTLE... IT'S NOT VERY PLEASANT.
I'LL TAKE THE GENERAL ANESTHESIA.
YOU CAN MAKE UP YOUR MIND ON THE DAY...IT HAS TO BE DONE ON AN EMPTY STOMACH.

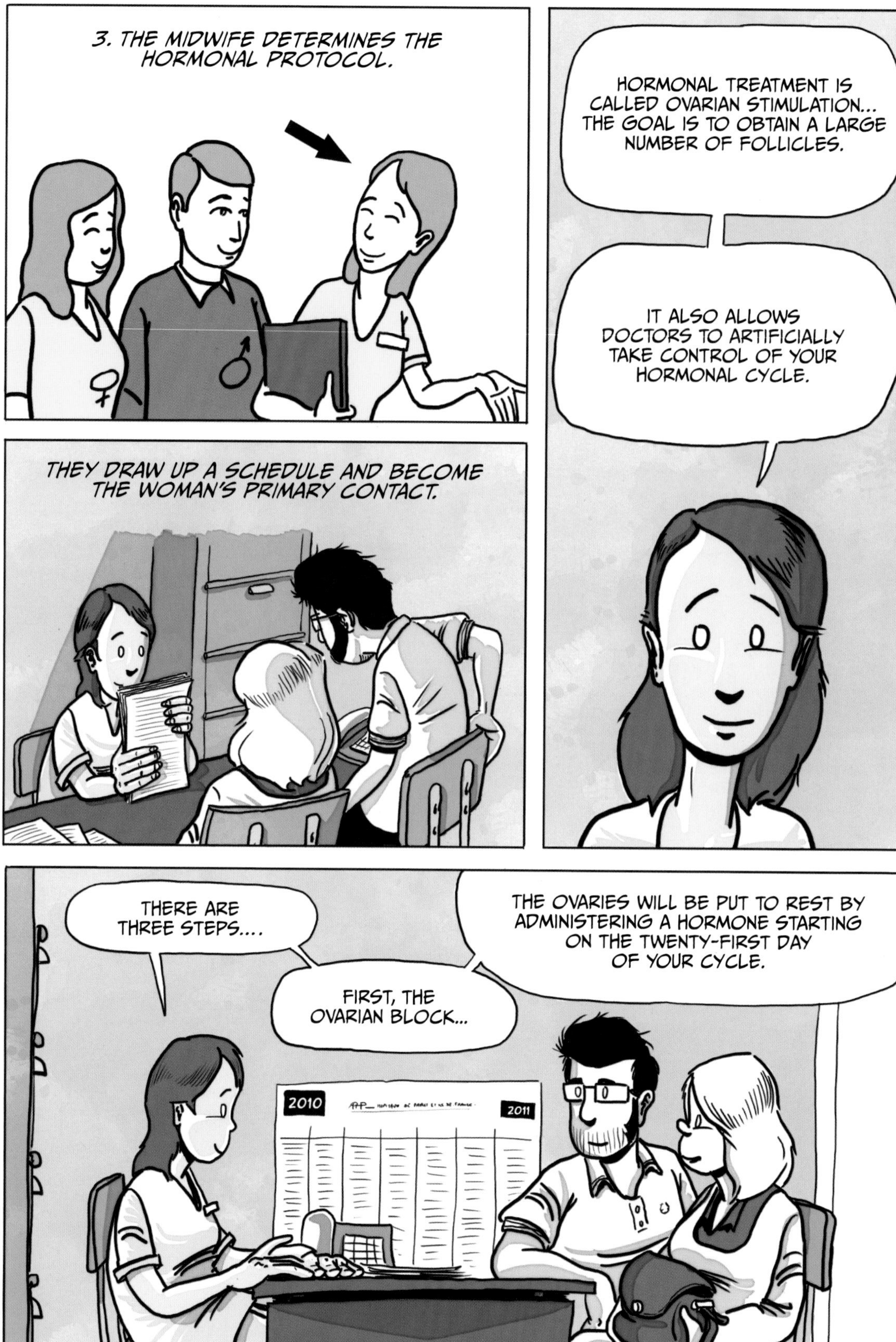
3. THE MIDWIFE DETERMINES THE HORMONAL PROTOCOL.
HORMONAL TREATMENT IS CALLED OVARIAN STIMULATION... THE GOAL IS TO OBTAIN A LARGE NUMBER OF FOLLICLES.
IT ALSO ALLOWS DOCTORS TO ARTIFICIALLY TAKE CONTROL OF YOUR HORMONAL CYCLE.
THEY DRAW UP A SCHEDULE AND BECOME THE WOMAN'S PRIMARY CONTACT.
THERE ARE THREE STEPS....
FIRST, THE OVARIAN BLOCK...
THE OVARIES WILL BE PUT TO REST BY ADMINISTERING A HORMONE STARTING ON THE TWENTY-FIRST DAY OF YOUR CYCLE.
2010
2011

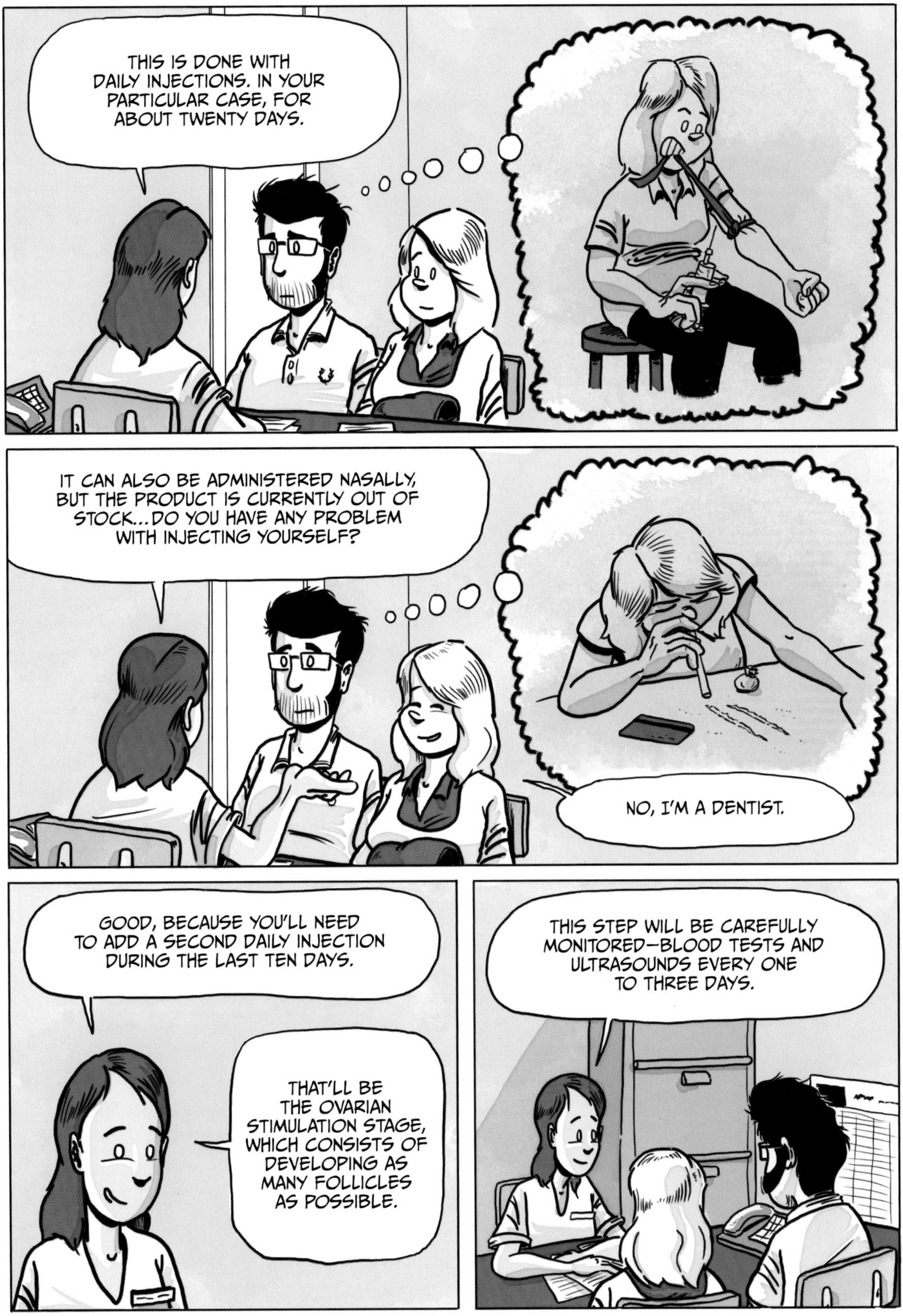
THIS IS DONE WITH DAILY INJECTIONS. IN YOUR PARTICULAR CASE, FOR ABOUT TWENTY DAYS.
IT CAN ALSO BE ADMINISTERED NASALLY, BUT THE PRODUCT IS CURRENTLY OUT OF STOCK...DO YOU HAVE ANY PROBLEM WITH INJECTING YOURSELF?
NO, I'M A DENTIST.
GOOD, BECAUSE YOU'LL NEED TO ADD A SECOND DAILY INJECTION DURING THE LAST TEN DAYS.
THAT'LL BE THE OVARIAN STIMULATION STAGE, WHICH CONSISTS OF DEVELOPING AS MANY FOLLICLES AS POSSIBLE.
THIS STEP WILL BE CAREFULLY MONITORED—BLOOD TESTS AND ULTRASOUNDS EVERY ONE TO THREE DAYS.

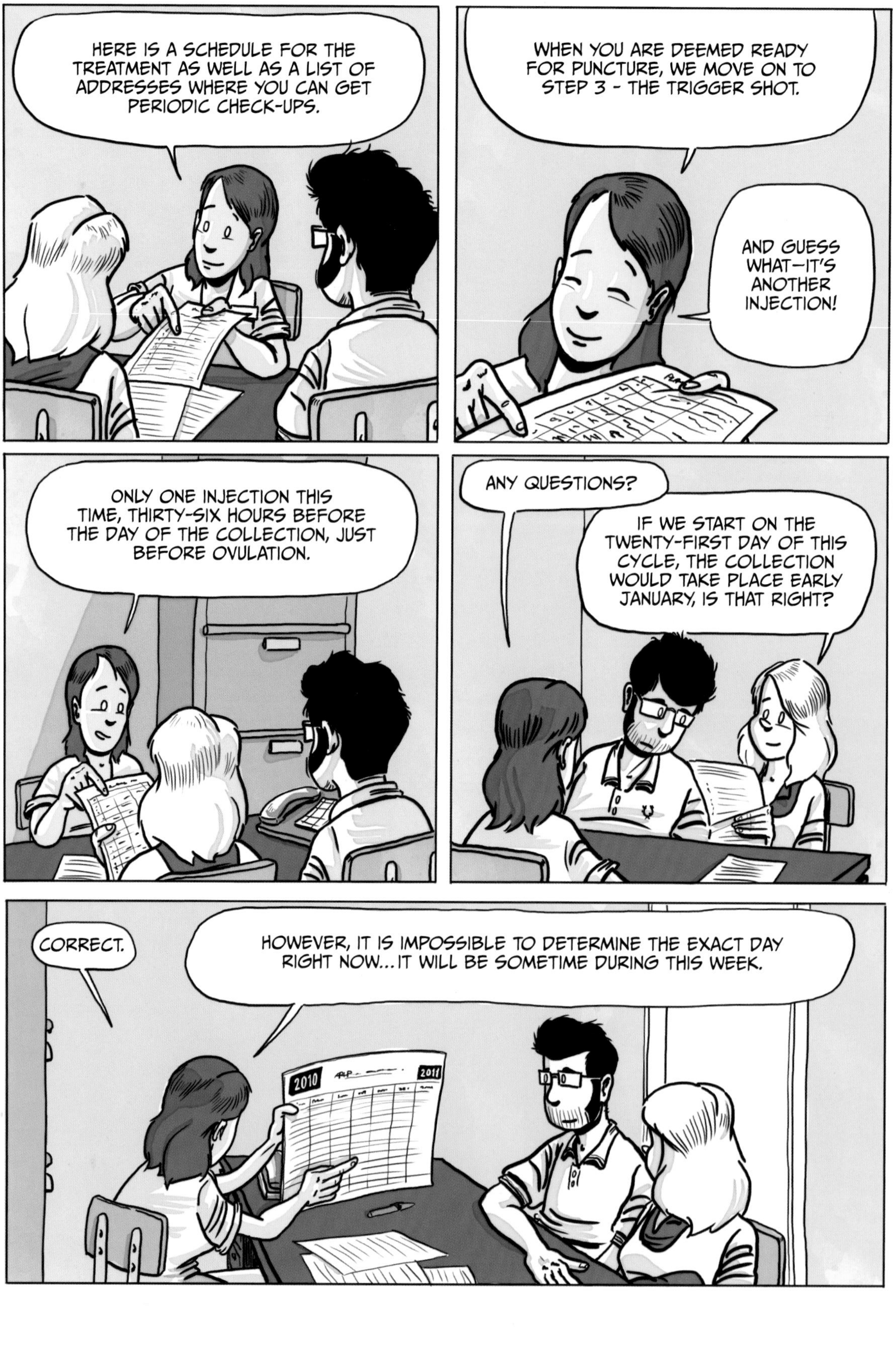
HERE IS A SCHEDULE FOR THE TREATMENT AS WELL AS A LIST OF ADDRESSES WHERE YOU CAN GET PERIODIC CHECK-UPS.
WHEN YOU ARE DEEMED READY FOR PUNCTURE, WE MOVE ON TO STEP 3 - THE TRIGGER SHOT.
AND GUESS WHAT—IT'S ANOTHER INJECTION!
ONLY ONE INJECTION THIS TIME, THIRTY-SIX HOURS BEFORE THE DAY OF THE COLLECTION, JUST BEFORE OVULATION.
ANY QUESTIONS?
IF WE START ON THE TWENTY-FIRST DAY OF THIS CYCLE, THE COLLECTION WOULD TAKE PLACE EARLY JANUARY, IS THAT RIGHT?
CORRECT.
HOWEVER, IT IS IMPOSSIBLE TO DETERMINE THE EXACT DAY RIGHT NOW... IT WILL BE SOMETIME DURING THIS WEEK.
2010
2011

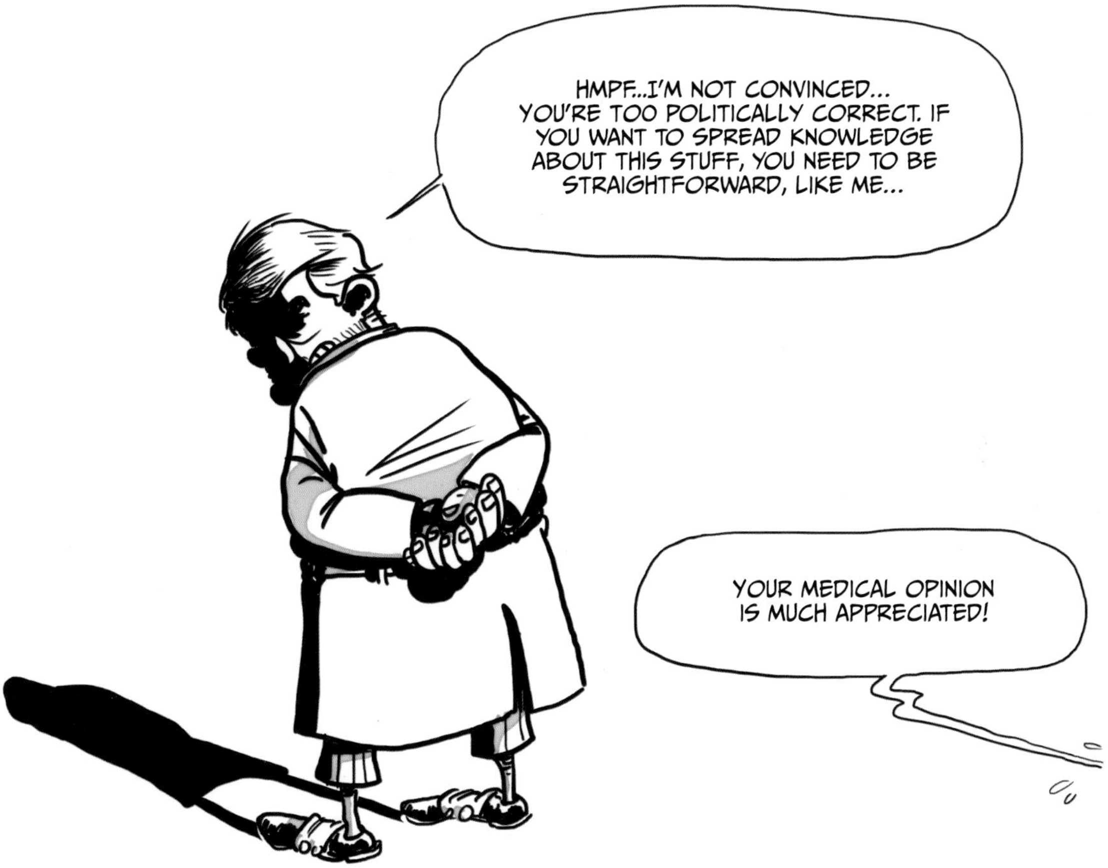
HMPF...I'M NOT CONVINCED... YOU'RE TOO POLITICALLY CORRECT. IF YOU WANT TO SPREAD KNOWLEDGE ABOUT THIS STUFF, YOU NEED TO BE STRAIGHTFORWARD, LIKE ME...
YOUR MEDICAL OPINION IS MUCH APPRECIATED!

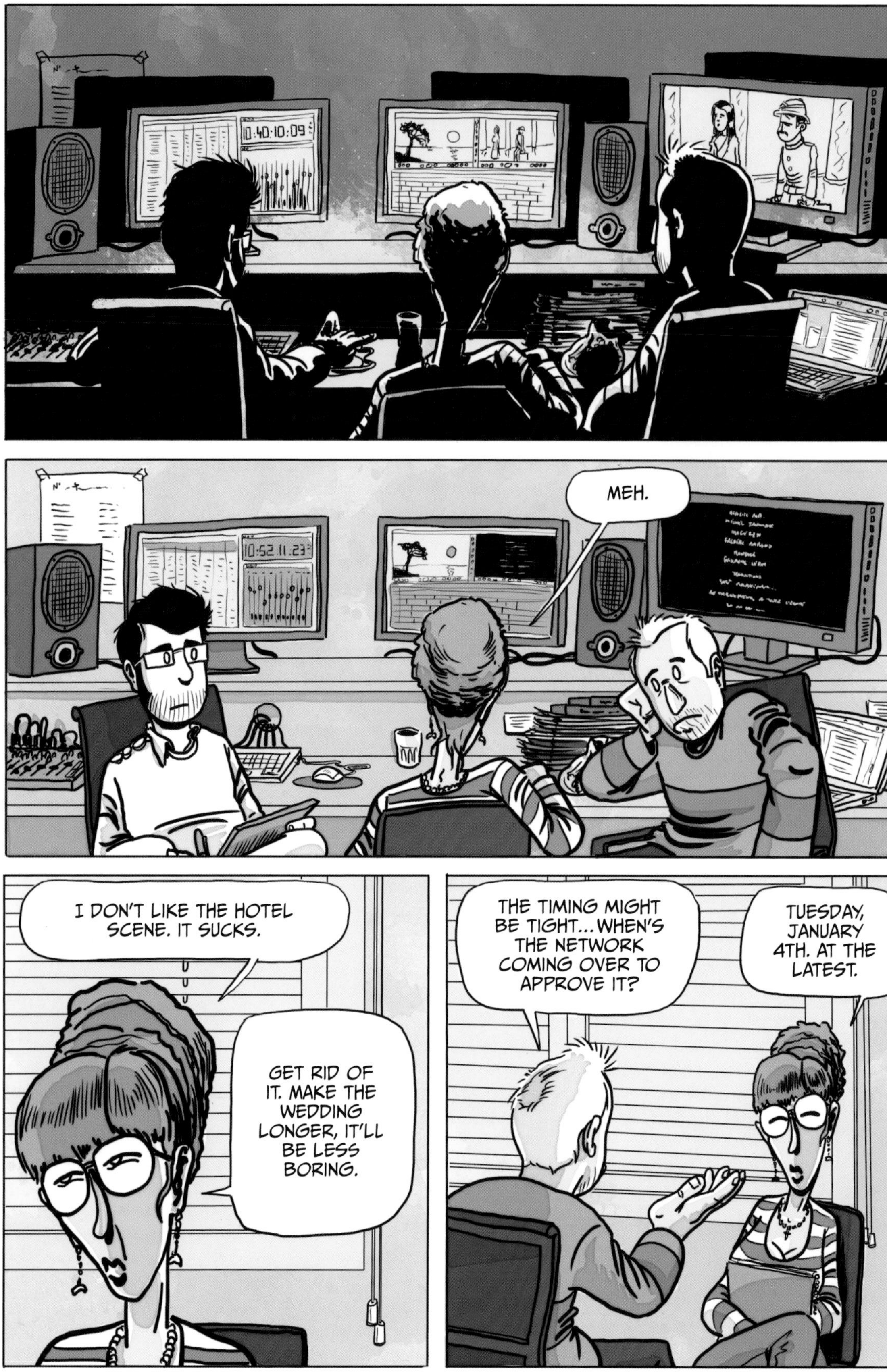
10:40:10:09
MEH.
I DON'T LIKE THE HOTEL SCENE. IT SUCKS.
GET RID OF IT. MAKE THE WEDDING LONGER, IT'LL BE LESS BORING.
THE TIMING MIGHT BE TIGHT...WHEN'S THE NETWORK COMING OVER TO APPROVE IT?
TUESDAY, JANUARY 4TH. AT THE LATEST.

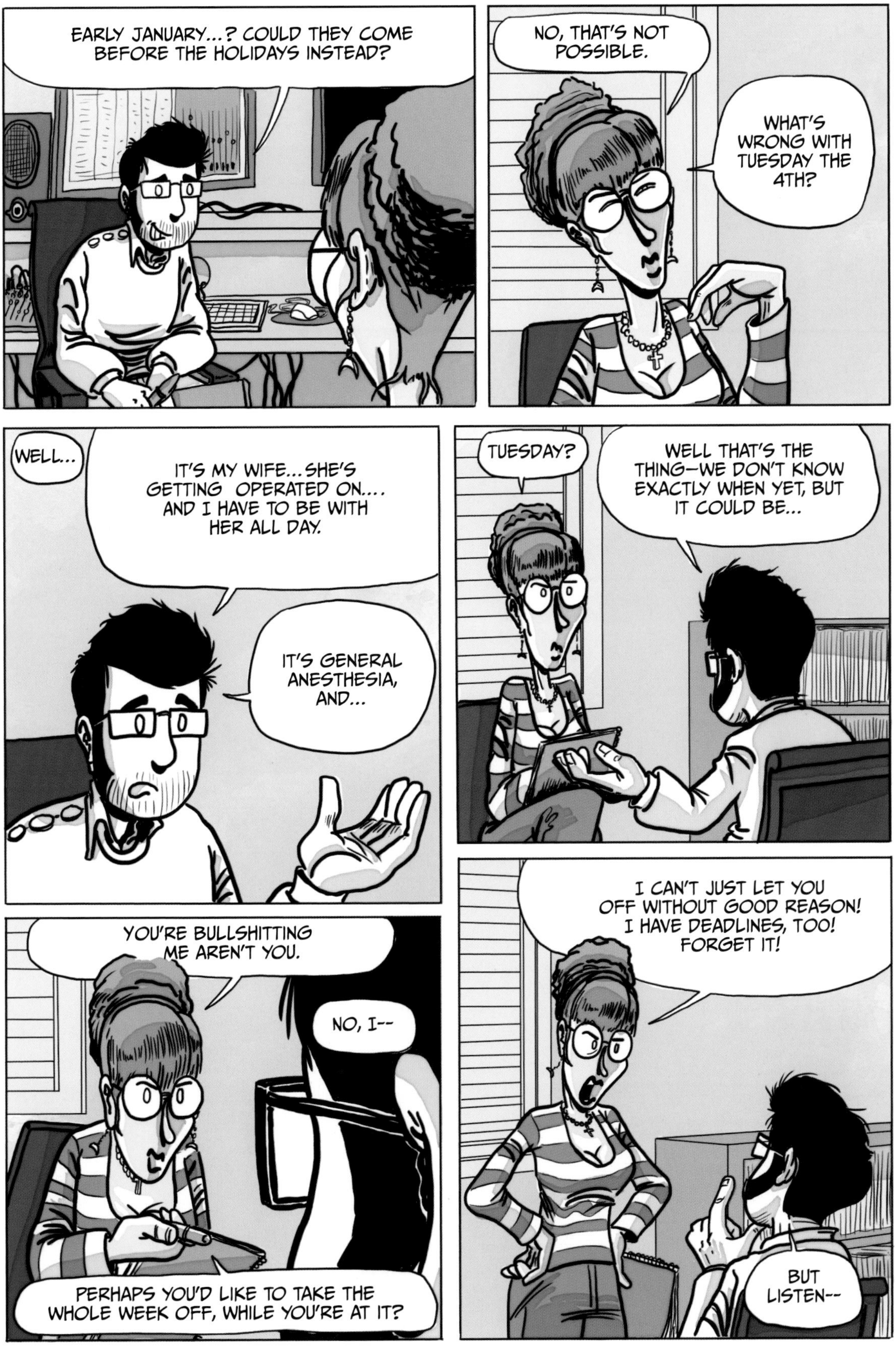
EARLY JANUARY...? COULD THEY COME BEFORE THE HOLIDAYS INSTEAD?
NO, THAT'S NOT POSSIBLE.
WHAT'S WRONG WITH TUESDAY THE 4TH?
WELL...
IT'S MY WIFE... SHE'S GETTING OPERATED ON.... AND I HAVE TO BE WITH HER ALL DAY.
IT'S GENERAL ANESTHESIA, AND...
TUESDAY?
WELL THAT'S THE THING—WE DON'T KNOW EXACTLY WHEN YET, BUT IT COULD BE...
YOU'RE BULLSHITTING ME AREN'T YOU.
NO, I--
PERHAPS YOU'D LIKE TO TAKE THE WHOLE WEEK OFF, WHILE YOU'RE AT IT?
I CAN'T JUST LET YOU OFF WITHOUT GOOD REASON! I HAVE DEADLINES, TOO! FORGET IT!
BUT LISTEN--

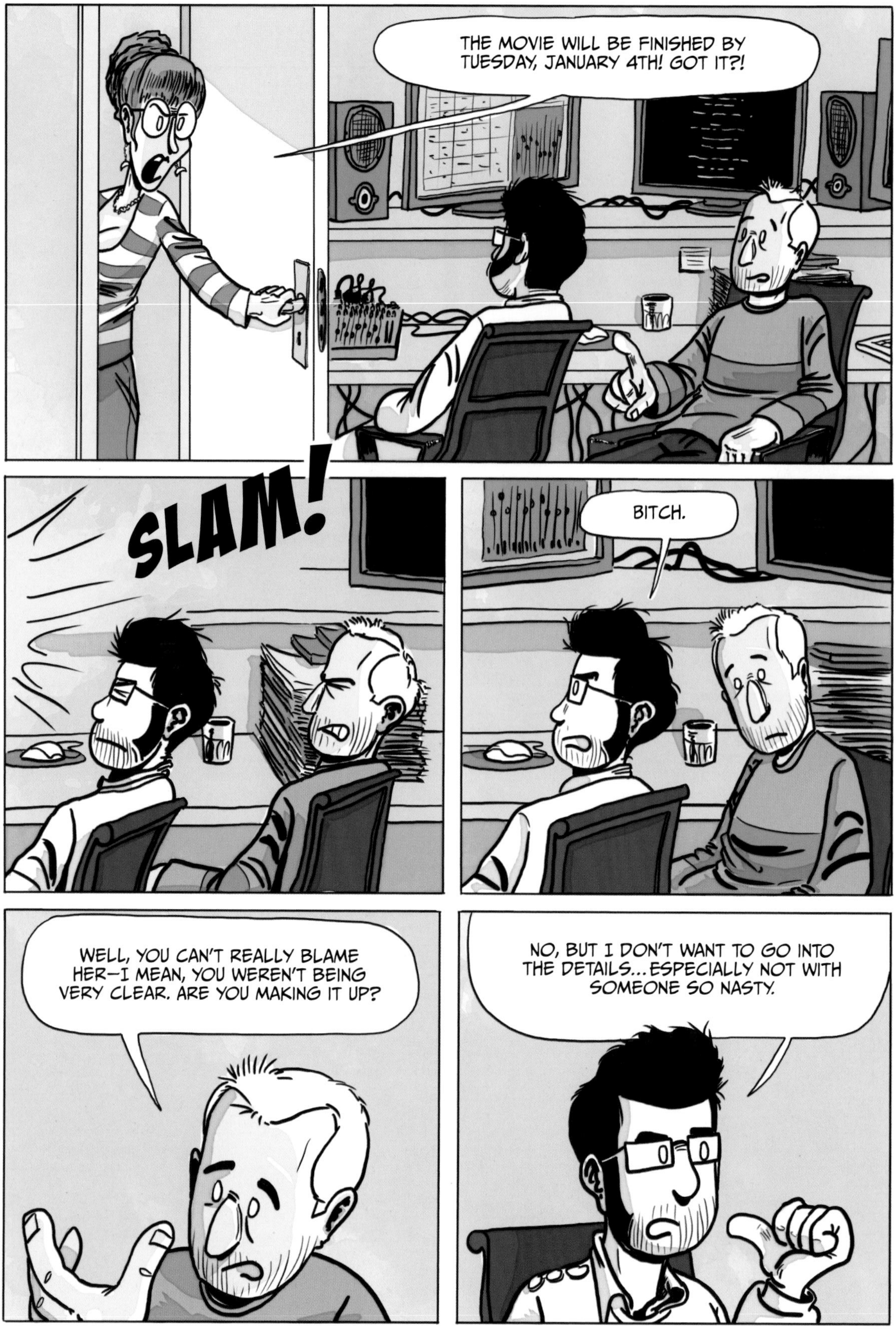
THE MOVIE WILL BE FINISHED BY TUESDAY, JANUARY 4TH! GOT IT?!
SLAM!
BITCH.
WELL, YOU CAN'T REALLY BLAME HER—I MEAN, YOU WEREN'T BEING VERY CLEAR. ARE YOU MAKING IT UP?
NO, BUT I DON'T WANT TO GO INTO THE DETAILS...ESPECIALLY NOT WITH SOMEONE SO NASTY.

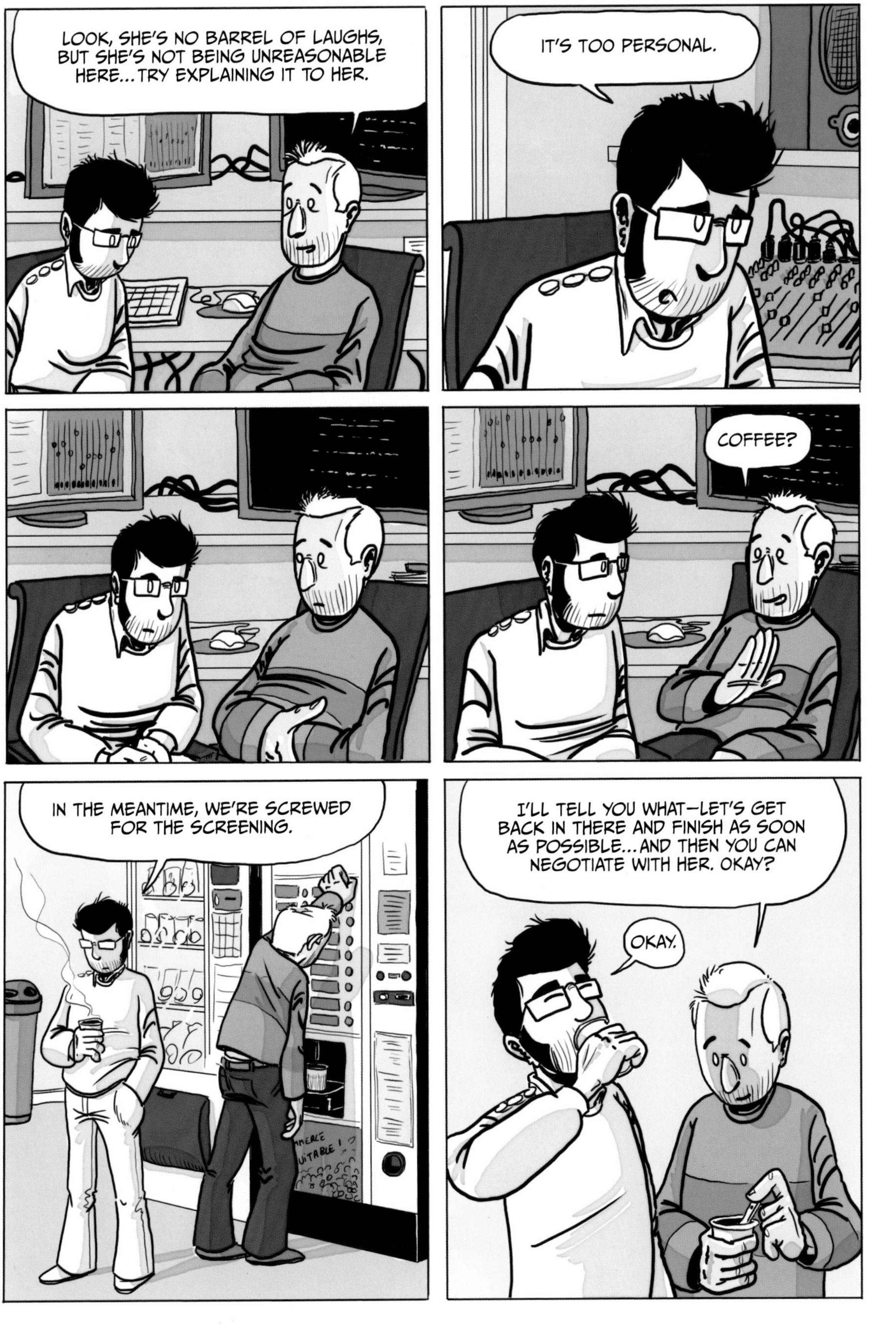
LOOK, SHE'S NO BARREL OF LAUGHS, BUT SHE'S NOT BEING UNREASONABLE HERE...TRY EXPLAINING IT TO HER.
IT'S TOO PERSONAL.
COFFEE?
IN THE MEANTIME, WE'RE SCREWED FOR THE SCREENING.
I'LL TELL YOU WHAT—LET'S GET BACK IN THERE AND FINISH AS SOON AS POSSIBLE...AND THEN YOU CAN NEGOTIATE WITH HER. OKAY?
OKAY.

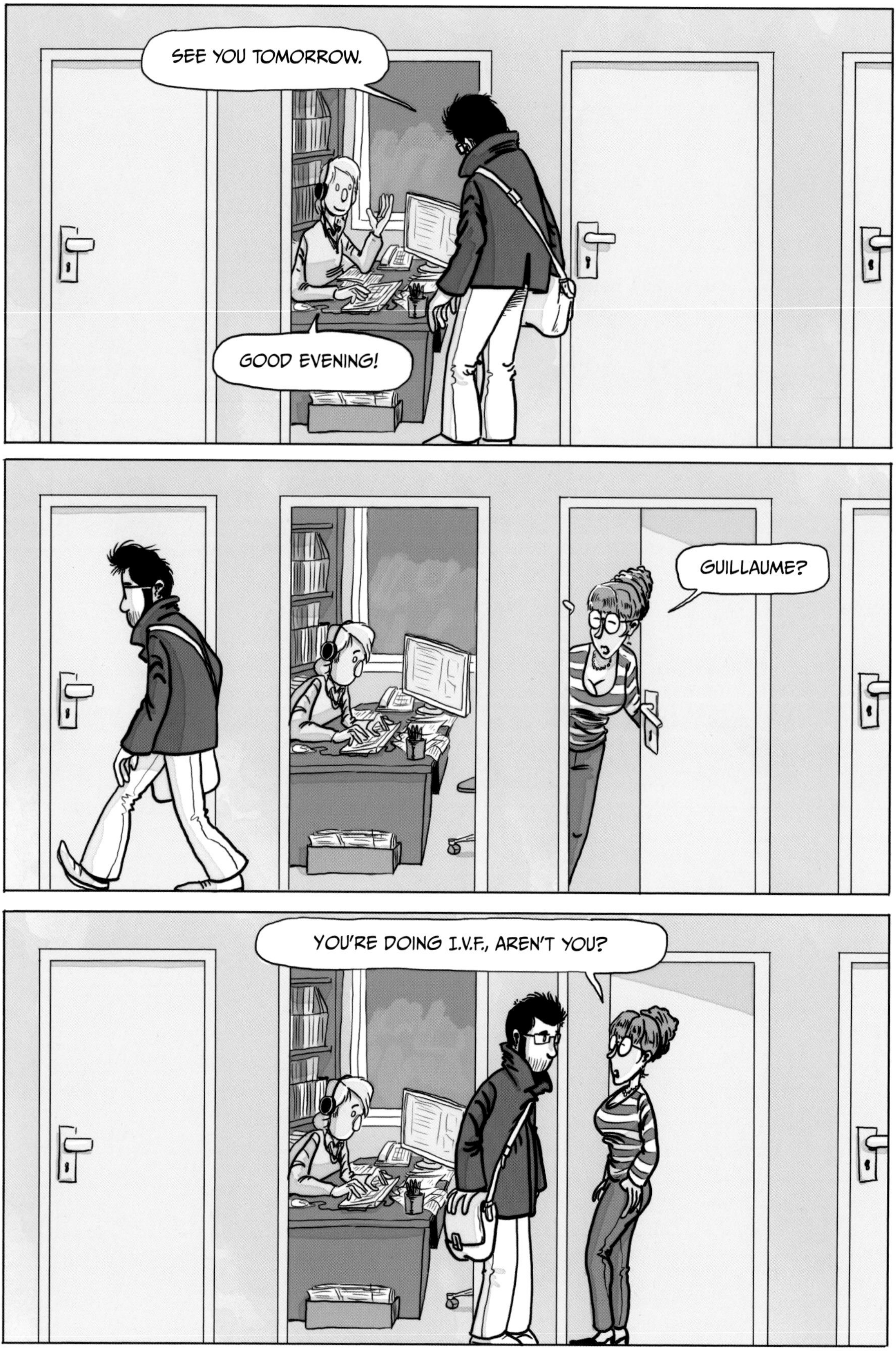
SEE YOU TOMORROW.
GOOD EVENING!
GUILLAUME?
YOU'RE DOING I.V.F., AREN'T YOU?

I TRIED THREE TIMES BEFORE IT WORKED.
CONCERT CHEVEU
LUNCH MENU 12€
APPETIZERS
- GOATS CHEESE + PARMA HAM SALAD
- SOUP OF THE DAY
- SALMON TARTAR
- HOUSE TARTAR
WHAT'S WRONG WITH YOUR WIFE?
ACTUALLY, *I'M* THE ONE WITH THE PROBLEM.
OH... WHAT IS IT?
SORRY, THAT'S INTRUSIVE.
IT'S HARD FOR ME TO LIVE WITH THE FACT THAT, ALTHOUGH I'M THE ONE WITH THE PROBLEM, ***SHE*** HAS TO DEAL WITH ALL THE MEDICAL STUFF IN ORDER TO HAVE A CHILD.

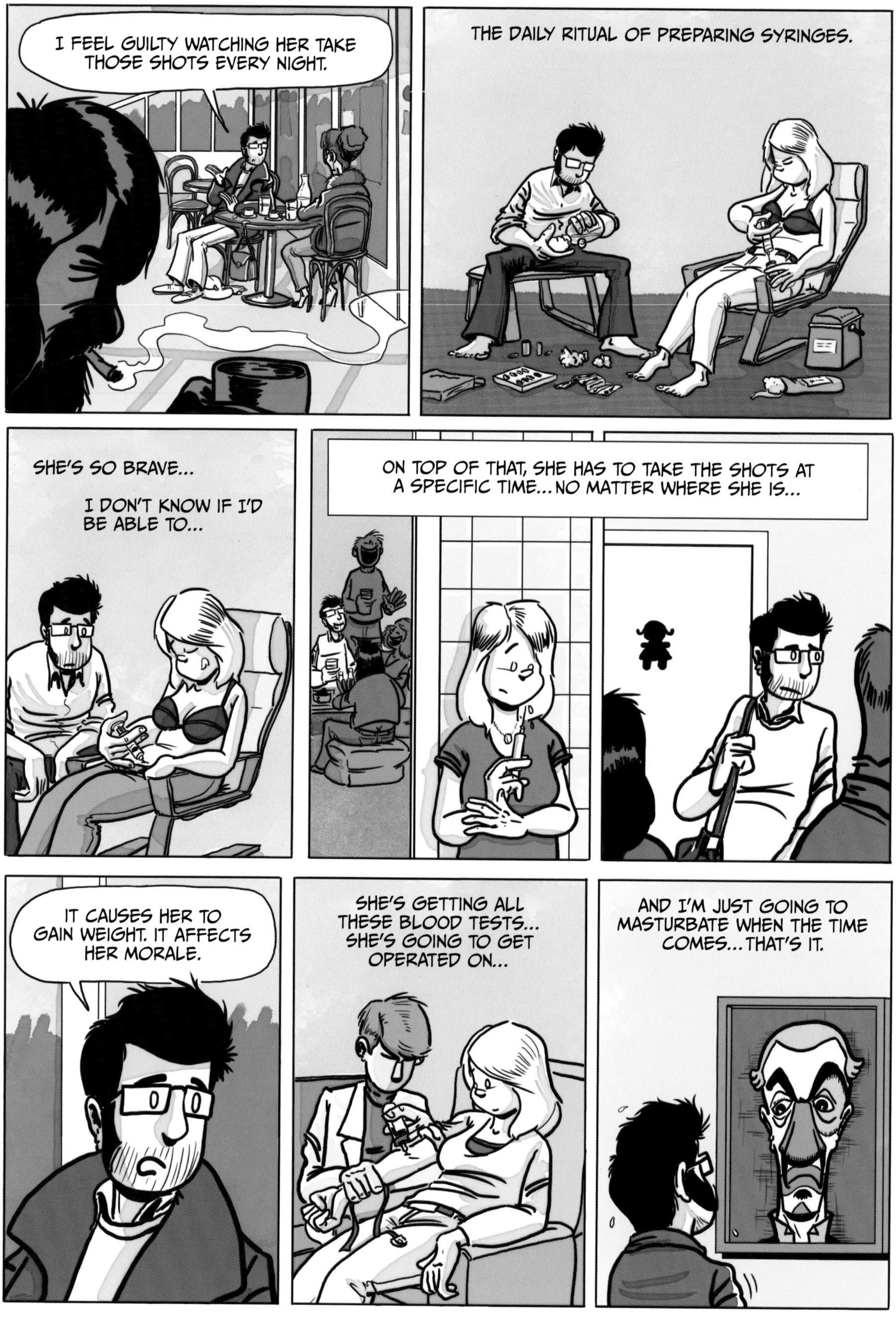
I FEEL GUILTY WATCHING HER TAKE THOSE SHOTS EVERY NIGHT.
THE DAILY RITUAL OF PREPARING SYRINGES.
SHE'S SO BRAVE...
I DON'T KNOW IF I'D BE ABLE TO...
ON TOP OF THAT, SHE HAS TO TAKE THE SHOTS AT A SPECIFIC TIME... NO MATTER WHERE SHE IS...
IT CAUSES HER TO GAIN WEIGHT. IT AFFECTS HER MORALE.
SHE'S GETTING ALL THESE BLOOD TESTS... SHE'S GOING TO GET OPERATED ON...
AND I'M JUST GOING TO MASTURBATE WHEN THE TIME COMES... THAT'S IT.

SOMETIMES I THINK SHE'D BE RIGHT TO LEAVE ME... TO FIND SOMEONE ELSE.

I.V.F. IS THE ULTIMATE TEST FOR A COUPLE...

THIS ICY, CLINICAL PROCESS INTRUDES ON YOUR INTIMACY.

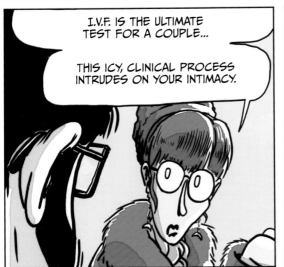

BUT ONCE ALL THIS IS OVER, YOU'LL SEE THAT IT WAS REALLY WORTH IT.

AS SOON AS YOU SET THE DATE, YOU TELL ME. I'LL WORK IT OUT WITH THE NETWORK, OKAY?

YOUR FATHER'S HERE, GUILLAUME. HE'S IN YOUR ROOM.

WE LOOKED ALL OVER FOR YOU.

AND SLOW DOWN!

HI, DEAR.

OH, ITS YOU...THE NURSE CONFUSED BERNARD WITH DAD.

DIDN'T HE COME BY LAST NIGHT?

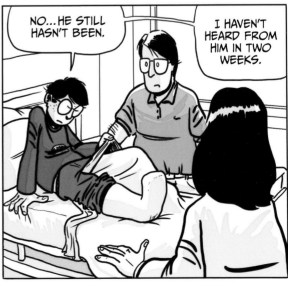

NO...HE STILL HASN'T BEEN.

I HAVEN'T HEARD FROM HIM IN TWO WEEKS.

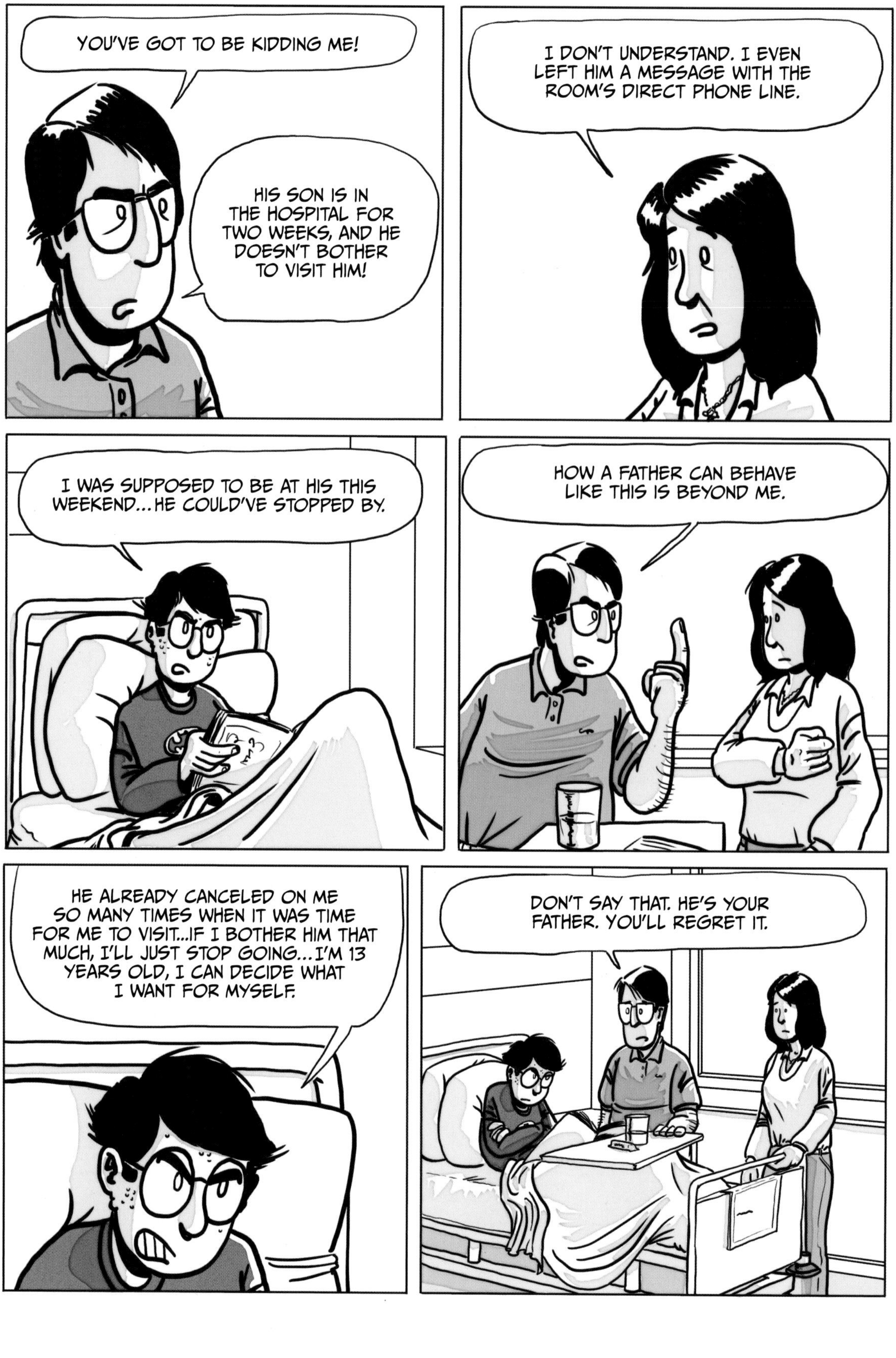
YOU'VE GOT TO BE KIDDING ME!
HIS SON IS IN THE HOSPITAL FOR TWO WEEKS, AND HE DOESN'T BOTHER TO VISIT HIM!
I DON'T UNDERSTAND. I EVEN LEFT HIM A MESSAGE WITH THE ROOM'S DIRECT PHONE LINE.
I WAS SUPPOSED TO BE AT HIS THIS WEEKEND... HE COULD'VE STOPPED BY.
HOW A FATHER CAN BEHAVE LIKE THIS IS BEYOND ME.
HE ALREADY CANCELED ON ME SO MANY TIMES WHEN IT WAS TIME FOR ME TO VISIT...IF I BOTHER HIM THAT MUCH, I'LL JUST STOP GOING... I'M 13 YEARS OLD, I CAN DECIDE WHAT I WANT FOR MYSELF.
DON'T SAY THAT. HE'S YOUR FATHER. YOU'LL REGRET IT.

HE MUST HAVE A GOOD REASON...

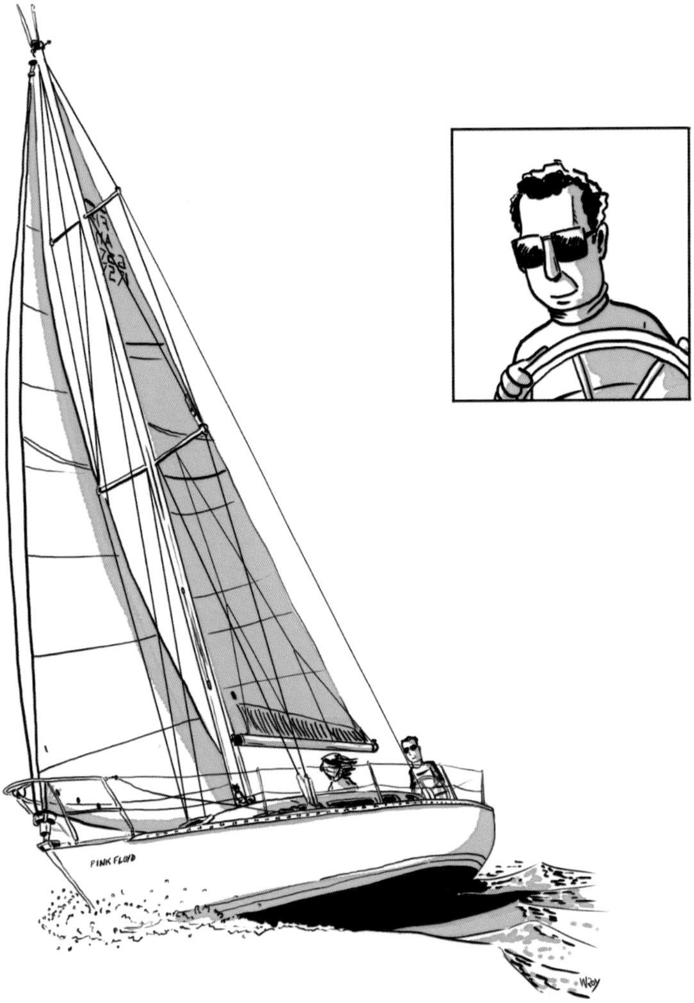
PINK FLOYD

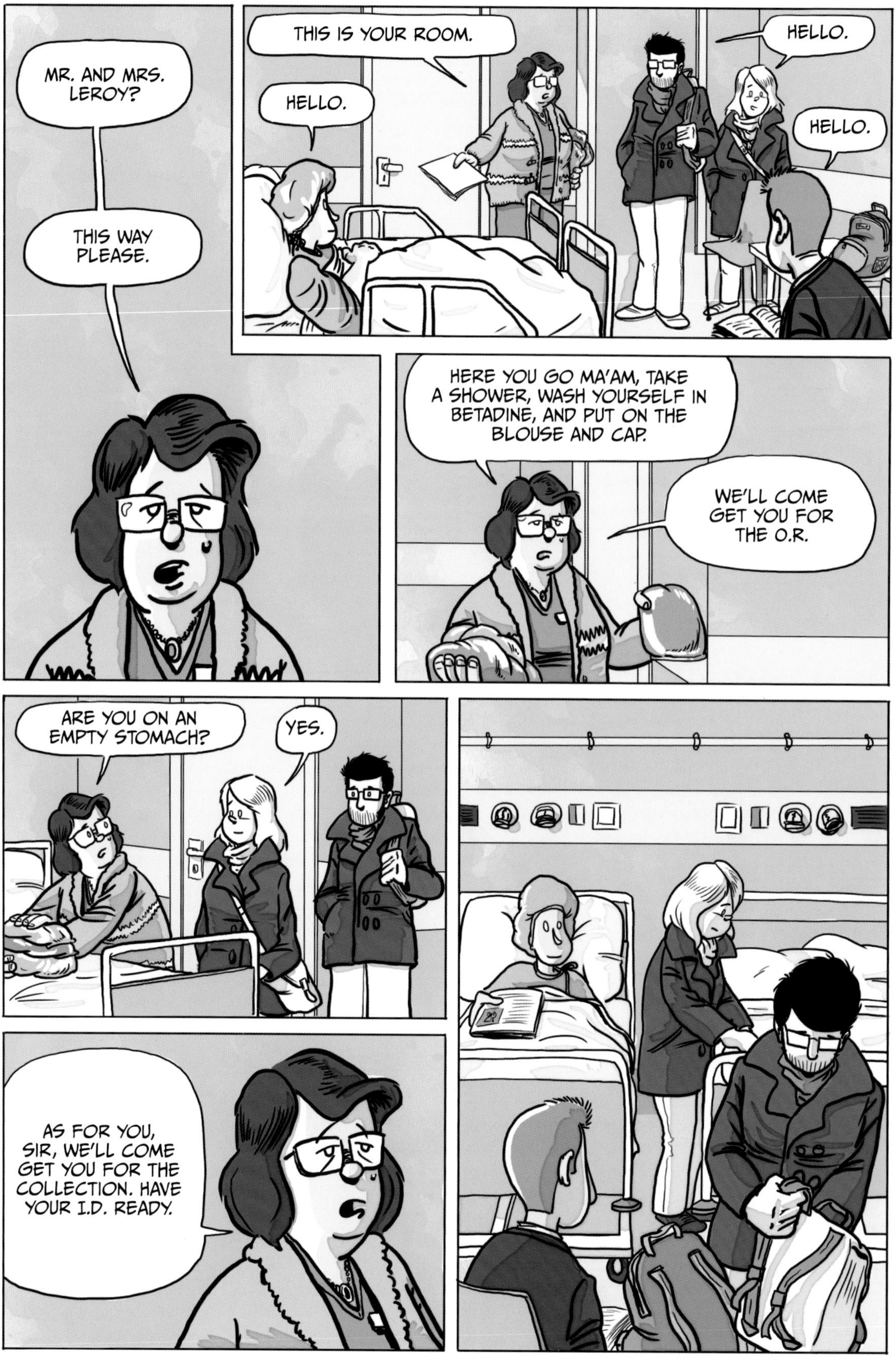
MR. AND MRS. LEROY?
THIS WAY PLEASE.
THIS IS YOUR ROOM.
HELLO.
HELLO.
HELLO.
HERE YOU GO MA'AM, TAKE A SHOWER, WASH YOURSELF IN BETADINE, AND PUT ON THE BLOUSE AND CAP.
WE'LL COME GET YOU FOR THE O.R.
ARE YOU ON AN EMPTY STOMACH?
YES.
AS FOR YOU, SIR, WE'LL COME GET YOU FOR THE COLLECTION. HAVE YOUR I.D. READY.

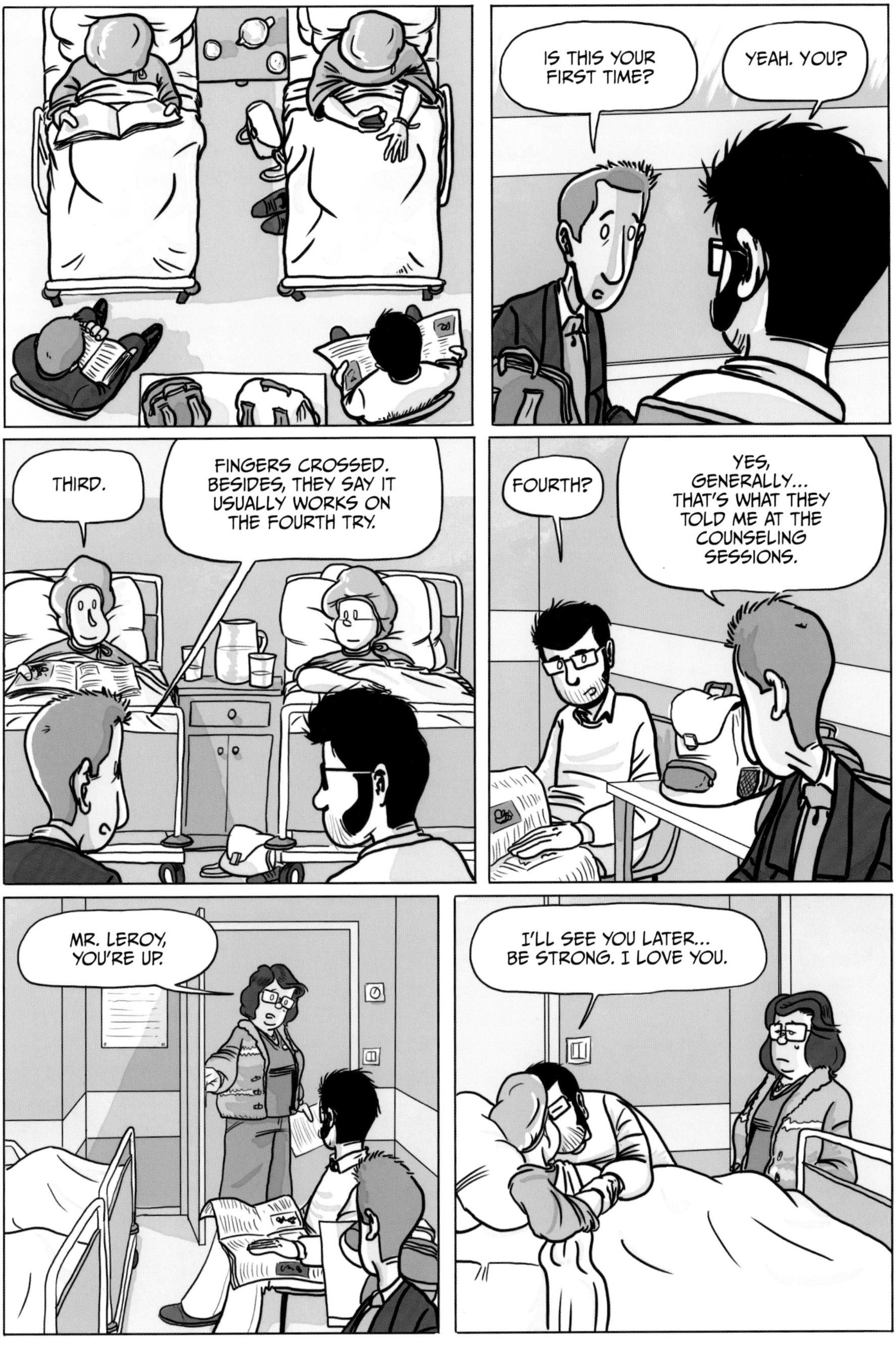
IS THIS YOUR FIRST TIME?
YEAH. YOU?
THIRD.
FINGERS CROSSED. BESIDES, THEY SAY IT USUALLY WORKS ON THE FOURTH TRY.
FOURTH?
YES, GENERALLY... THAT'S WHAT THEY TOLD ME AT THE COUNSELING SESSIONS.
MR. LEROY, YOU'RE UP.
I'LL SEE YOU LATER... BE STRONG. I LOVE YOU.

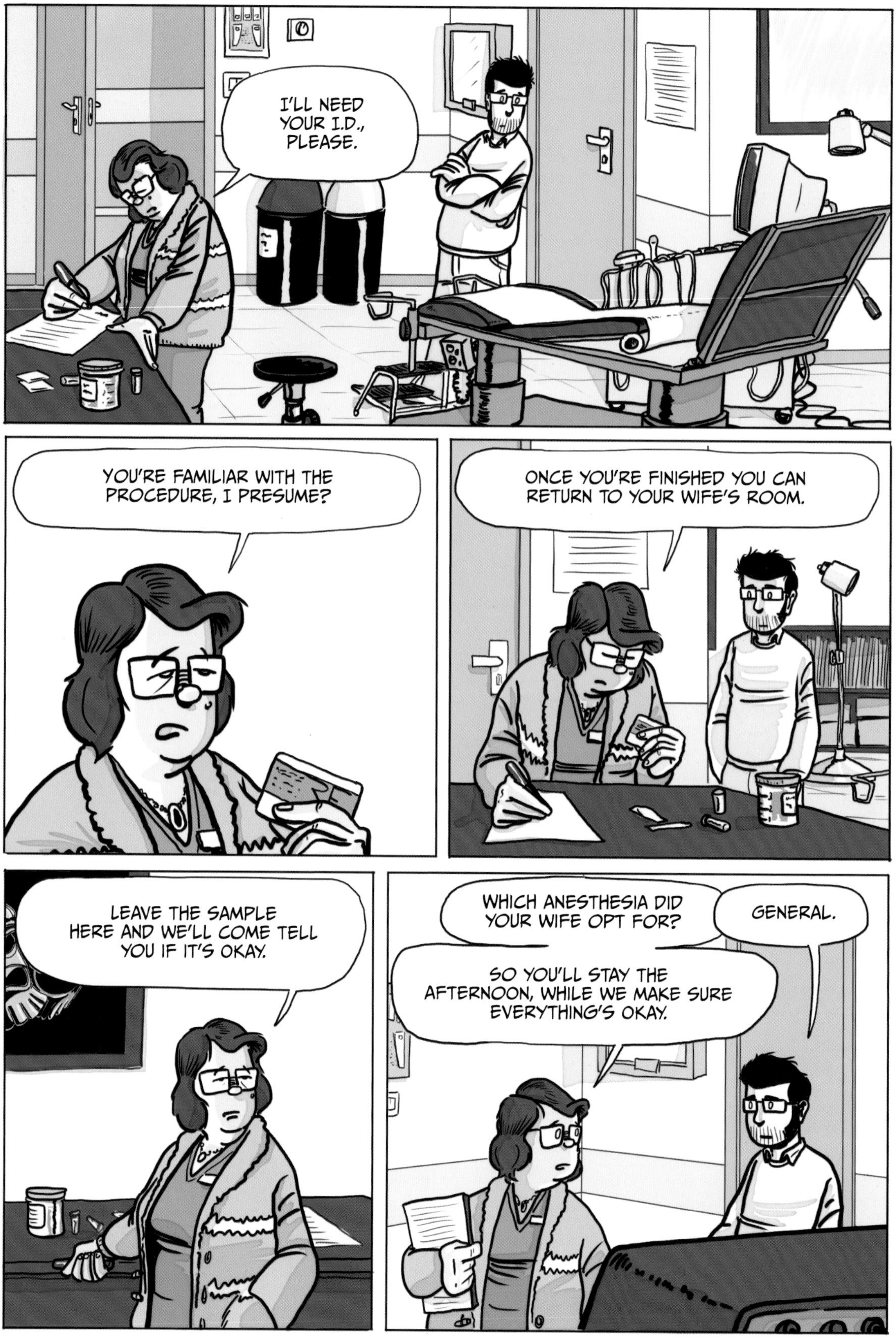
I'LL NEED YOUR I.D., PLEASE.
YOU'RE FAMILIAR WITH THE PROCEDURE, I PRESUME?
ONCE YOU'RE FINISHED YOU CAN RETURN TO YOUR WIFE'S ROOM.
LEAVE THE SAMPLE HERE AND WE'LL COME TELL YOU IF IT'S OKAY.
WHICH ANESTHESIA DID YOUR WIFE OPT FOR?
GENERAL.
SO YOU'LL STAY THE AFTERNOON, WHILE WE MAKE SURE EVERYTHING'S OKAY.

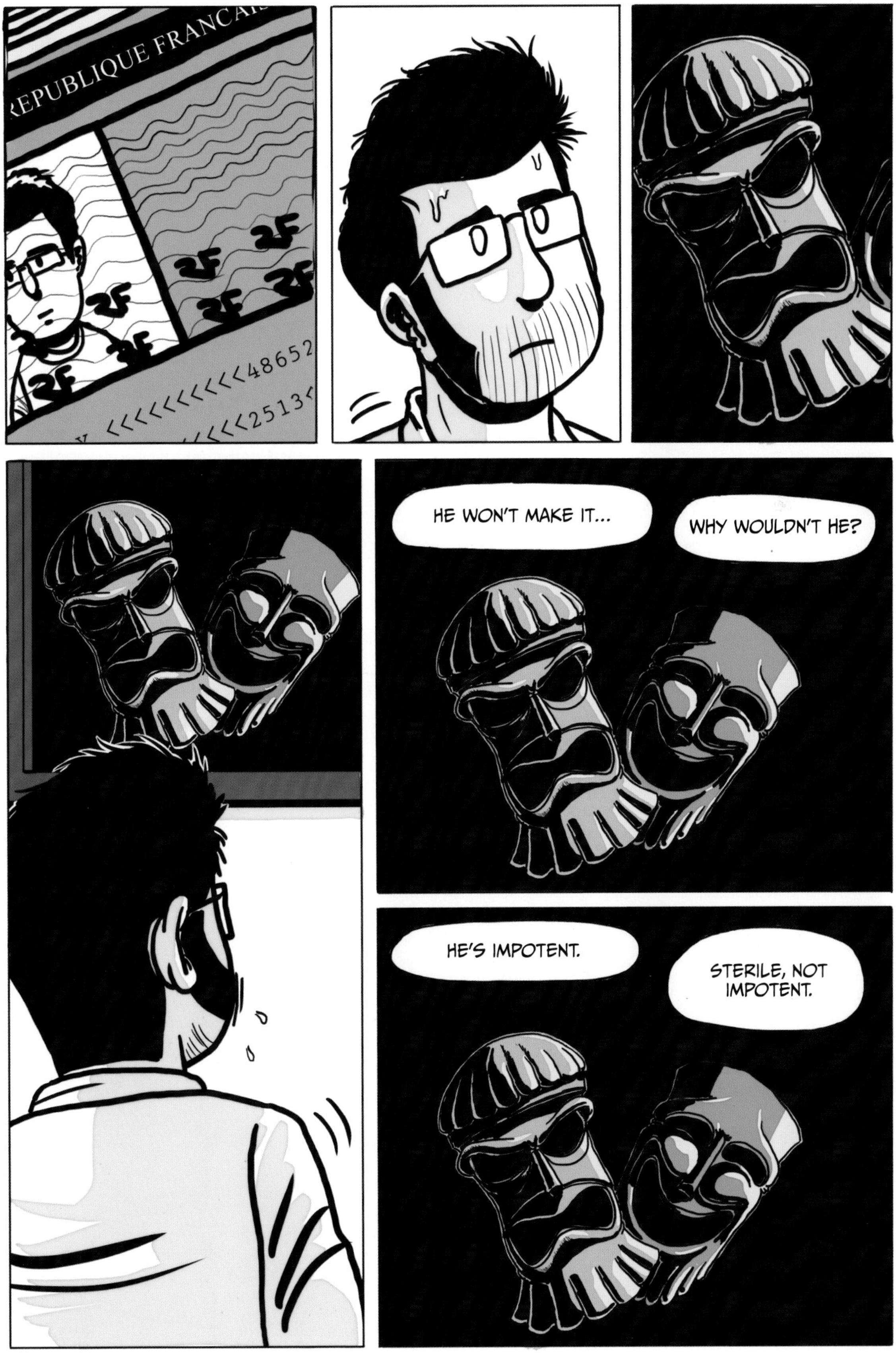
HE WON'T MAKE IT...
WHY WOULDN'T HE?
HE'S IMPOTENT.
STERILE, NOT IMPOTENT.

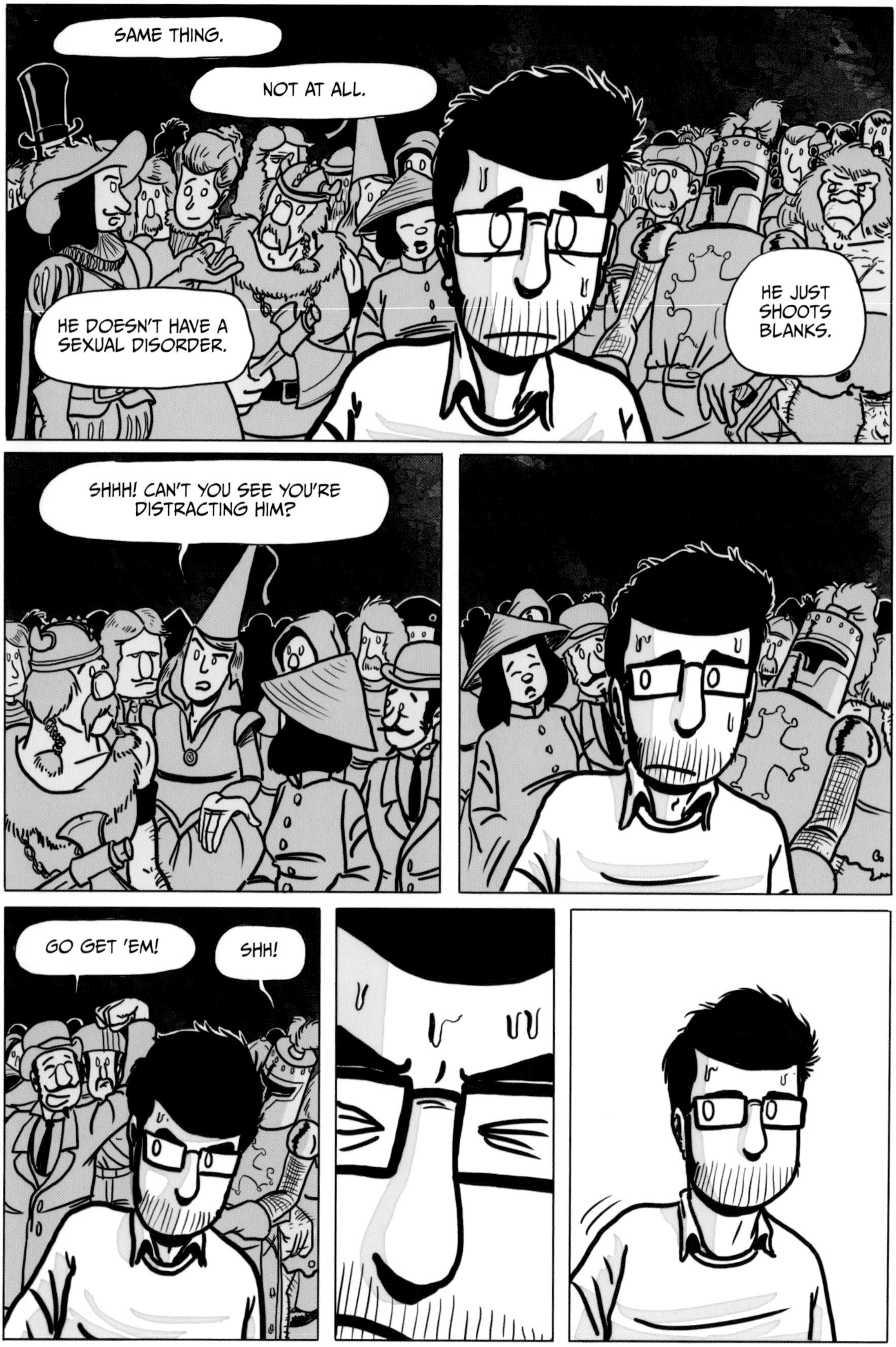
SAME THING.
NOT AT ALL.
HE DOESN'T HAVE A SEXUAL DISORDER.
HE JUST SHOOTS BLANKS.
SHHH! CAN'T YOU SEE YOU'RE DISTRACTING HIM?
GO GET 'EM!
SHH!

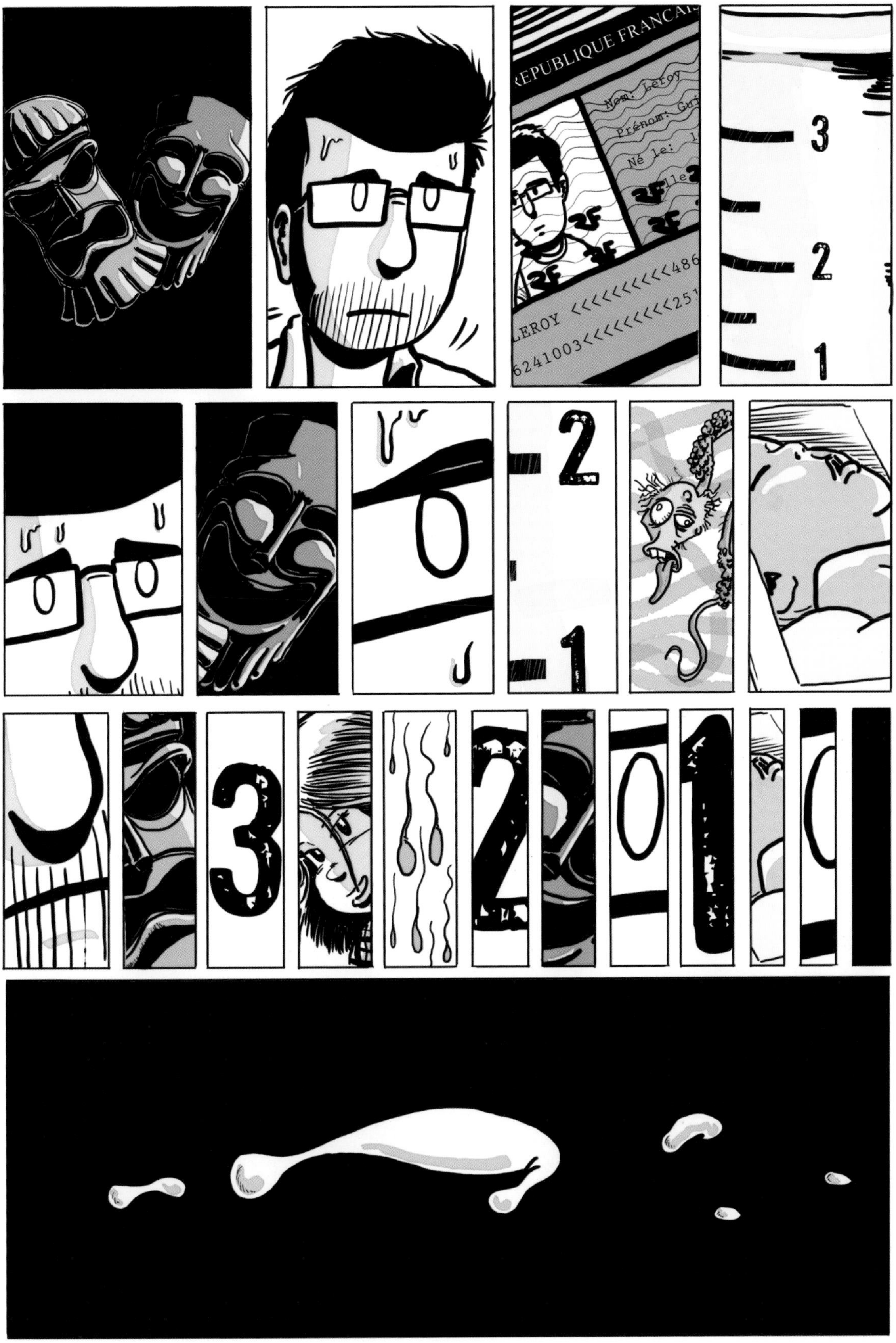

Nom: Leroy
Prénom:
Né le:
LEROY

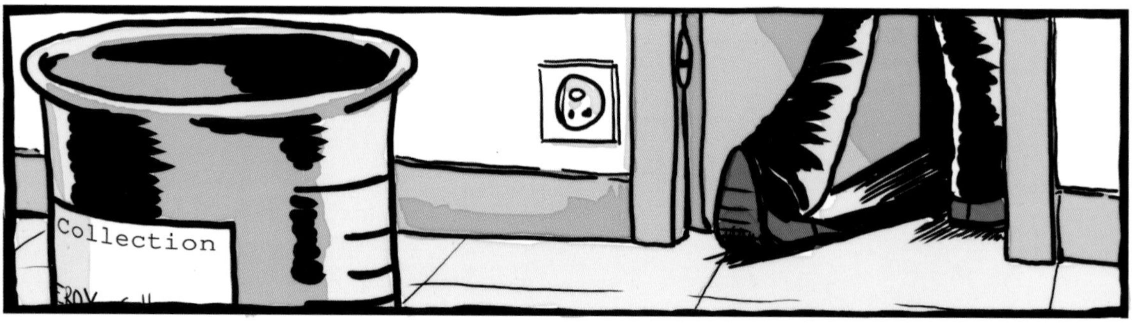
Collection

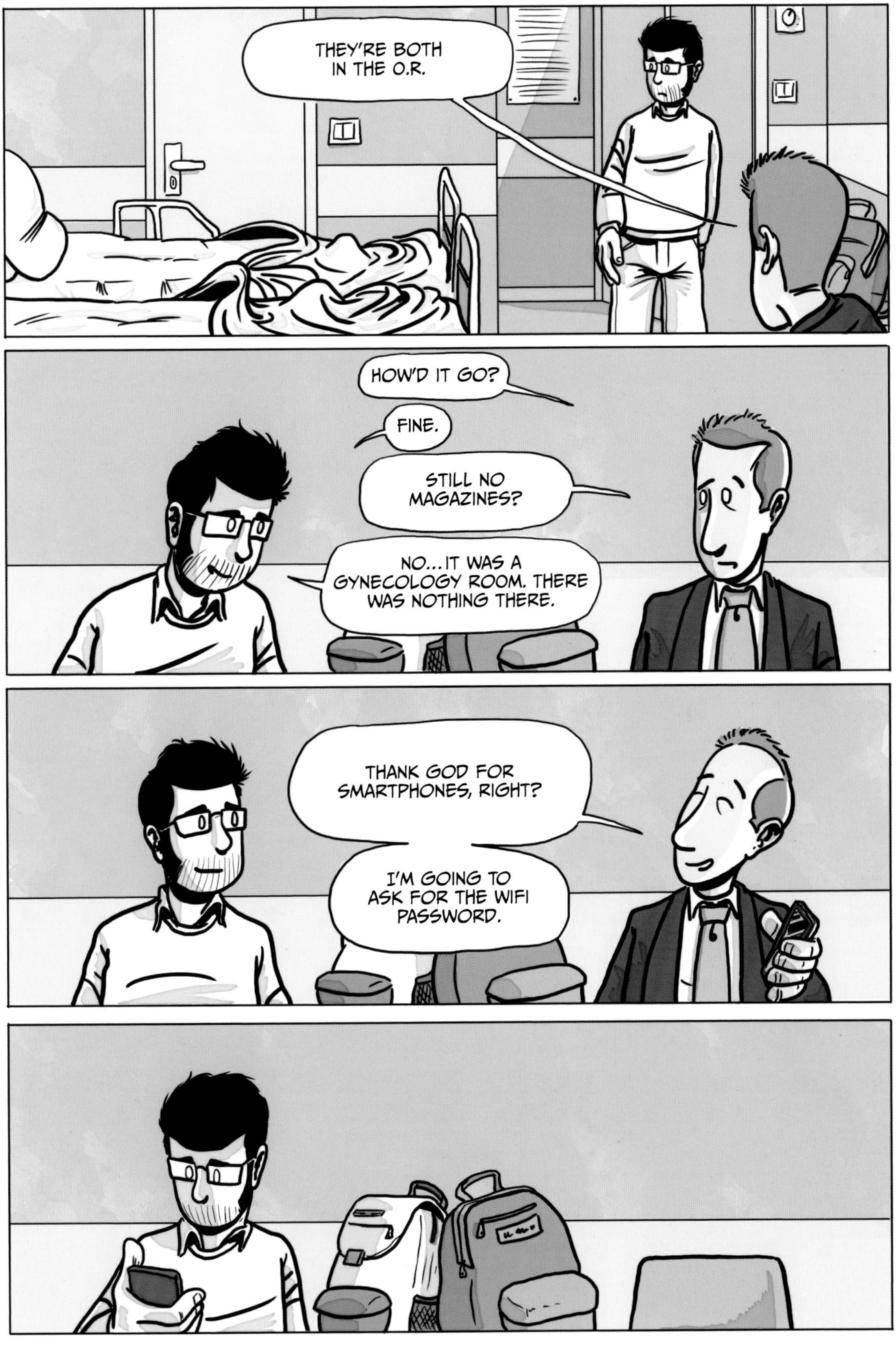
THEY'RE BOTH IN THE O.R.
HOW'D IT GO?
FINE.
STILL NO MAGAZINES?
NO... IT WAS A GYNECOLOGY ROOM. THERE WAS NOTHING THERE.
THANK GOD FOR SMARTPHONES, RIGHT?
I'M GOING TO ASK FOR THE WIFI PASSWORD.

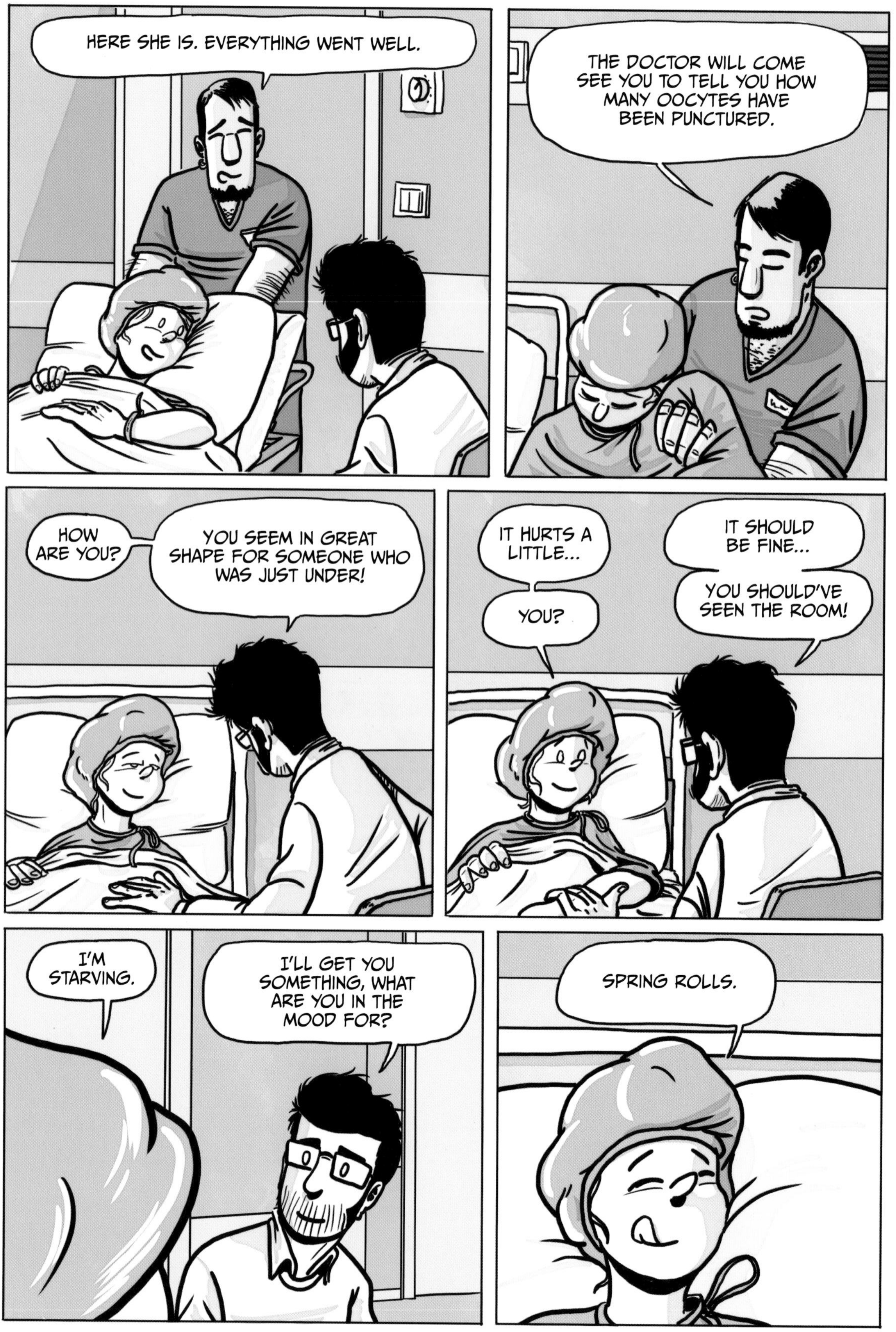
HERE SHE IS. EVERYTHING WENT WELL.
THE DOCTOR WILL COME SEE YOU TO TELL YOU HOW MANY OOCYTES HAVE BEEN PUNCTURED.
HOW ARE YOU?
YOU SEEM IN GREAT SHAPE FOR SOMEONE WHO WAS JUST UNDER!
IT HURTS A LITTLE...
YOU?
IT SHOULD BE FINE...
YOU SHOULD'VE SEEN THE ROOM!
I'M STARVING.
I'LL GET YOU SOMETHING, WHAT ARE YOU IN THE MOOD FOR?
SPRING ROLLS.

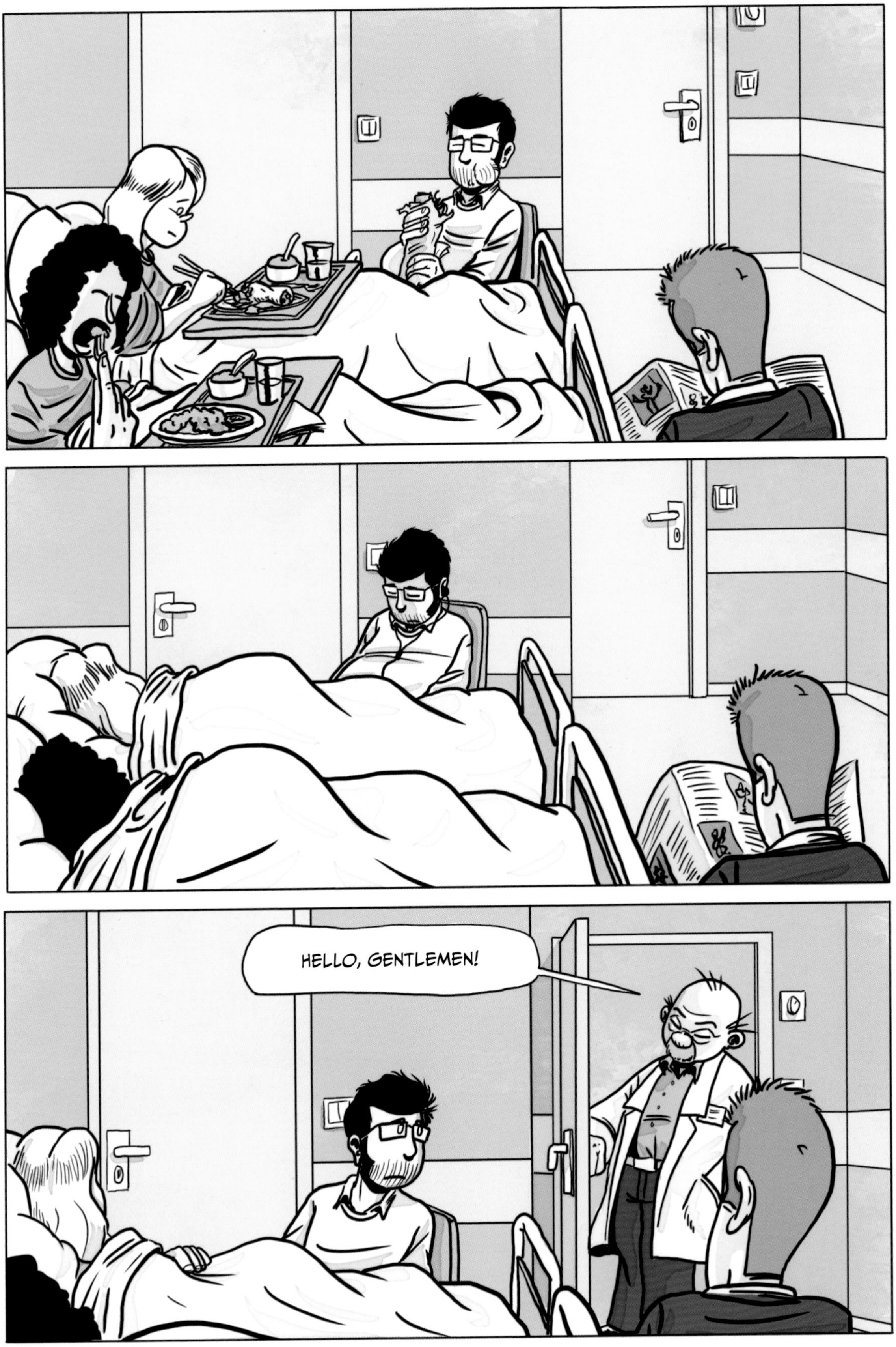
HELLO, GENTLEMEN!

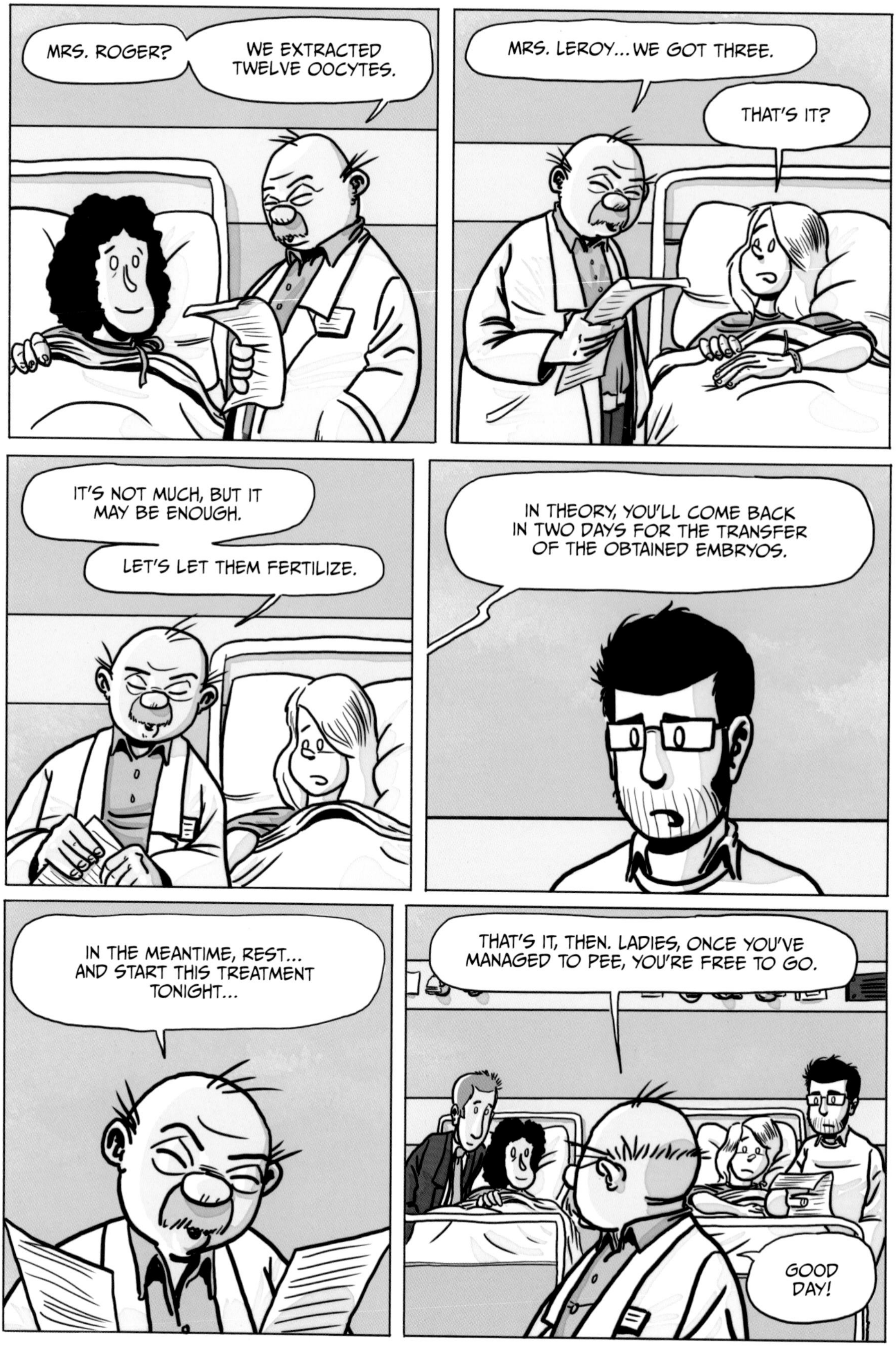
MRS. ROGER?
WE EXTRACTED TWELVE OOCYTES.
MRS. LEROY... WE GOT THREE.
THAT'S IT?
IT'S NOT MUCH, BUT IT MAY BE ENOUGH.
LET'S LET THEM FERTILIZE.
IN THEORY, YOU'LL COME BACK IN TWO DAYS FOR THE TRANSFER OF THE OBTAINED EMBRYOS.
IN THE MEANTIME, REST... AND START THIS TREATMENT TONIGHT...
THAT'S IT, THEN. LADIES, ONCE YOU'VE MANAGED TO PEE, YOU'RE FREE TO GO.
GOOD DAY!

"HELLO, MRS. LEROY?"

"YES?"

"WE PRODUCED AN EMBRYO. IT'S NOT PERFECT, BUT WE MADE THE DECISION TO TRANSFER IT TO YOU TOMORROW MORNING AT 10 AM."

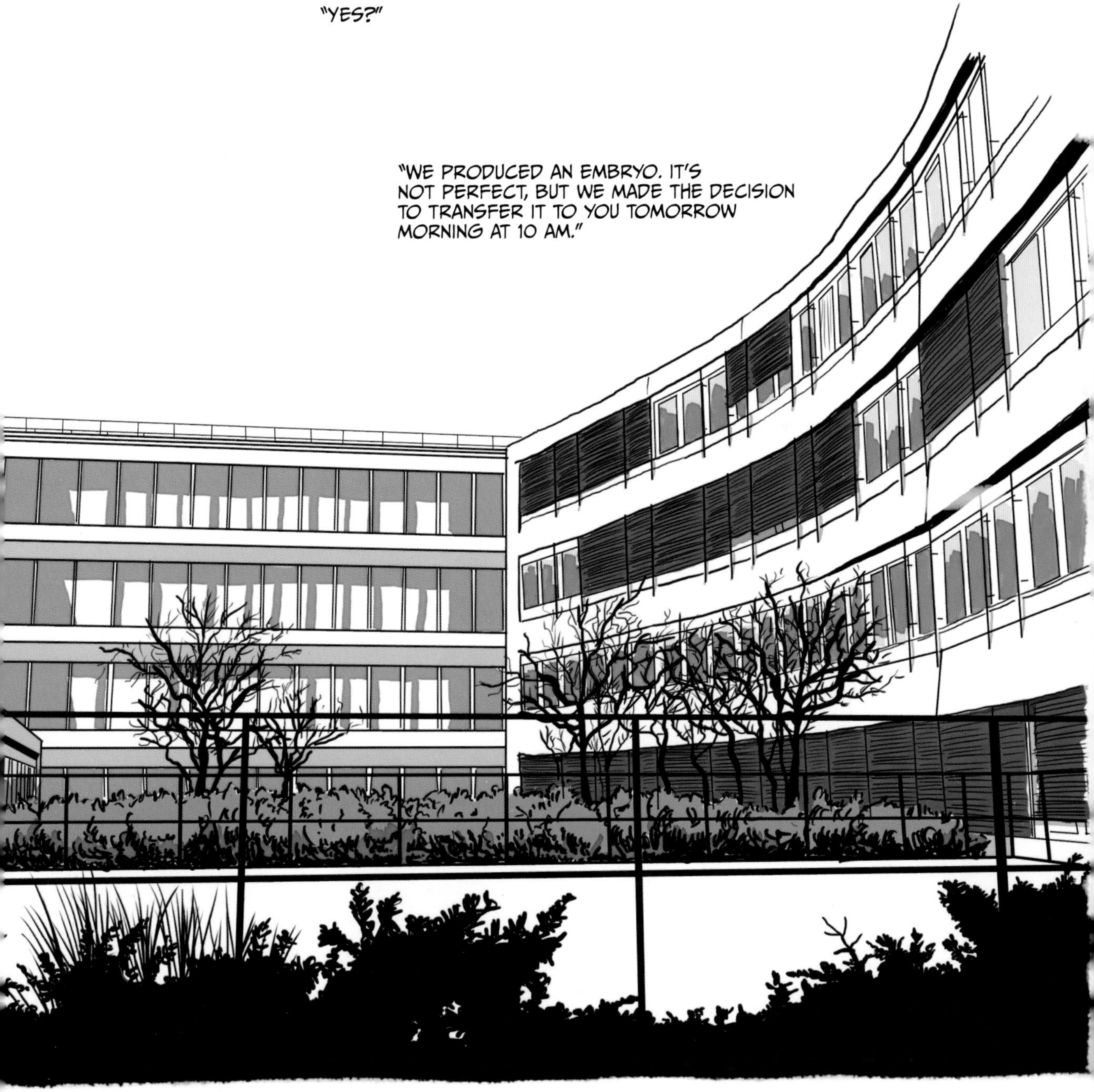

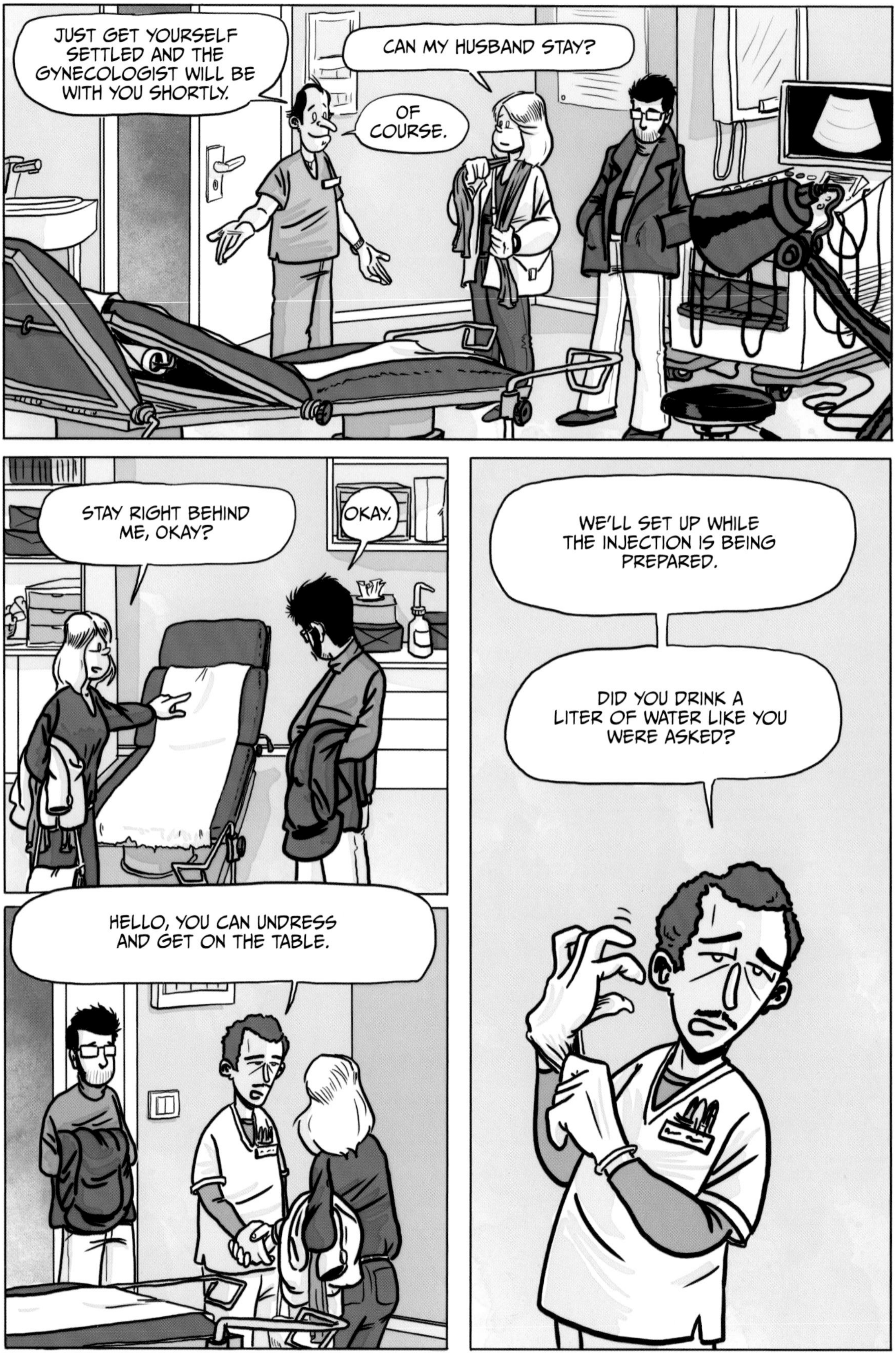
JUST GET YOURSELF SETTLED AND THE GYNECOLOGIST WILL BE WITH YOU SHORTLY.
CAN MY HUSBAND STAY?
OF COURSE.
STAY RIGHT BEHIND ME, OKAY?
OKAY.
HELLO, YOU CAN UNDRESS AND GET ON THE TABLE.
WE'LL SET UP WHILE THE INJECTION IS BEING PREPARED.
DID YOU DRINK A LITER OF WATER LIKE YOU WERE ASKED?

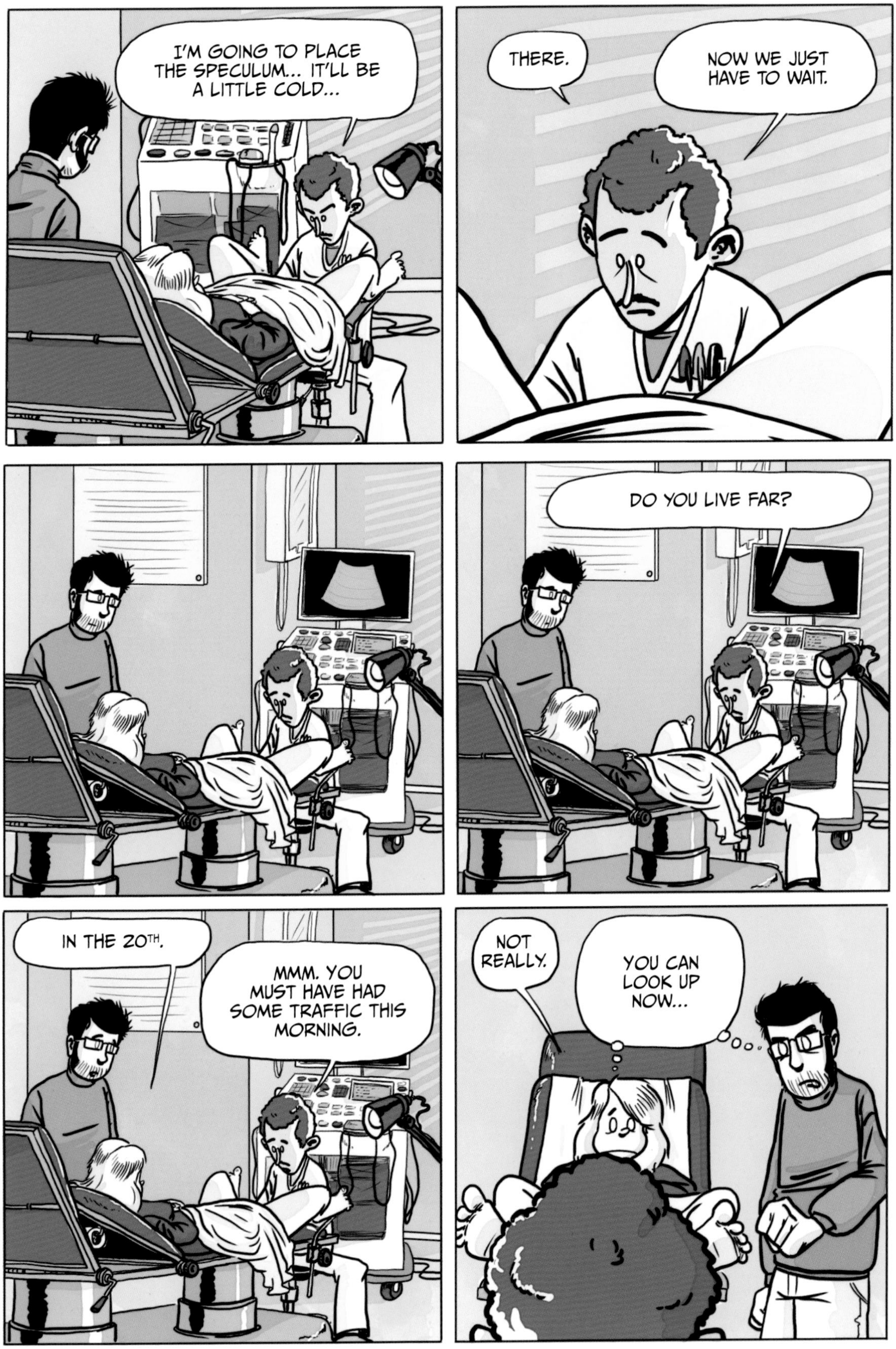
I'M GOING TO PLACE THE SPECULUM... IT'LL BE A LITTLE COLD...
THERE.
NOW WE JUST HAVE TO WAIT.
DO YOU LIVE FAR?
IN THE 20TH.
MMM. YOU MUST HAVE HAD SOME TRAFFIC THIS MORNING.
NOT REALLY.
YOU CAN LOOK UP NOW...

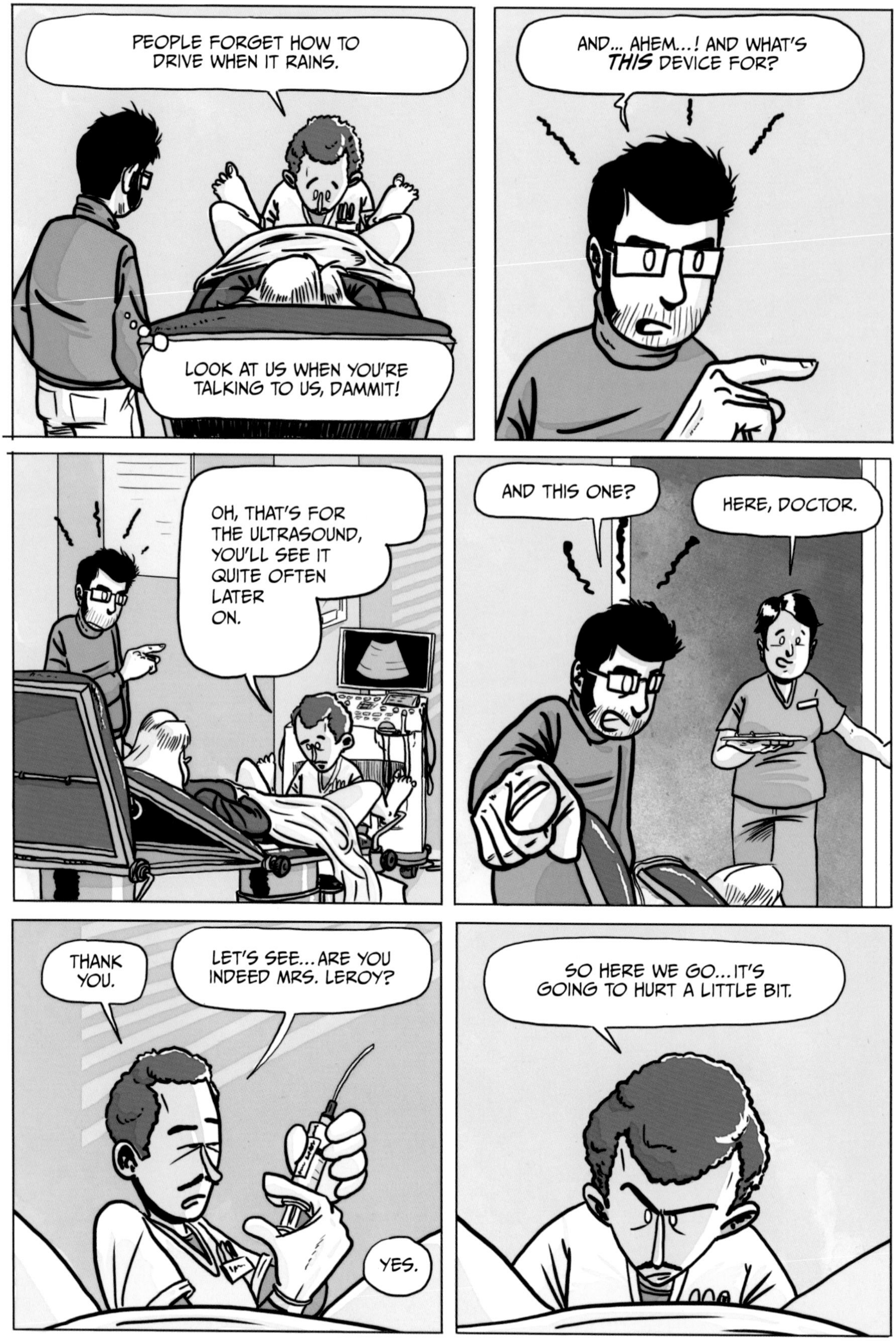
PEOPLE FORGET HOW TO DRIVE WHEN IT RAINS.
LOOK AT US WHEN YOU'RE TALKING TO US, DAMMIT!
AND... AHEM...! AND WHAT'S *THIS* DEVICE FOR?
OH, THAT'S FOR THE ULTRASOUND, YOU'LL SEE IT QUITE OFTEN LATER ON.
AND THIS ONE?
HERE, DOCTOR.
THANK YOU.
LET'S SEE... ARE YOU INDEED MRS. LEROY?
YES.
SO HERE WE GO... IT'S GOING TO HURT A LITTLE BIT.

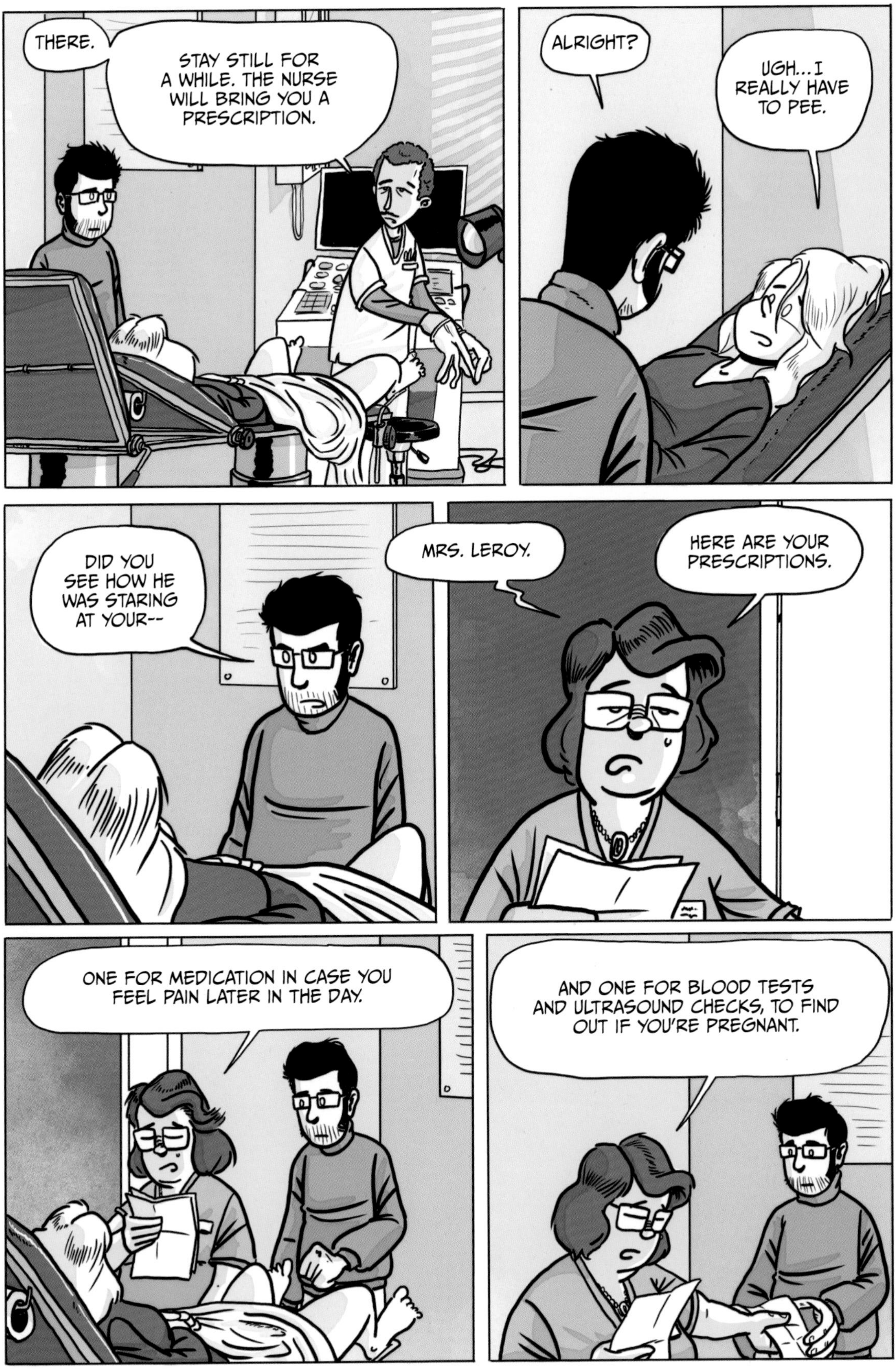
THERE.
STAY STILL FOR A WHILE. THE NURSE WILL BRING YOU A PRESCRIPTION.
ALRIGHT?
UGH... I REALLY HAVE TO PEE.
DID YOU SEE HOW HE WAS STARING AT YOUR--
MRS. LEROY.
HERE ARE YOUR PRESCRIPTIONS.
ONE FOR MEDICATION IN CASE YOU FEEL PAIN LATER IN THE DAY.
AND ONE FOR BLOOD TESTS AND ULTRASOUND CHECKS, TO FIND OUT IF YOU'RE PREGNANT.

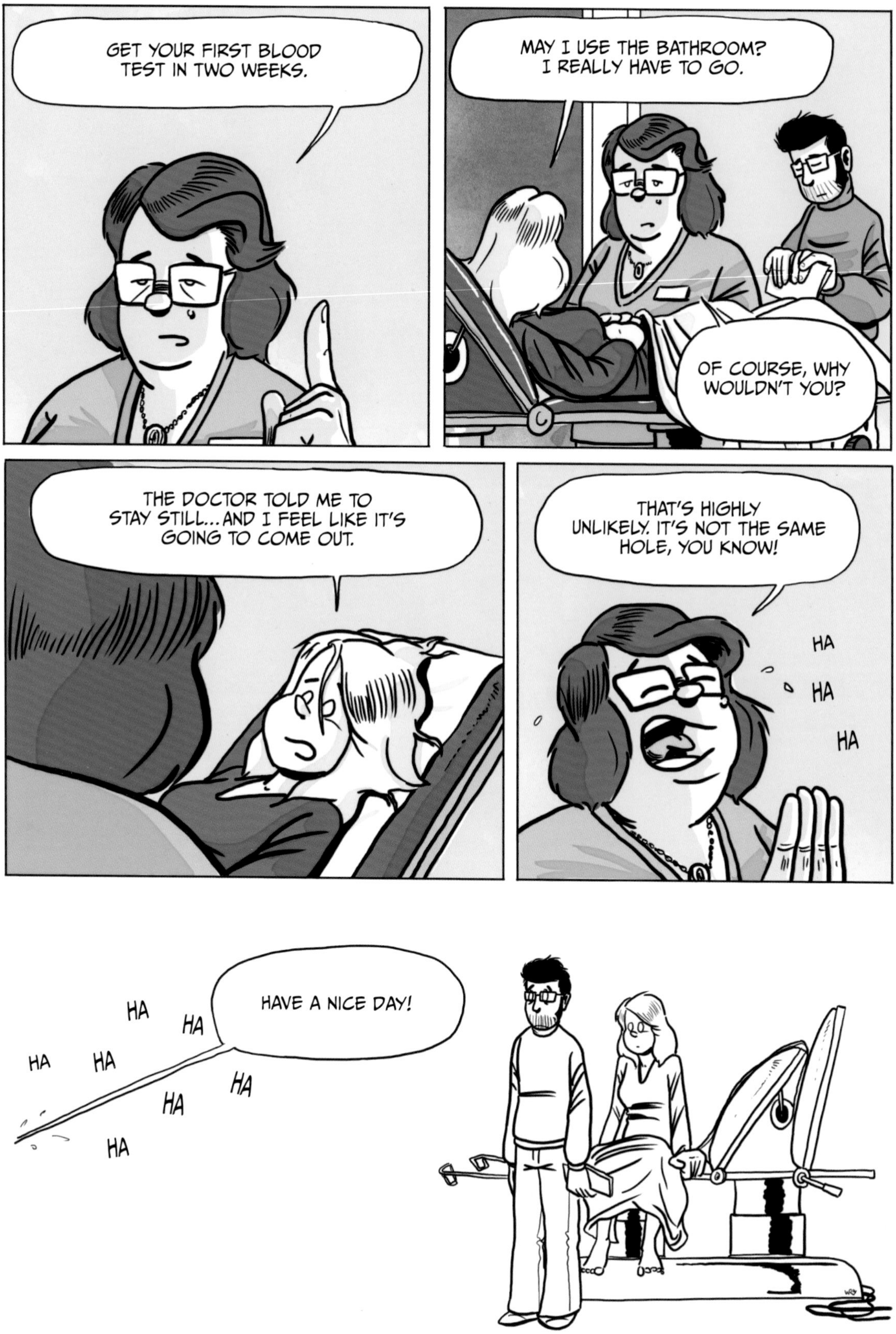
GET YOUR FIRST BLOOD TEST IN TWO WEEKS.
MAY I USE THE BATHROOM? I REALLY HAVE TO GO.
OF COURSE, WHY WOULDN'T YOU?
THE DOCTOR TOLD ME TO STAY STILL...AND I FEEL LIKE IT'S GOING TO COME OUT.
THAT'S HIGHLY UNLIKELY. IT'S NOT THE SAME HOLE, YOU KNOW!
HA
HA
HA
HA
HA
HA
HA
HA
HA
HA
HAVE A NICE DAY!

UGH... THERE'S NOTHING ON TV.

YOU WANNA GO FOR A WALK?

PING!

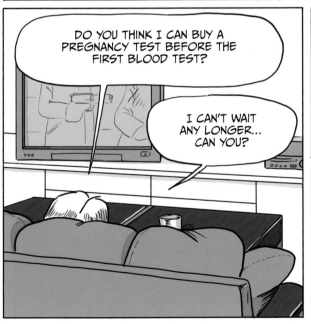

DO YOU THINK I CAN BUY A PREGNANCY TEST BEFORE THE FIRST BLOOD TEST?

I CAN'T WAIT ANY LONGER... CAN YOU?

GUILLAUME?

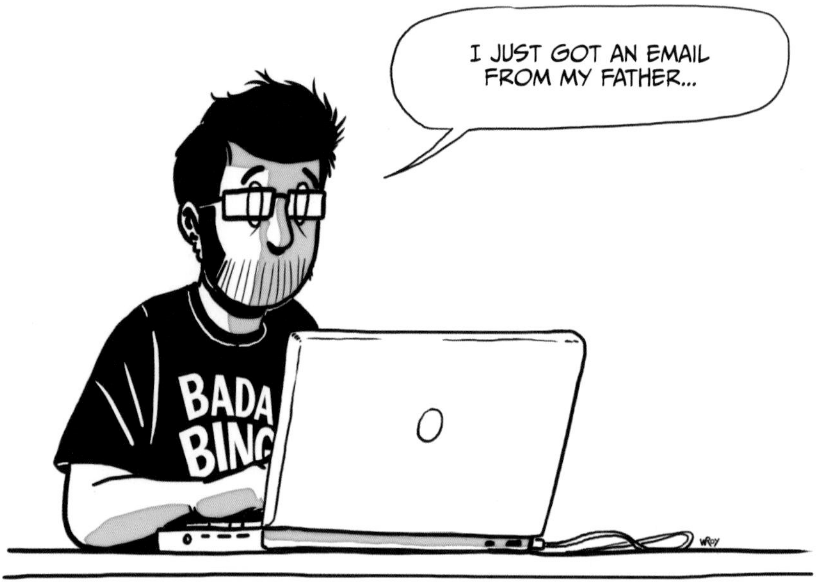
I JUST GOT AN EMAIL FROM MY FATHER...
BADA BING

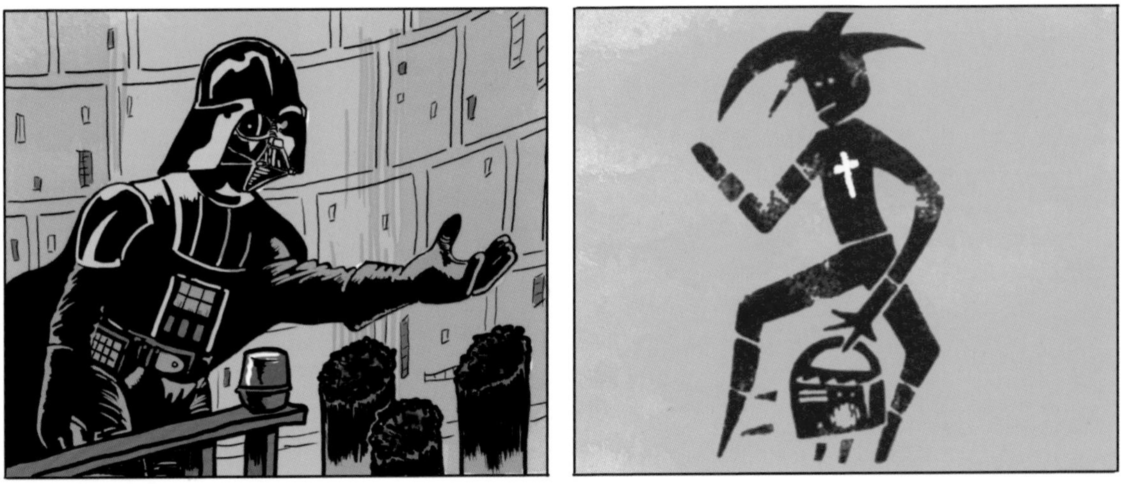

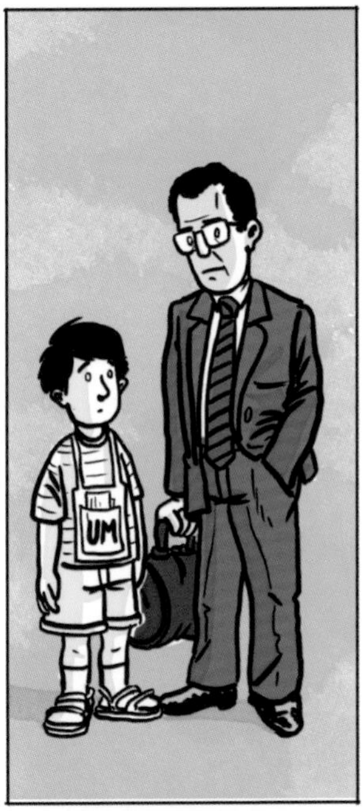
UM

2.
I.V.F.
ROULETTE

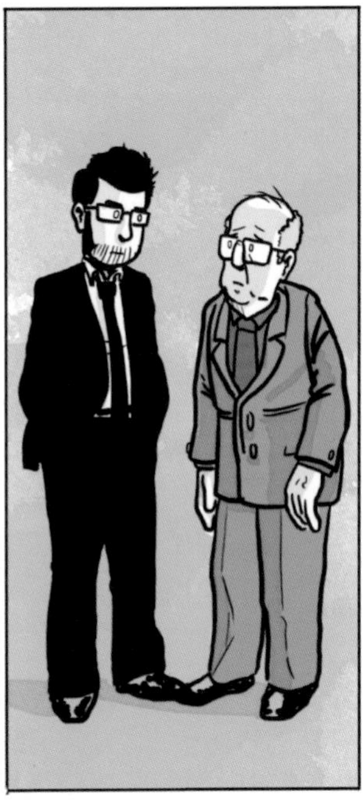

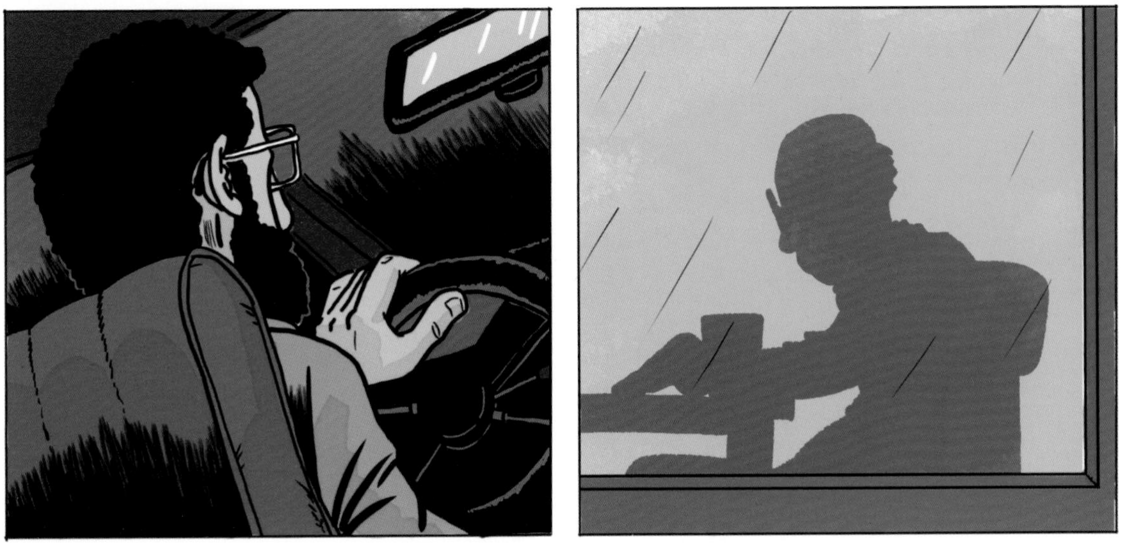

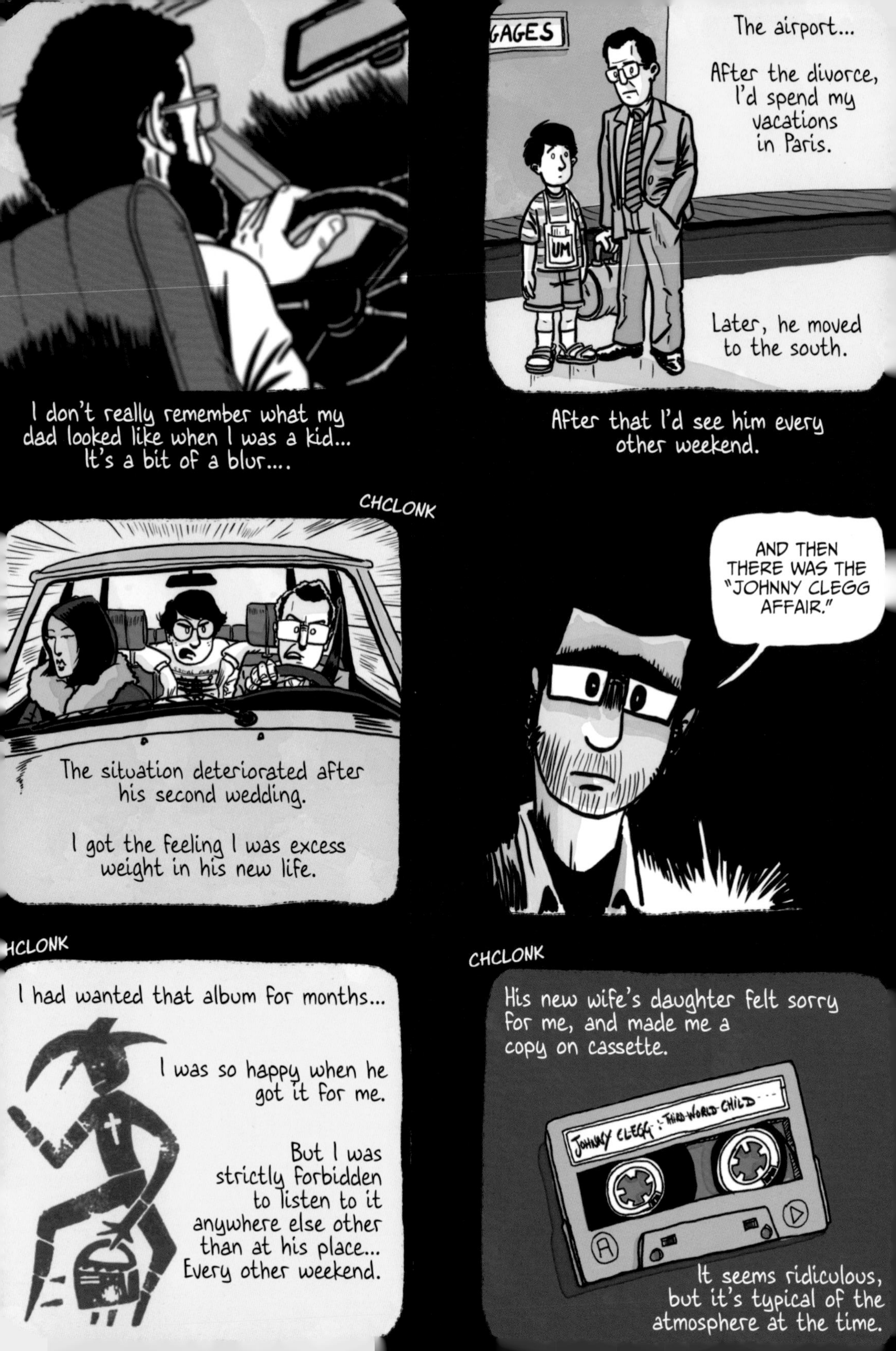

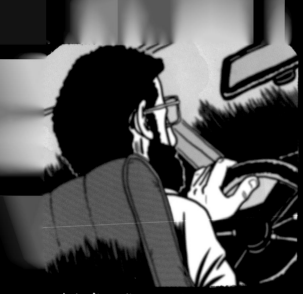

I don't really remember what my dad looked like when I was a kid... It's a bit of a blur....
GAGES
The airport...
After the divorce, I'd spend my vacations in Paris.
UM
Later, he moved to the south.
After that I'd see him every other weekend.
CHCLONK
The situation deteriorated after his second wedding.
I got the feeling I was excess weight in his new life.
AND THEN THERE WAS THE "JOHNNY CLEGG AFFAIR."
CHCLONK
I had wanted that album for months...
I was so happy when he got it for me.
But I was strictly forbidden to listen to it anywhere else other than at his place... Every other weekend.
CHCLONK
His new wife's daughter felt sorry for me, and made me a copy on cassette.
JOHNNY CLEGG - THIRD WORLD CHILD
A
It seems ridiculous, but it's typical of the atmosphere at the time.

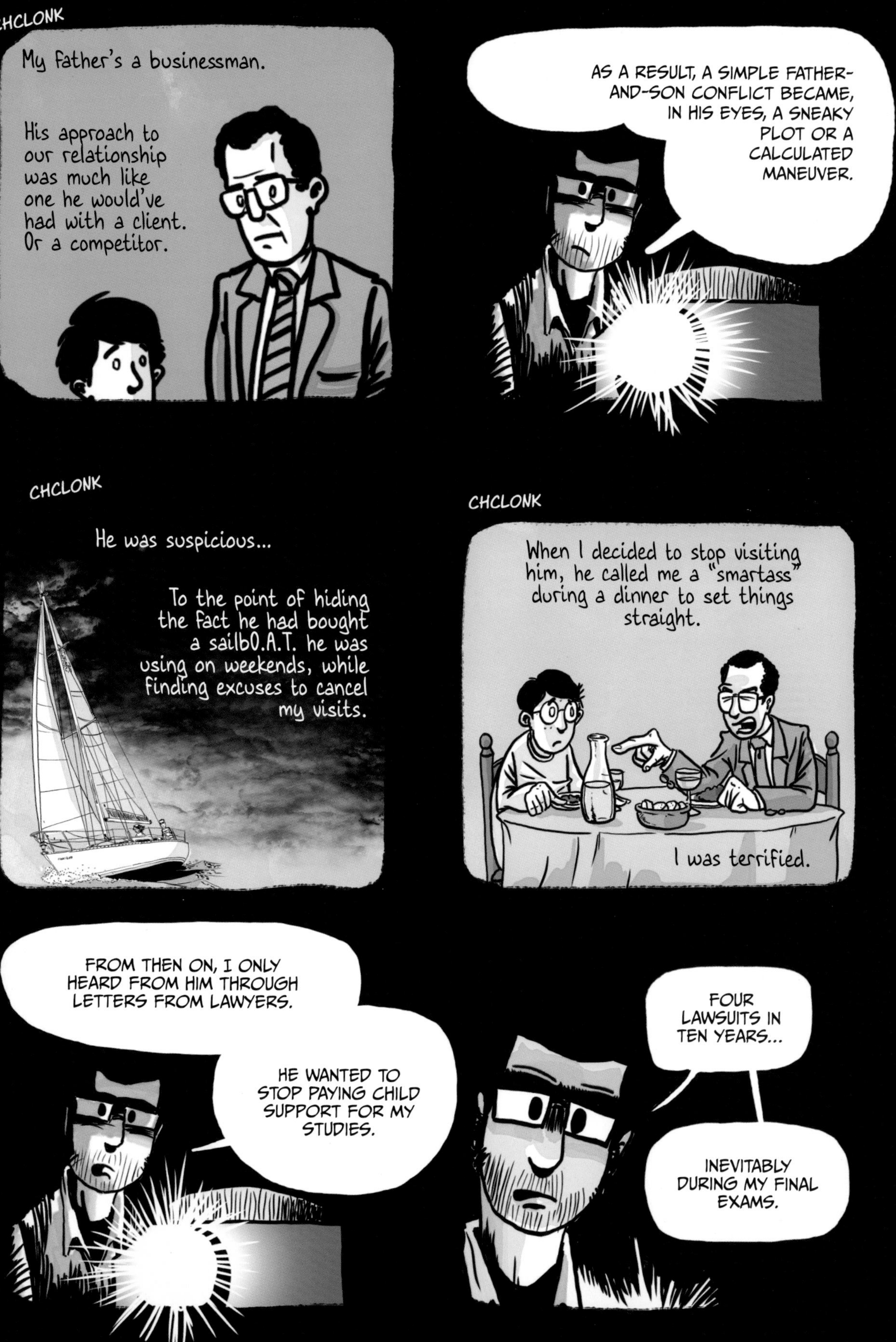
CHCLONK
My father's a businessman.
His approach to our relationship was much like one he would've had with a client. Or a competitor.
AS A RESULT, A SIMPLE FATHER-AND-SON CONFLICT BECAME, IN HIS EYES, A SNEAKY PLOT OR A CALCULATED MANEUVER.
CHCLONK
He was suspicious...
To the point of hiding the fact he had bought a sailbO.A.T. he was using on weekends, while finding excuses to cancel my visits.
CHCLONK
When I decided to stop visiting him, he called me a "smartass" during a dinner to set things straight.
I was terrified.
FROM THEN ON, I ONLY HEARD FROM HIM THROUGH LETTERS FROM LAWYERS.
HE WANTED TO STOP PAYING CHILD SUPPORT FOR MY STUDIES.
FOUR LAWSUITS IN TEN YEARS...
INEVITABLY DURING MY FINAL EXAMS.

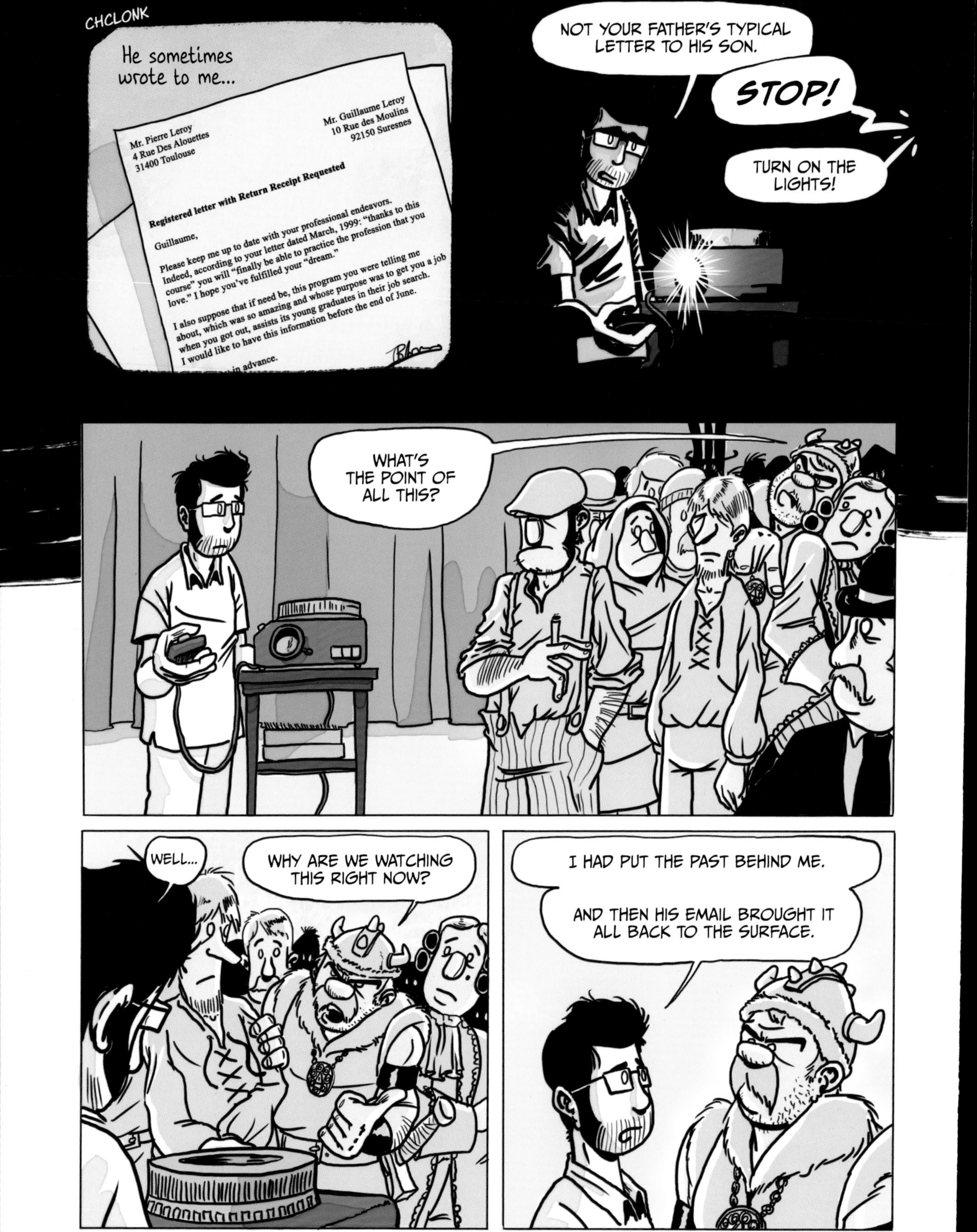
CHCLONK
He sometimes wrote to me...
Mr. Pierre Leroy
4 Rue Des Alouettes
31400 Toulouse
Mr. Guillaume Leroy
10 Rue des Moulins
92150 Suresnes
Registered letter with Return Receipt Requested
Guillaume,
Please keep me up to date with your professional endeavors. Indeed, according to your letter dated March, 1999: "thanks to this course" you will "finally be able to practice the profession that you love." I hope you've fulfilled your "dream."
I also suppose that if need be, this program you were telling me about, which was so amazing and whose purpose was to get you a job when you got out, assists its young graduates in their job search. I would like to have this information before the end of June.
in advance.
NOT YOUR FATHER'S TYPICAL LETTER TO HIS SON.
STOP!
TURN ON THE LIGHTS!
WHAT'S THE POINT OF ALL THIS?
WELL...
WHY ARE WE WATCHING THIS RIGHT NOW?
I HAD PUT THE PAST BEHIND ME.
AND THEN HIS EMAIL BROUGHT IT ALL BACK TO THE SURFACE.

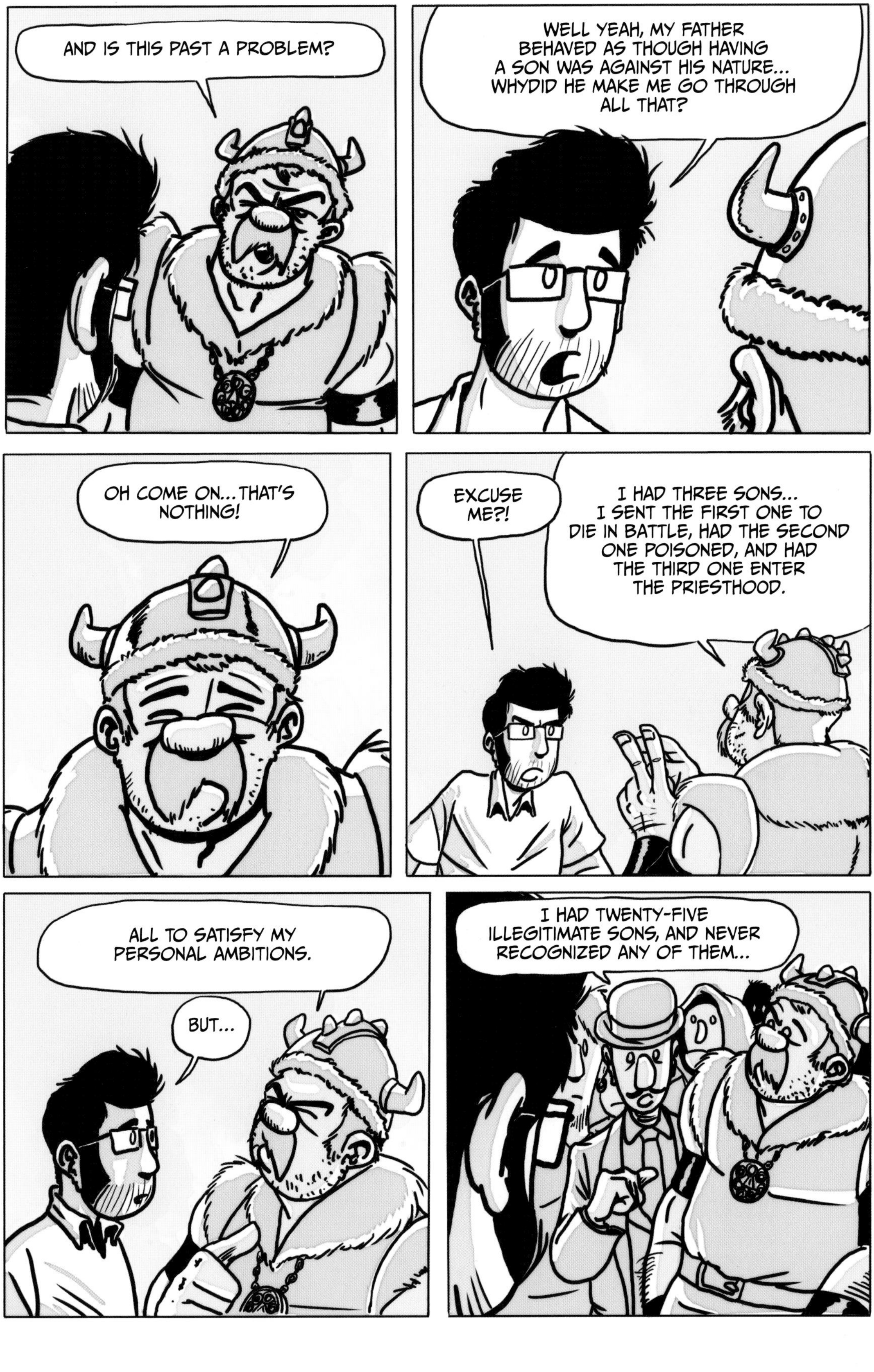
AND IS THIS PAST A PROBLEM?
WELL YEAH, MY FATHER BEHAVED AS THOUGH HAVING A SON WAS AGAINST HIS NATURE... WHYDID HE MAKE ME GO THROUGH ALL THAT?
OH COME ON...THAT'S NOTHING!
EXCUSE ME?!
I HAD THREE SONS... I SENT THE FIRST ONE TO DIE IN BATTLE, HAD THE SECOND ONE POISONED, AND HAD THE THIRD ONE ENTER THE PRIESTHOOD.
ALL TO SATISFY MY PERSONAL AMBITIONS.
BUT...
I HAD TWENTY-FIVE ILLEGITIMATE SONS, AND NEVER RECOGNIZED ANY OF THEM...

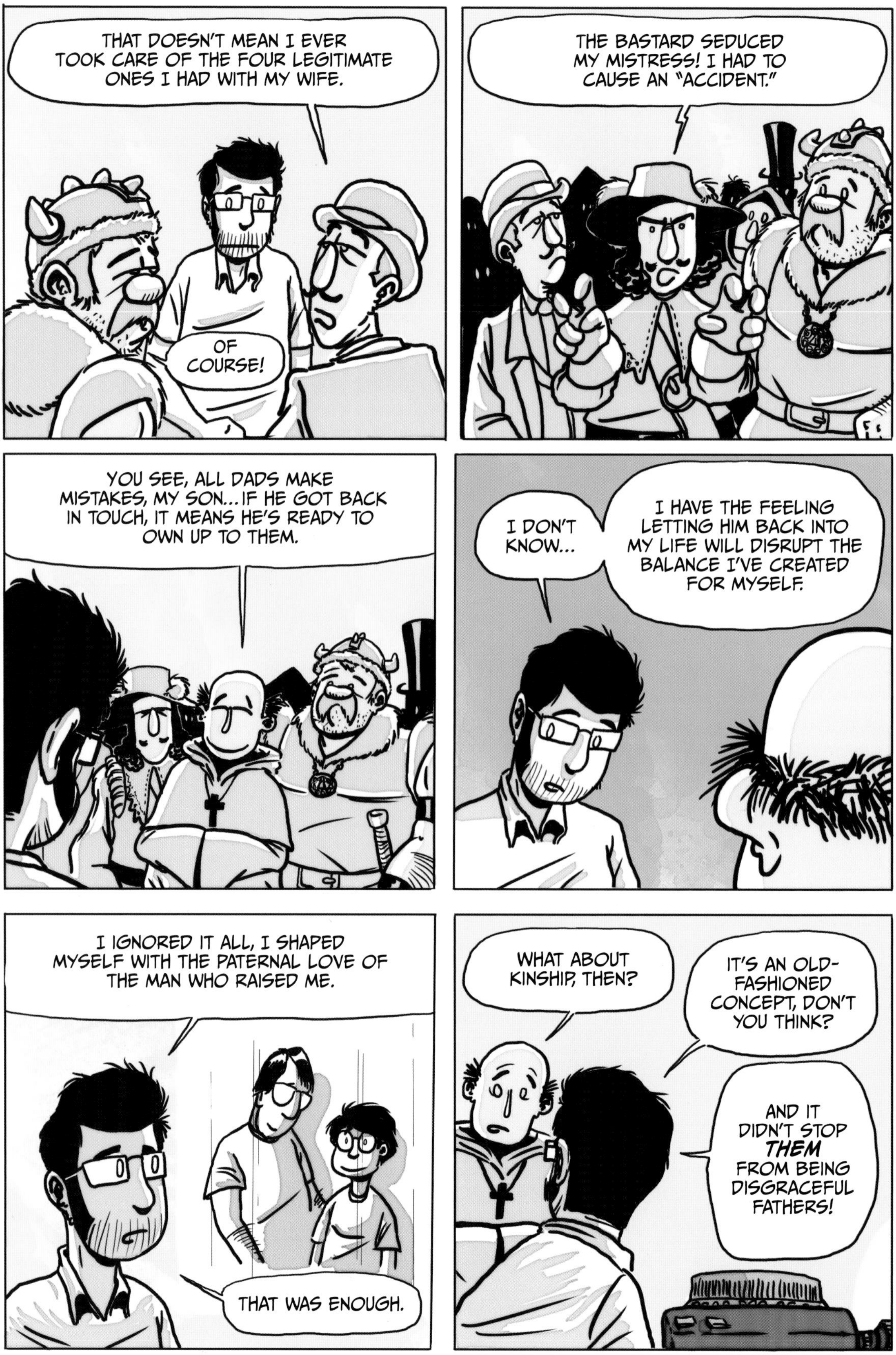
THAT DOESN'T MEAN I EVER TOOK CARE OF THE FOUR LEGITIMATE ONES I HAD WITH MY WIFE.
OF COURSE!
THE BASTARD SEDUCED MY MISTRESS! I HAD TO CAUSE AN "ACCIDENT."
YOU SEE, ALL DADS MAKE MISTAKES, MY SON... IF HE GOT BACK IN TOUCH, IT MEANS HE'S READY TO OWN UP TO THEM.
I DON'T KNOW...
I HAVE THE FEELING LETTING HIM BACK INTO MY LIFE WILL DISRUPT THE BALANCE I'VE CREATED FOR MYSELF.
I IGNORED IT ALL, I SHAPED MYSELF WITH THE PATERNAL LOVE OF THE MAN WHO RAISED ME.
THAT WAS ENOUGH.
WHAT ABOUT KINSHIP, THEN?
IT'S AN OLD-FASHIONED CONCEPT, DON'T YOU THINK?
AND IT DIDN'T STOP ***THEM*** FROM BEING DISGRACEFUL FATHERS!

IT IS ESSENTIAL TO FORGIVE.
I WISH MY SON WOULD HAVE FORGIVEN ME.
YOU HAVE KIDS?
IN AN ESOTERIC SENSE, OF COURSE... AHEM...
IN A WHAT?!

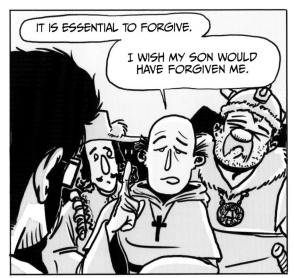

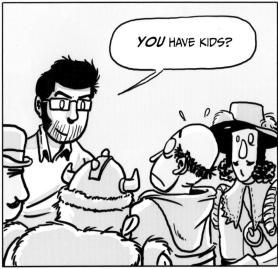

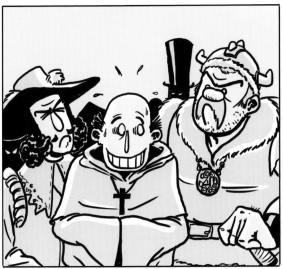

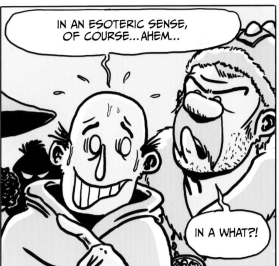

WELL... DON'T YOU CALL ME ***FATHER***?

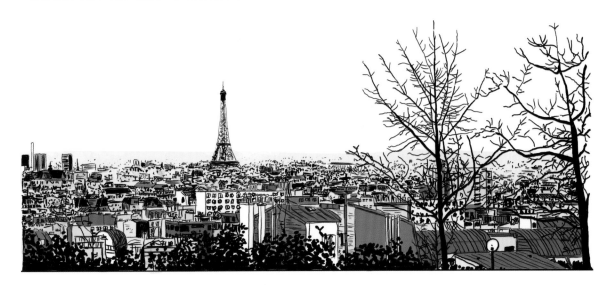

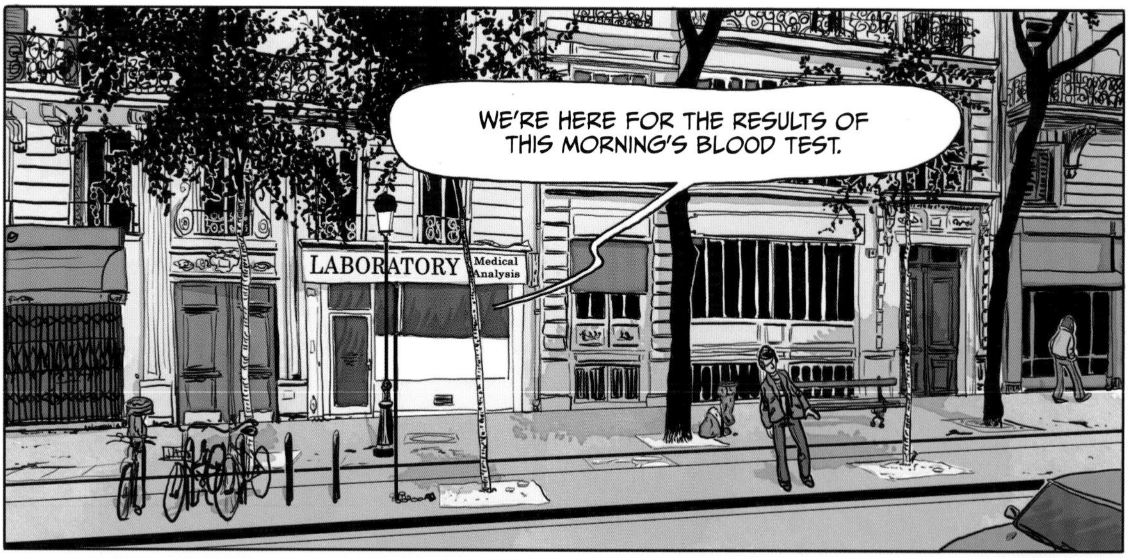
WE'RE HERE FOR THE RESULTS OF THIS MORNING'S BLOOD TEST.
LABORATORY
Medical Analysis

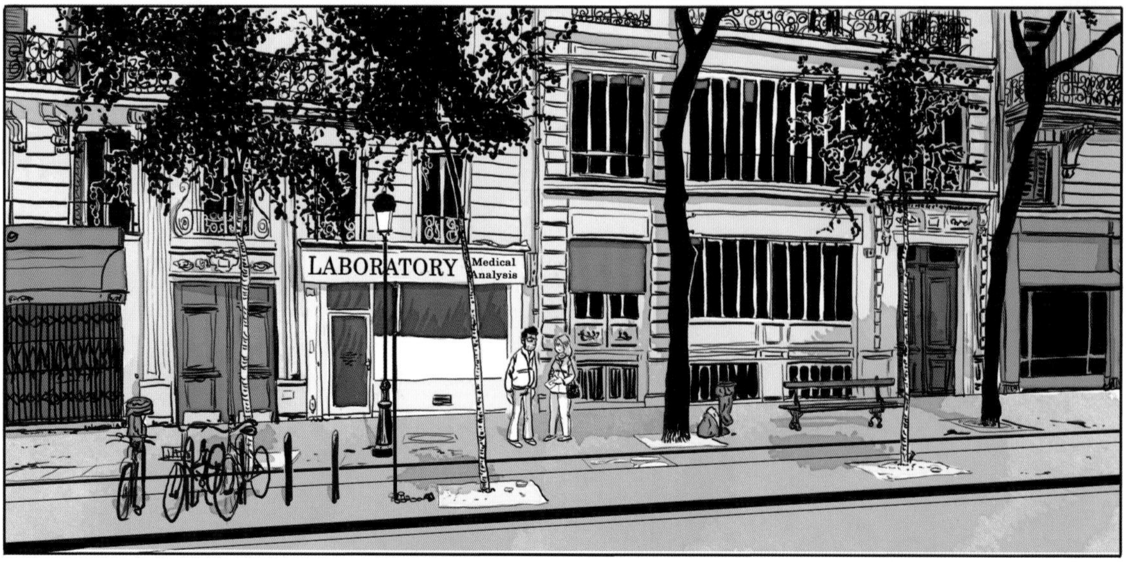
LABORATORY
Medical Analysis

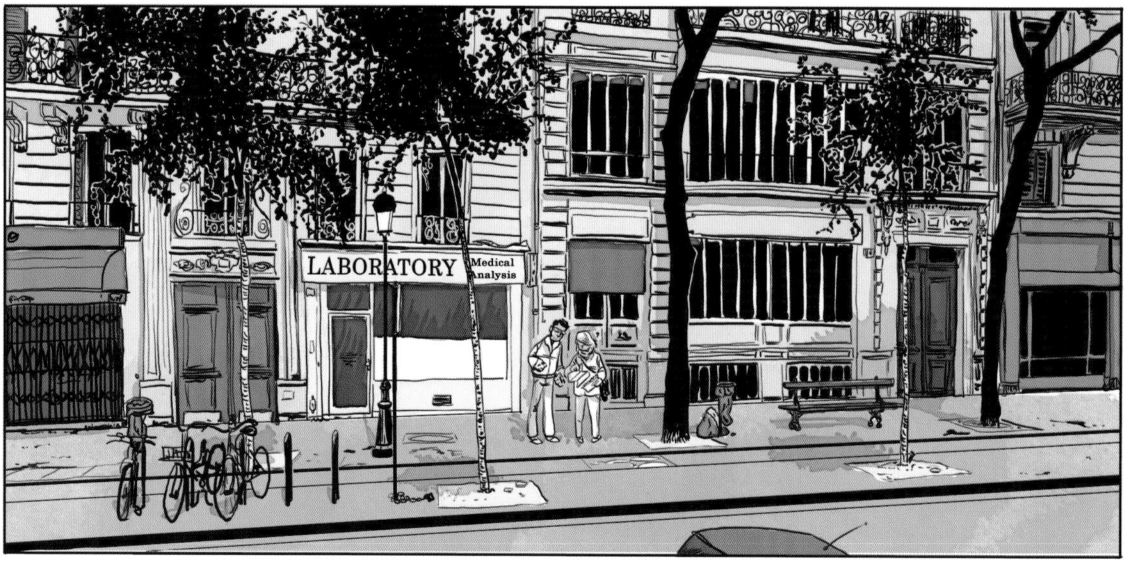
LABORATORY
Medical Analysis

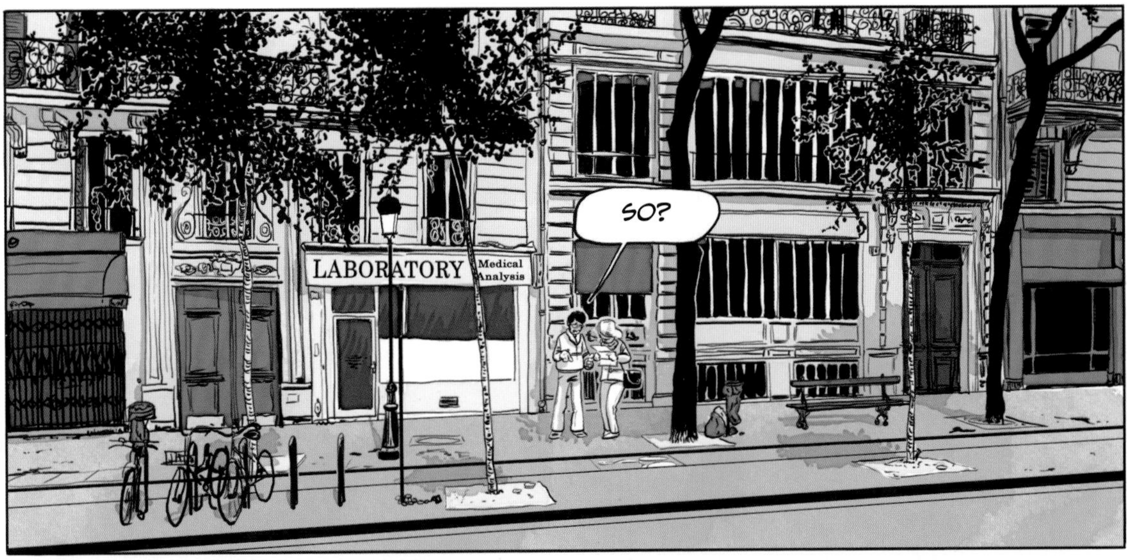
SO?
LABORATORY Medical Analysis

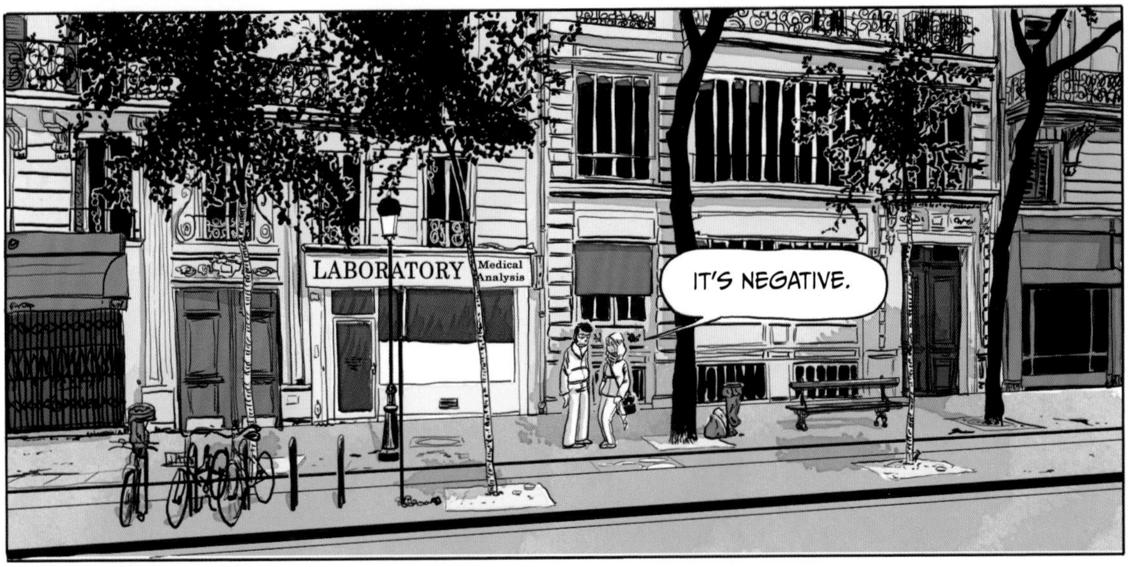
IT'S NEGATIVE.
LABORATORY Medical Analysis

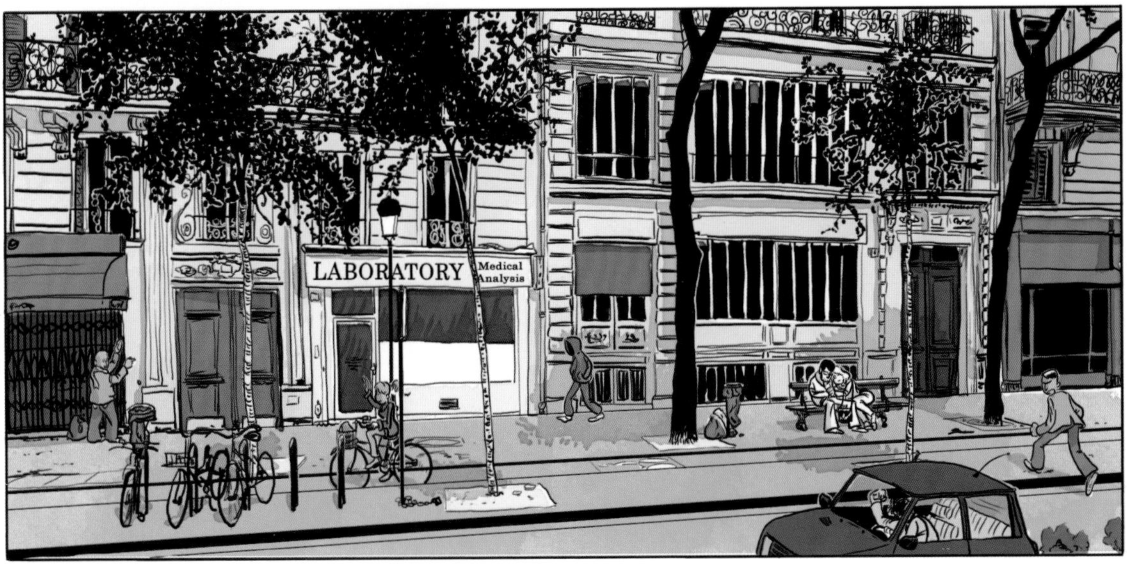
LABORATORY Medical Analysis

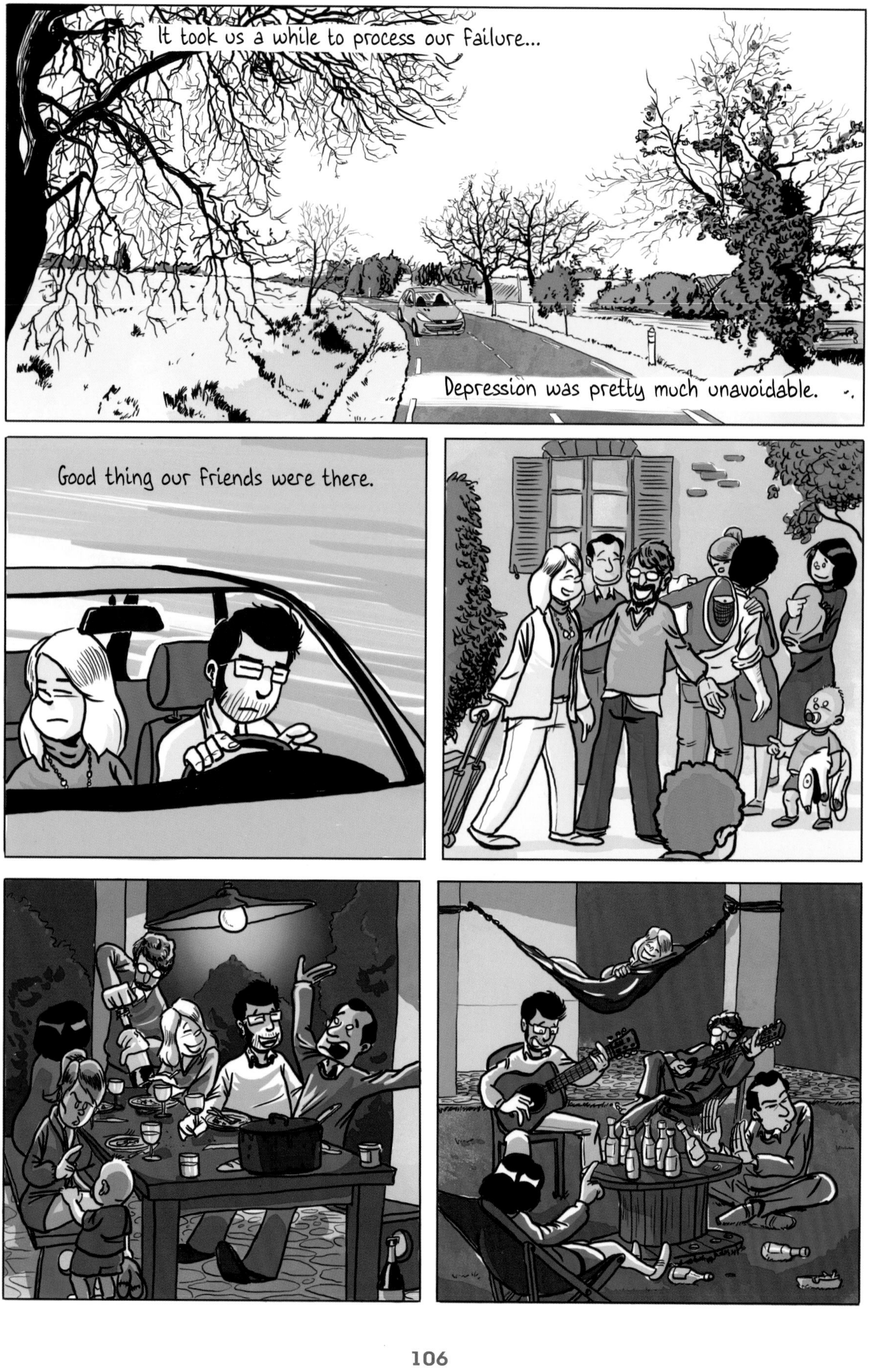
It took us a while to process our failure...
Depression was pretty much unavoidable.
Good thing our friends were there.

It gets hard to see so many children.

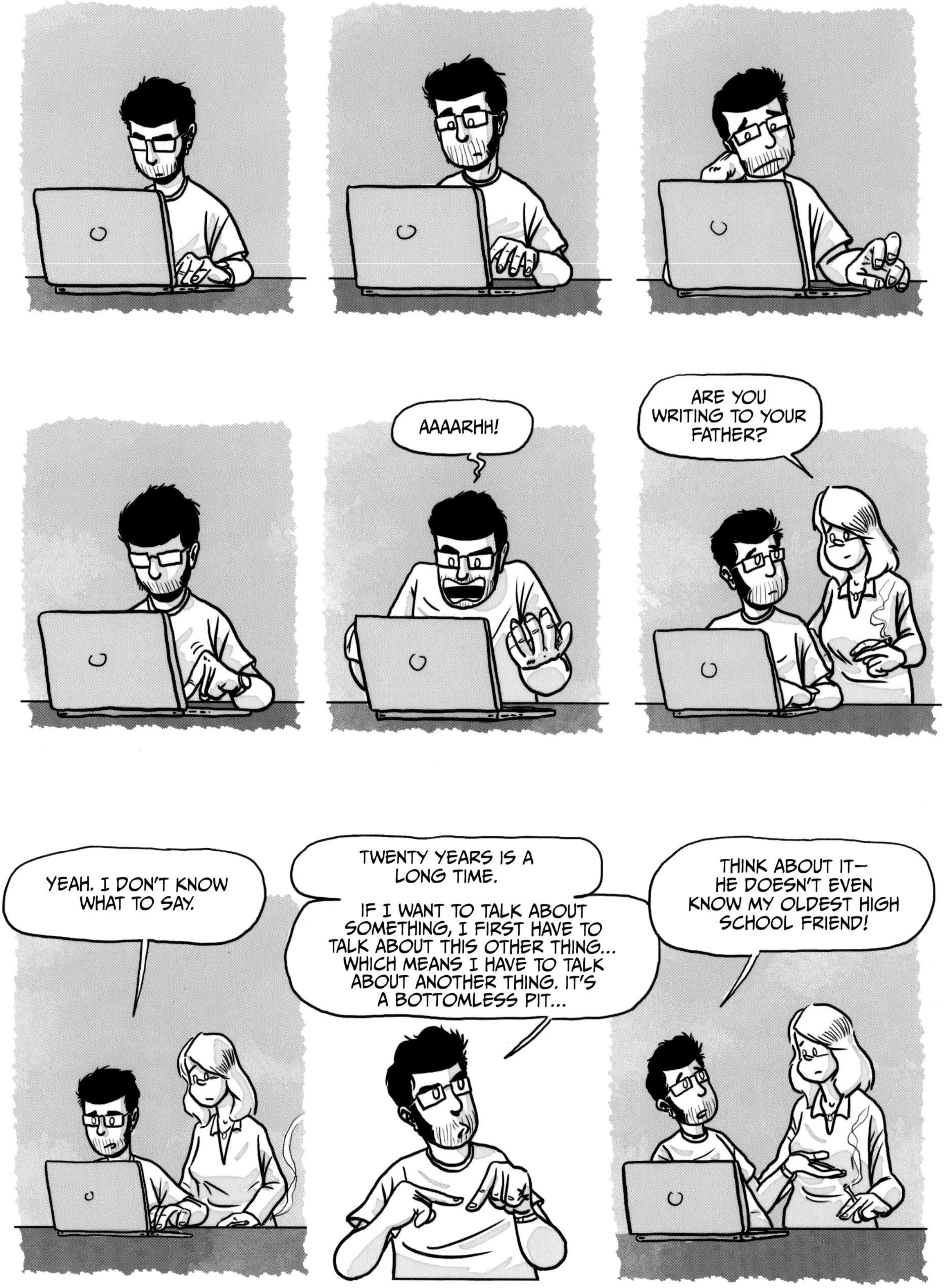
AAAARHH!
ARE YOU WRITING TO YOUR FATHER?
YEAH. I DON'T KNOW WHAT TO SAY.
TWENTY YEARS IS A LONG TIME.
IF I WANT TO TALK ABOUT SOMETHING, I FIRST HAVE TO TALK ABOUT THIS OTHER THING... WHICH MEANS I HAVE TO TALK ABOUT ANOTHER THING. IT'S A BOTTOMLESS PIT...
THINK ABOUT IT— HE DOESN'T EVEN KNOW MY OLDEST HIGH SCHOOL FRIEND!

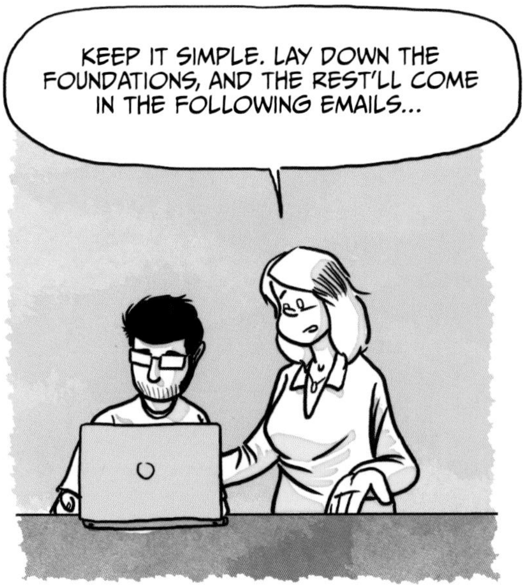
KEEP IT SIMPLE. LAY DOWN THE FOUNDATIONS, AND THE REST'LL COME IN THE FOLLOWING EMAILS...

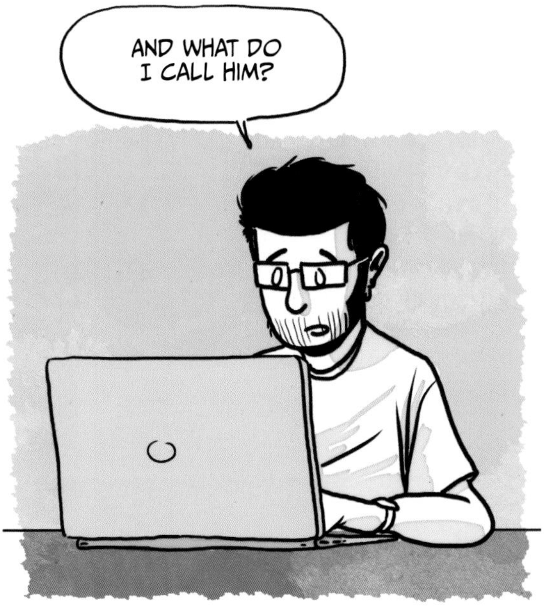
AND WHAT DO I CALL HIM?

From: Guillaume Leroy
Subject: Re: News?
Date: September 7, 2011 8:46:33 PM CET
To: Jean-Pierre Leroy

Dad,

It took me a while to respond to your email, which, you can imagine, caught me off guard. It's difficult to get back in touch after 20 years of silence, sometimes broken by the law suits you were filing…

Your request to meet me comes as a surprise. I don't think I'm ready to see you. It took me a long time to find a balance that suited me. We can, however, talk by email if that's OK with you. And see where it leads us…
I live in Paris. I'm married. Without children.

What's new on your end?

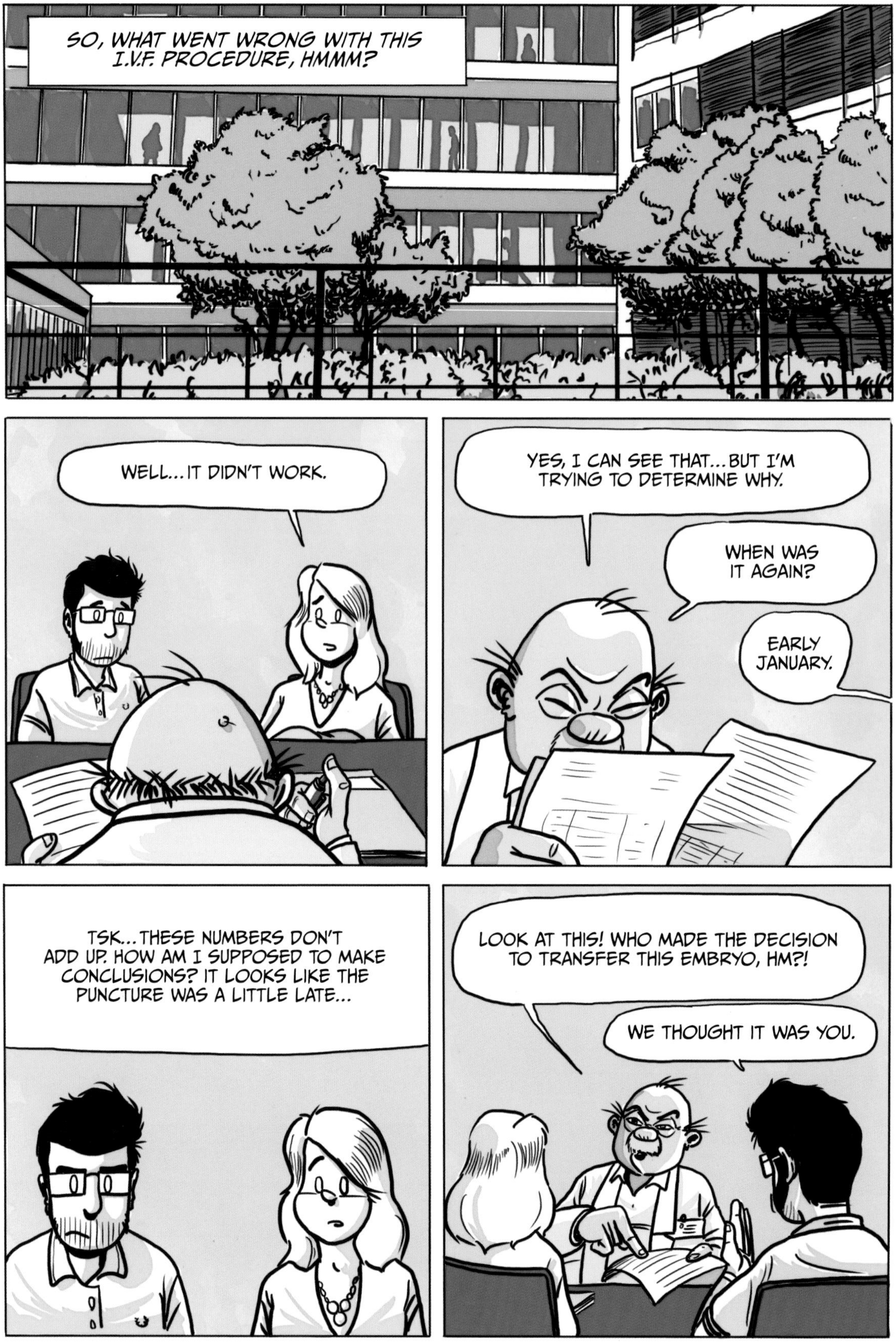
SO, WHAT WENT WRONG WITH THIS I.V.F. PROCEDURE, HMMM?
WELL... IT DIDN'T WORK.
YES, I CAN SEE THAT... BUT I'M TRYING TO DETERMINE WHY.
WHEN WAS IT AGAIN?
EARLY JANUARY.
TSK... THESE NUMBERS DON'T ADD UP. HOW AM I SUPPOSED TO MAKE CONCLUSIONS? IT LOOKS LIKE THE PUNCTURE WAS A LITTLE LATE...
LOOK AT THIS! WHO MADE THE DECISION TO TRANSFER THIS EMBRYO, HM?!
WE THOUGHT IT WAS YOU.

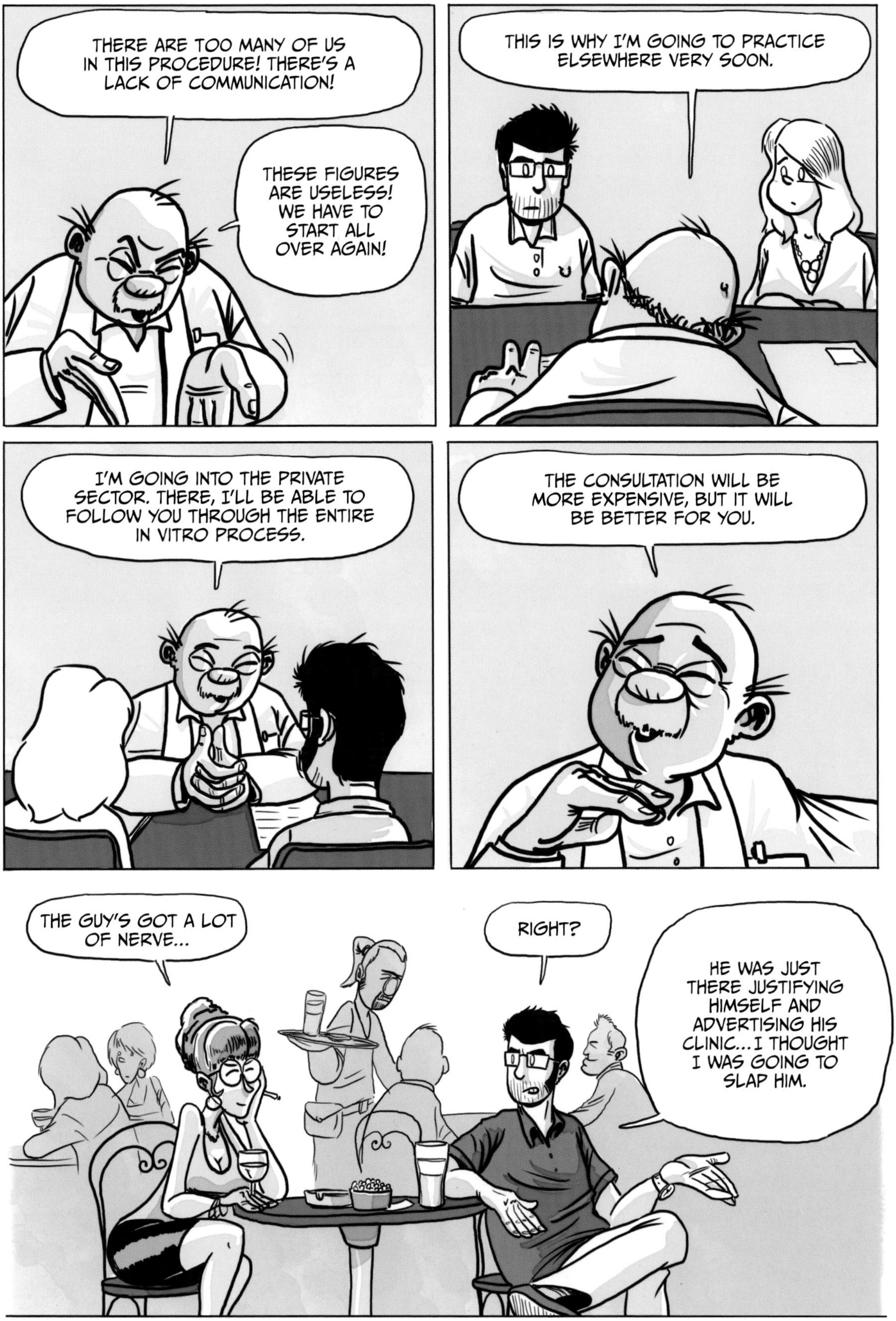
THERE ARE TOO MANY OF US IN THIS PROCEDURE! THERE'S A LACK OF COMMUNICATION!
THESE FIGURES ARE USELESS! WE HAVE TO START ALL OVER AGAIN!
THIS IS WHY I'M GOING TO PRACTICE ELSEWHERE VERY SOON.
I'M GOING INTO THE PRIVATE SECTOR. THERE, I'LL BE ABLE TO FOLLOW YOU THROUGH THE ENTIRE IN VITRO PROCESS.
THE CONSULTATION WILL BE MORE EXPENSIVE, BUT IT WILL BE BETTER FOR YOU.
THE GUY'S GOT A LOT OF NERVE...
RIGHT?
HE WAS JUST THERE JUSTIFYING HIMSELF AND ADVERTISING HIS CLINIC... I THOUGHT I WAS GOING TO SLAP HIM.

DID YOU TELL HIM TO GO TO HELL?

NOT EVEN.

THE PROBLEM IS THAT WE DON'T WANT TO WASTE ANY MORE TIME, YOU KNOW?

AND CHANGING DOCTORS MEANS STARTING OVER FROM SCRATCH AND LOSING SIX MONTHS.

SO WE TRIED AGAIN WITH HIM. WE WERE BACK AT IT—HORMONES, INJECTIONS, CHECK-UPS...THE SAME...ONLY WITH HIGHER DOSES.

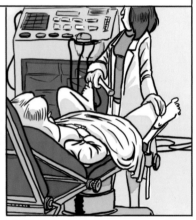

EVERYTHING WAS ALL GOING WELL, AND ONE MONTH IN, THE ULTRASOUND SCANNER GAVE US THE DATE OF THE COLLECTION, BASED ON THE EGG'S MATURITY...

YOU WON'T BELIEVE THIS—THE HOSPITAL WAS EMPTY THAT DAY... A NATIONAL HOLIDAY.

WHAT?!

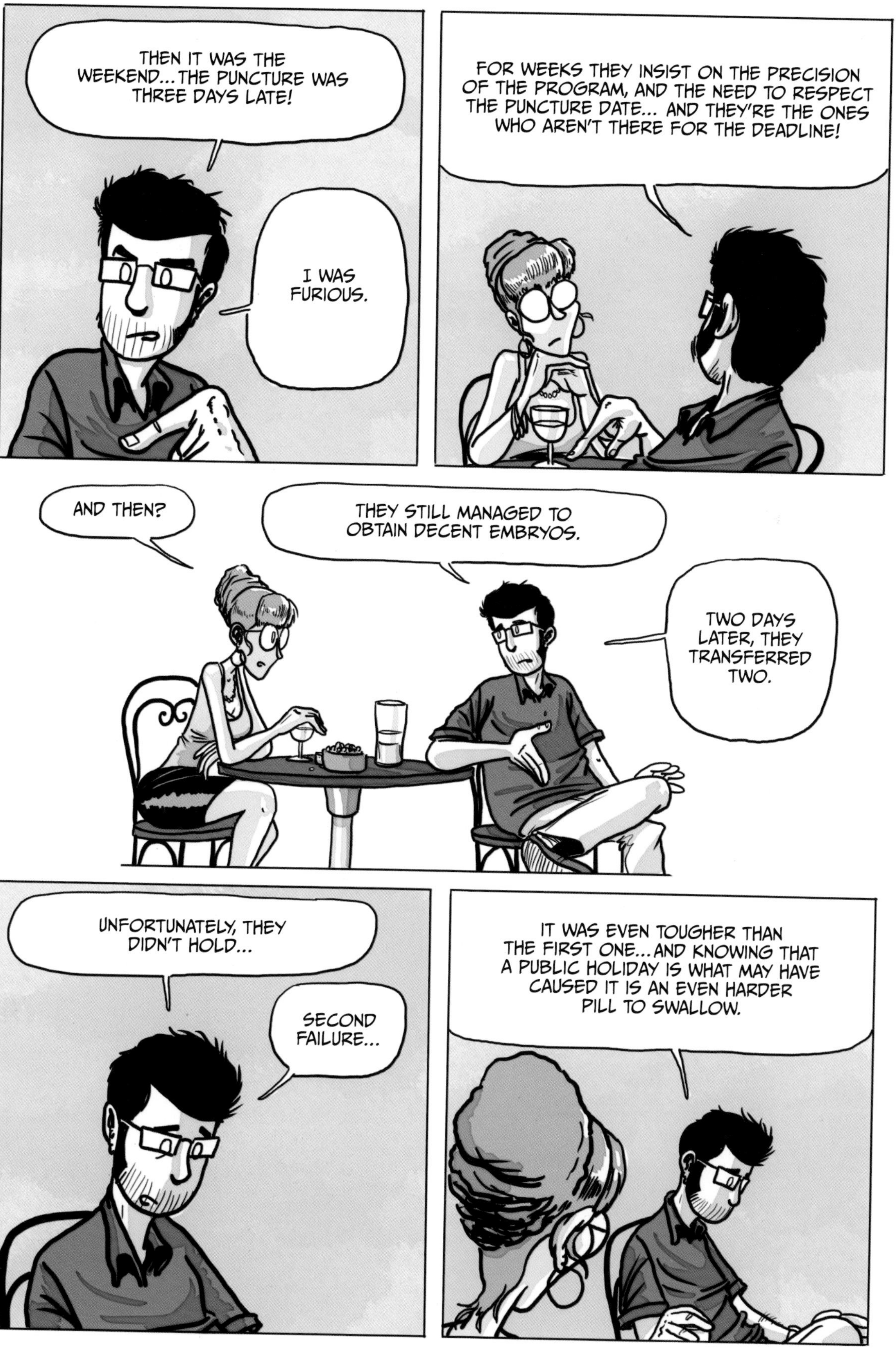
THEN IT WAS THE WEEKEND... THE PUNCTURE WAS THREE DAYS LATE!
I WAS FURIOUS.
FOR WEEKS THEY INSIST ON THE PRECISION OF THE PROGRAM, AND THE NEED TO RESPECT THE PUNCTURE DATE... AND THEY'RE THE ONES WHO AREN'T THERE FOR THE DEADLINE!
AND THEN?
THEY STILL MANAGED TO OBTAIN DECENT EMBRYOS.
TWO DAYS LATER, THEY TRANSFERRED TWO.
UNFORTUNATELY, THEY DIDN'T HOLD...
SECOND FAILURE...
IT WAS EVEN TOUGHER THAN THE FIRST ONE... AND KNOWING THAT A PUBLIC HOLIDAY IS WHAT MAY HAVE CAUSED IT IS AN EVEN HARDER PILL TO SWALLOW.

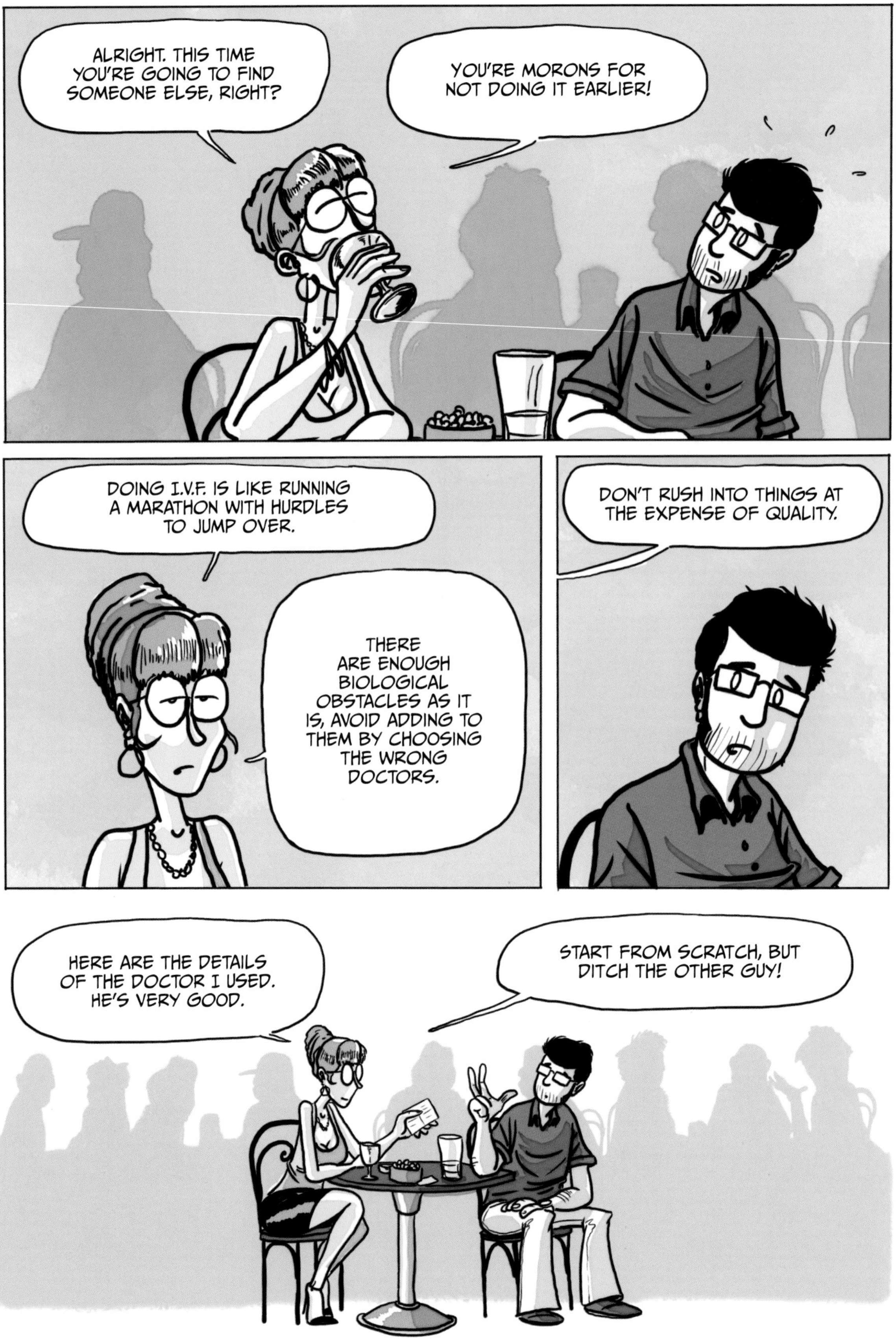
ALRIGHT. THIS TIME YOU'RE GOING TO FIND SOMEONE ELSE, RIGHT?
YOU'RE MORONS FOR NOT DOING IT EARLIER!
DOING I.V.F. IS LIKE RUNNING A MARATHON WITH HURDLES TO JUMP OVER.
THERE ARE ENOUGH BIOLOGICAL OBSTACLES AS IT IS, AVOID ADDING TO THEM BY CHOOSING THE WRONG DOCTORS.
DON'T RUSH INTO THINGS AT THE EXPENSE OF QUALITY.
HERE ARE THE DETAILS OF THE DOCTOR I USED. HE'S VERY GOOD.
START FROM SCRATCH, BUT DITCH THE OTHER GUY!

From: Jean-Pierre Leroy
Subject: Re: Re: News?
Date: May 25, 2012 8:11:56 PM CET
To: Guillaume Leroy

Guillaume,

I respect your decision not to see me, even if I find it incomprehensible. But I have a hard time accepting your apparent refusal to reply to my emails. I wrote to you almost three months ago and didn't get a reply.

You told me in a previous letter that you had shaped yourself by putting the past behind you. I really think it's time to forget about our small quarrels and put aside our pride if we want to successfully rebuild something.

I still hope we'll manage to meet face to face, so that you can have my personal answers to the questions you have asked only of others.

I believe it would make our situation more acceptable, even if it doesn't develop any further.

As I told you last time, I'm still in Toulouse. I'm widowed and have three grandchildren. I'm

---

From: Guillaume Leroy
Subject: Re: Re: Re: News?
Date: June 14, 2012 1:05:13 PM CET
To: Jean-Pierre Leroy

Dad,

Unfortunately, I've been very busy and didn't get a chance to answer you. Some priorities came first, before our correspondence.

I find your last email interesting in many respects, however.

To call the many lawsuits you have brought against me during my school years "small quarrels" reminds me of how little you appreciate me, still.

I get the impression that you got back in touch with me only because you need me to admit that I did something wrong, instead of admitting that you did.

I may have behaved impulsively and thoughtlessly. But bear in mind that I was 13 years old, and at that age, people react violently when they feel hurt. It seems worse for a mature adult to maintain such an unhealthy situation and to want to make his son pay for wounding his pride for so long.

Also know that no one tried to play me against you at that time, as you seem to think. On the contrary.

But since you expect me to ask you questions, here's one: grandchildren? Where from? Did I miss out on a brother or sister?

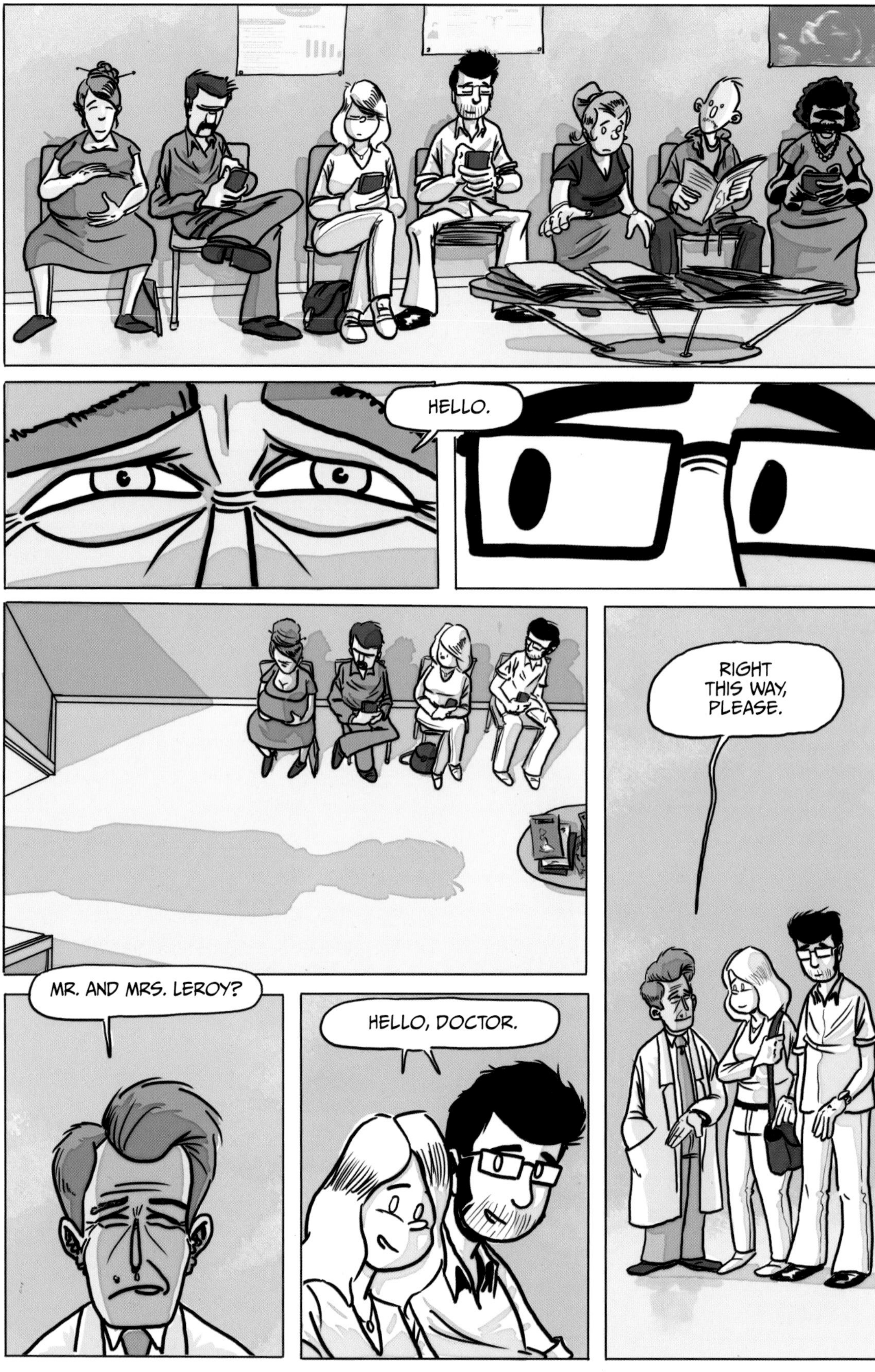
HELLO.
MR. AND MRS. LEROY?
HELLO, DOCTOR.
RIGHT THIS WAY, PLEASE.

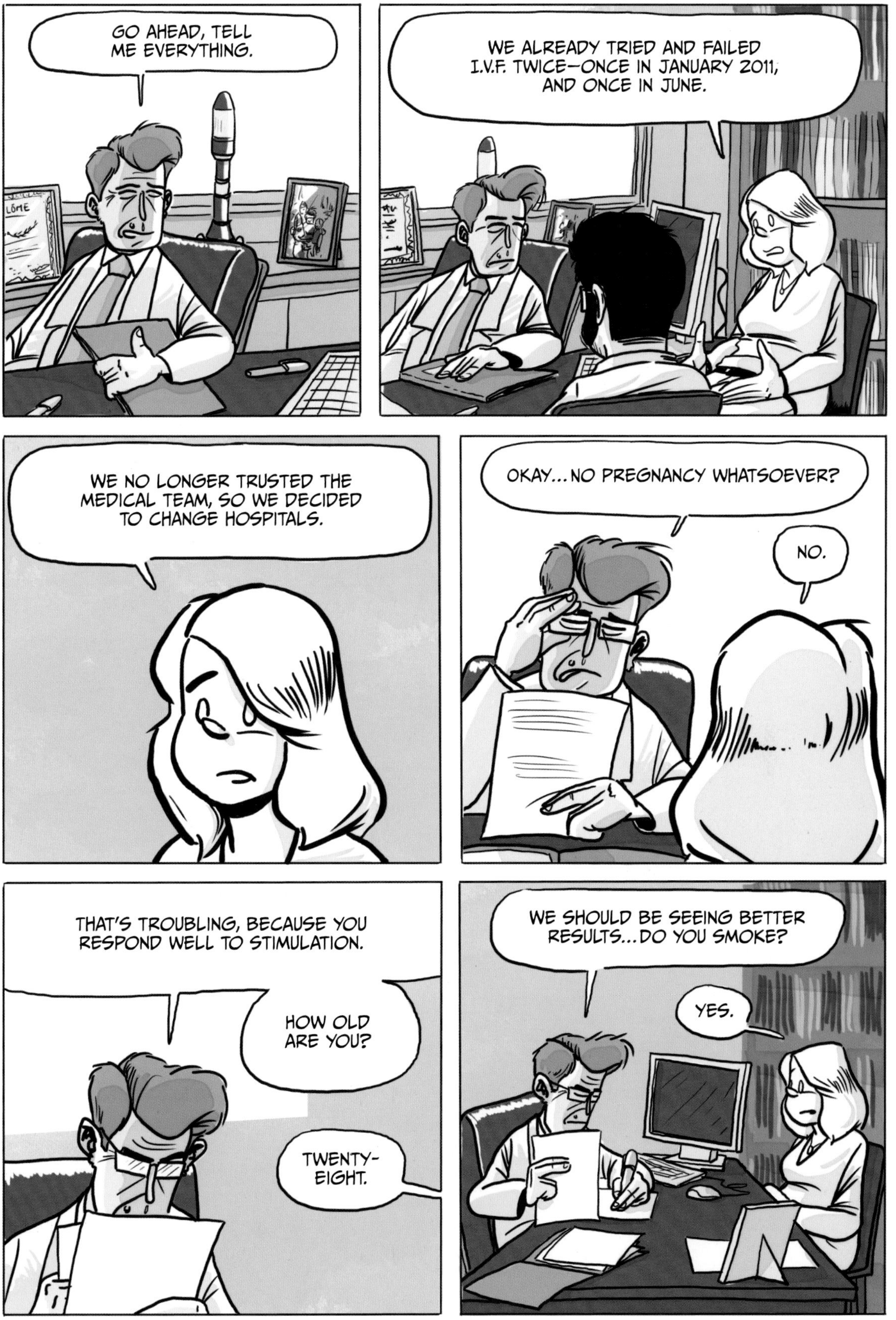
GO AHEAD, TELL ME EVERYTHING.
WE ALREADY TRIED AND FAILED I.V.F. TWICE—ONCE IN JANUARY 2011, AND ONCE IN JUNE.
WE NO LONGER TRUSTED THE MEDICAL TEAM, SO WE DECIDED TO CHANGE HOSPITALS.
OKAY... NO PREGNANCY WHATSOEVER?
NO.
THAT'S TROUBLING, BECAUSE YOU RESPOND WELL TO STIMULATION.
HOW OLD ARE YOU?
TWENTY-EIGHT.
WE SHOULD BE SEEING BETTER RESULTS... DO YOU SMOKE?
YES.

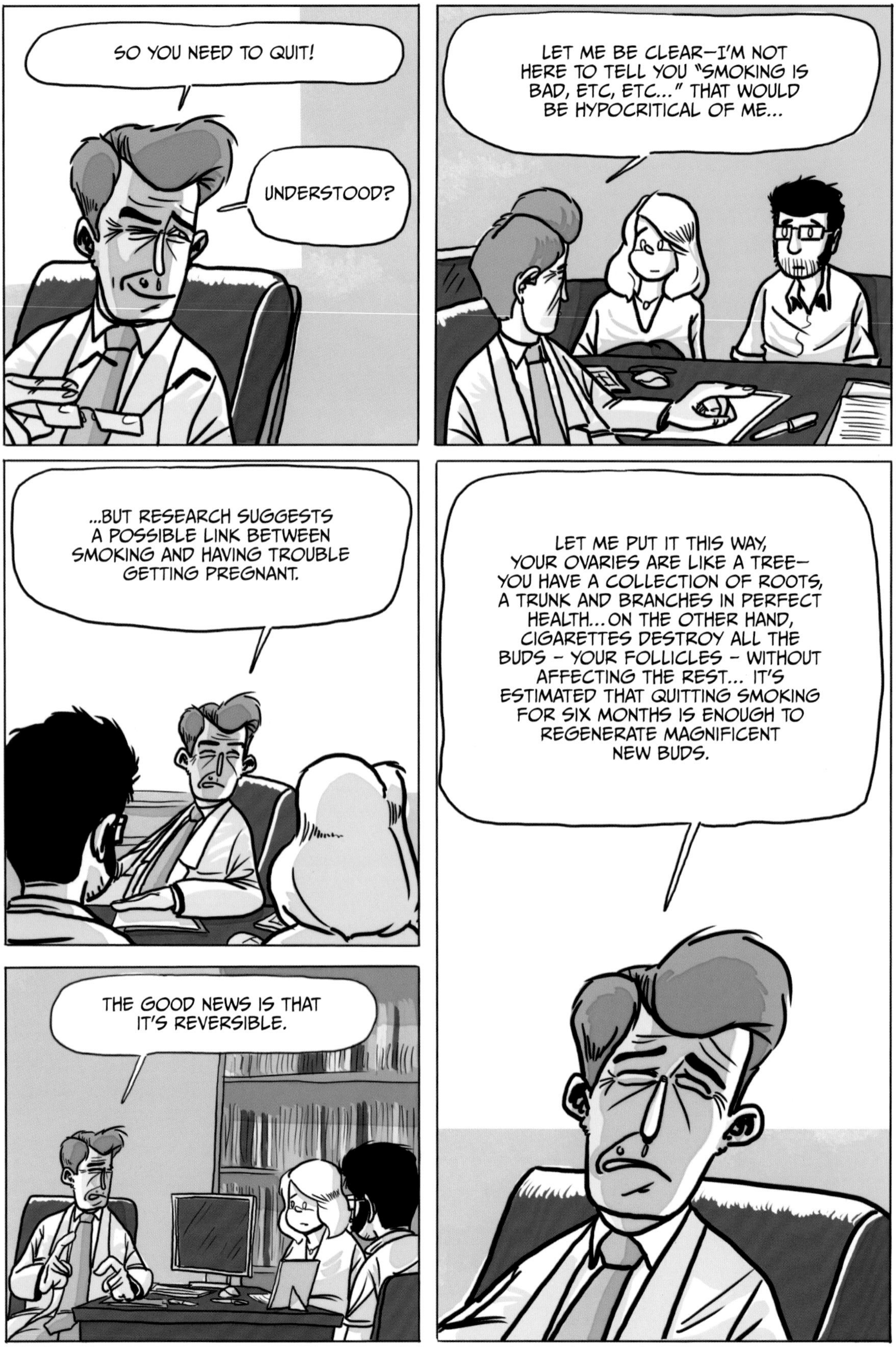
SO YOU NEED TO QUIT!
UNDERSTOOD?
LET ME BE CLEAR—I'M NOT HERE TO TELL YOU "SMOKING IS BAD, ETC, ETC..." THAT WOULD BE HYPOCRITICAL OF ME...
...BUT RESEARCH SUGGESTS A POSSIBLE LINK BETWEEN SMOKING AND HAVING TROUBLE GETTING PREGNANT.
THE GOOD NEWS IS THAT IT'S REVERSIBLE.
LET ME PUT IT THIS WAY, YOUR OVARIES ARE LIKE A TREE—YOU HAVE A COLLECTION OF ROOTS, A TRUNK AND BRANCHES IN PERFECT HEALTH...ON THE OTHER HAND, CIGARETTES DESTROY ALL THE BUDS - YOUR FOLLICLES - WITHOUT AFFECTING THE REST... IT'S ESTIMATED THAT QUITTING SMOKING FOR SIX MONTHS IS ENOUGH TO REGENERATE MAGNIFICENT NEW BUDS.

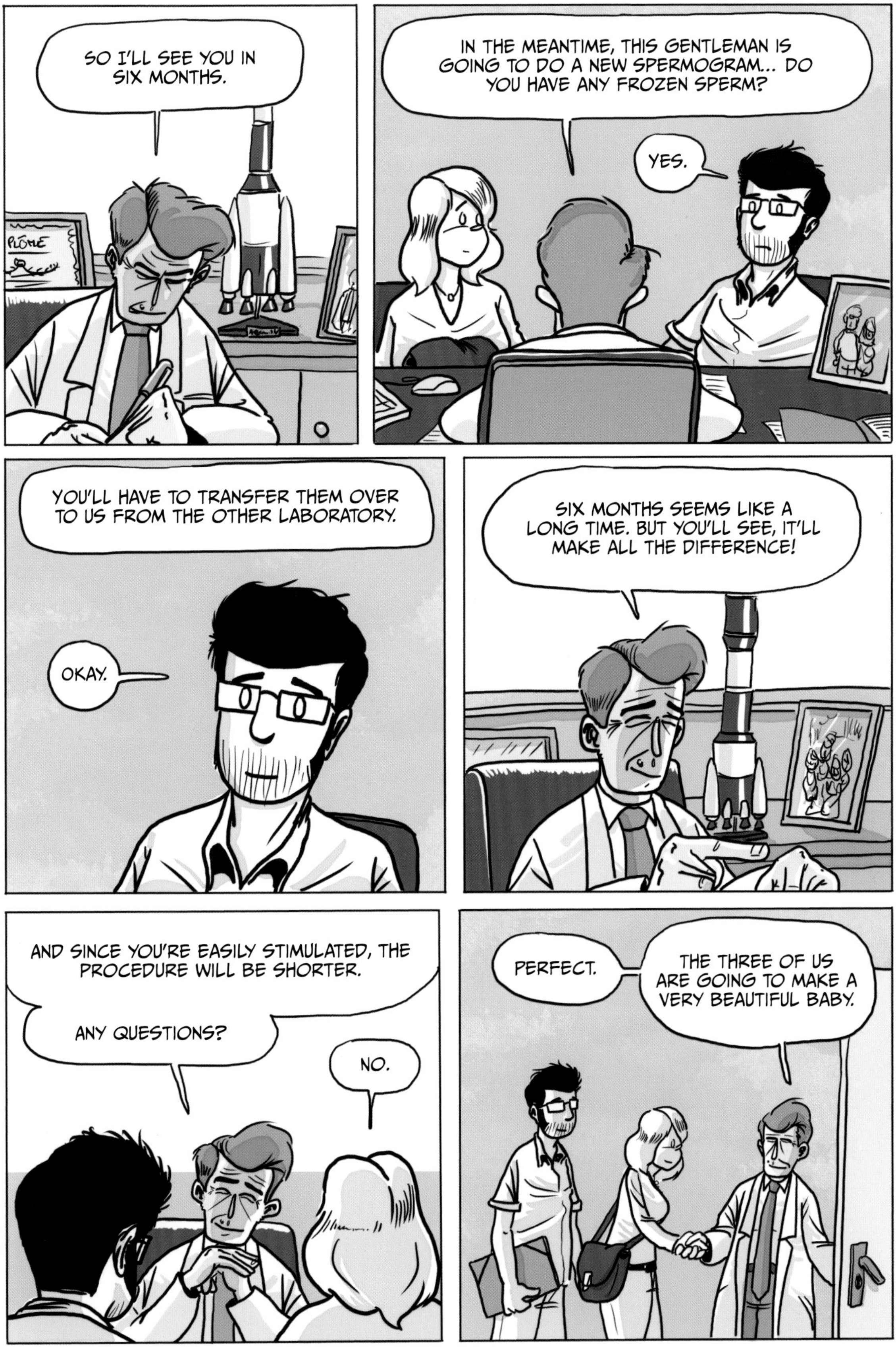
SO I'LL SEE YOU IN SIX MONTHS.
IN THE MEANTIME, THIS GENTLEMAN IS GOING TO DO A NEW SPERMOGRAM... DO YOU HAVE ANY FROZEN SPERM?
YES.
YOU'LL HAVE TO TRANSFER THEM OVER TO US FROM THE OTHER LABORATORY.
OKAY.
SIX MONTHS SEEMS LIKE A LONG TIME. BUT YOU'LL SEE, IT'LL MAKE ALL THE DIFFERENCE!
AND SINCE YOU'RE EASILY STIMULATED, THE PROCEDURE WILL BE SHORTER.
ANY QUESTIONS?
NO.
PERFECT.
THE THREE OF US ARE GOING TO MAKE A VERY BEAUTIFUL BABY.

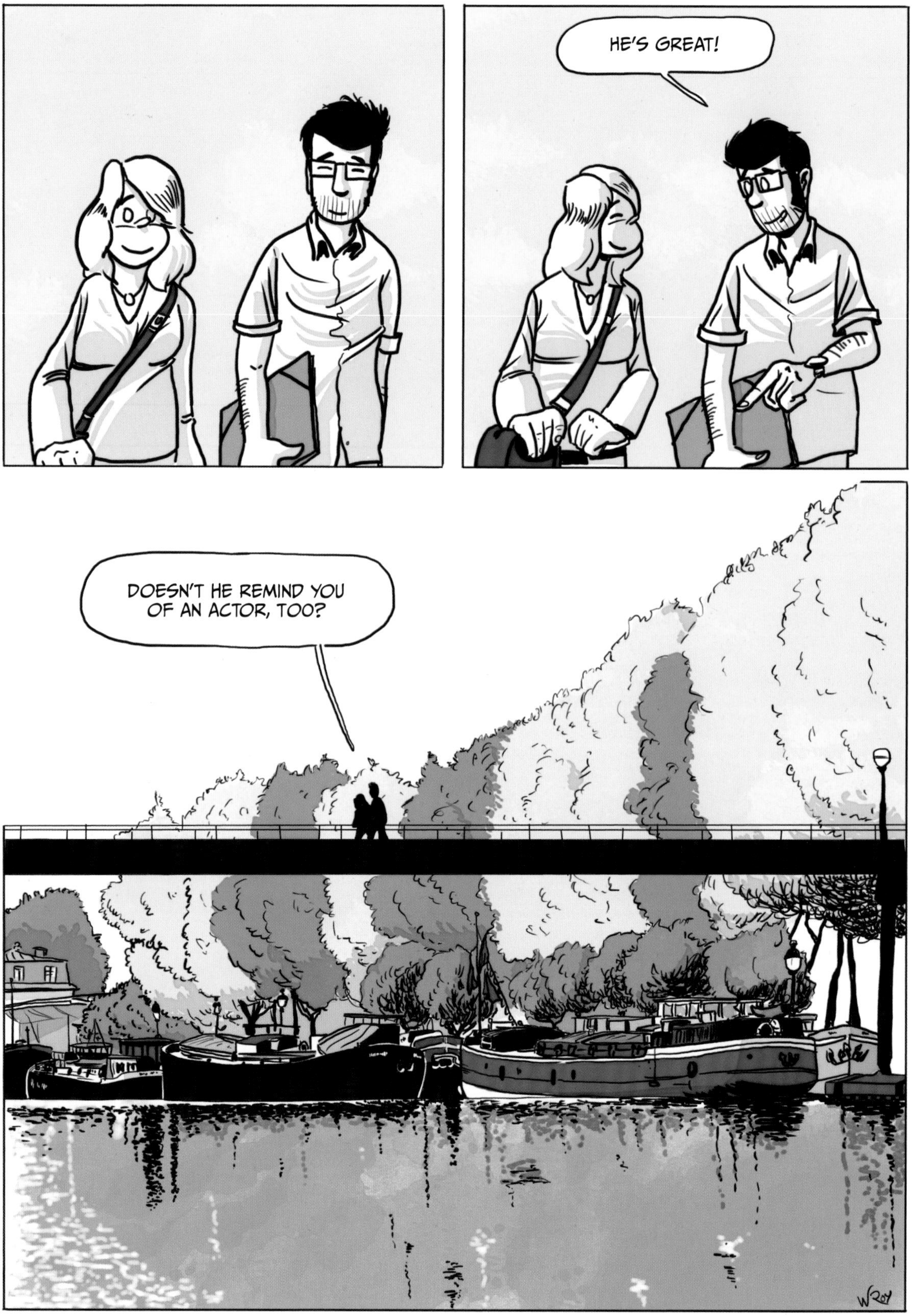
HE'S GREAT!
DOESN'T HE REMIND YOU OF AN ACTOR, TOO?

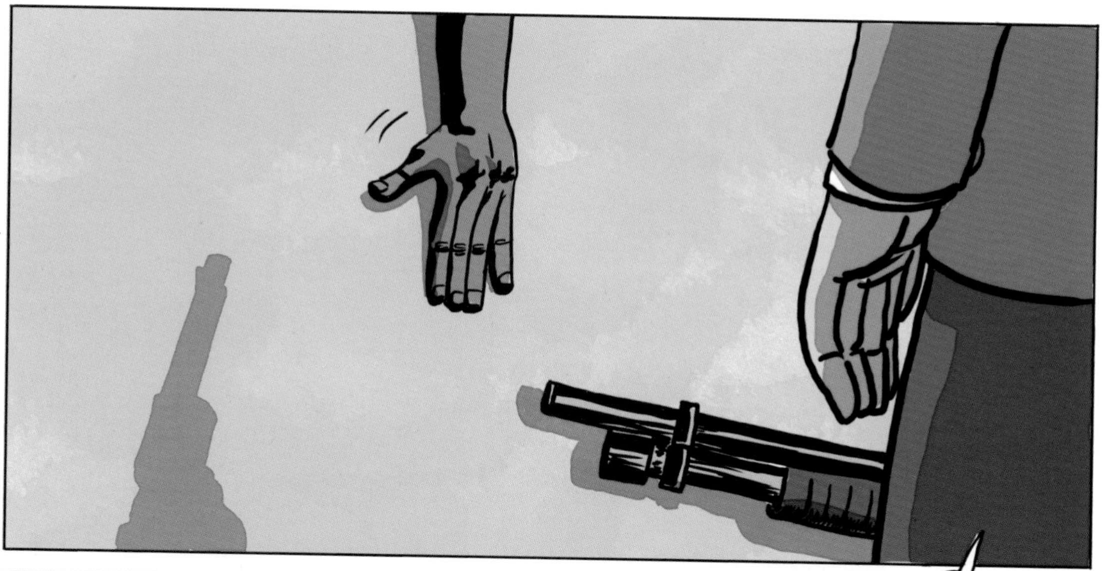

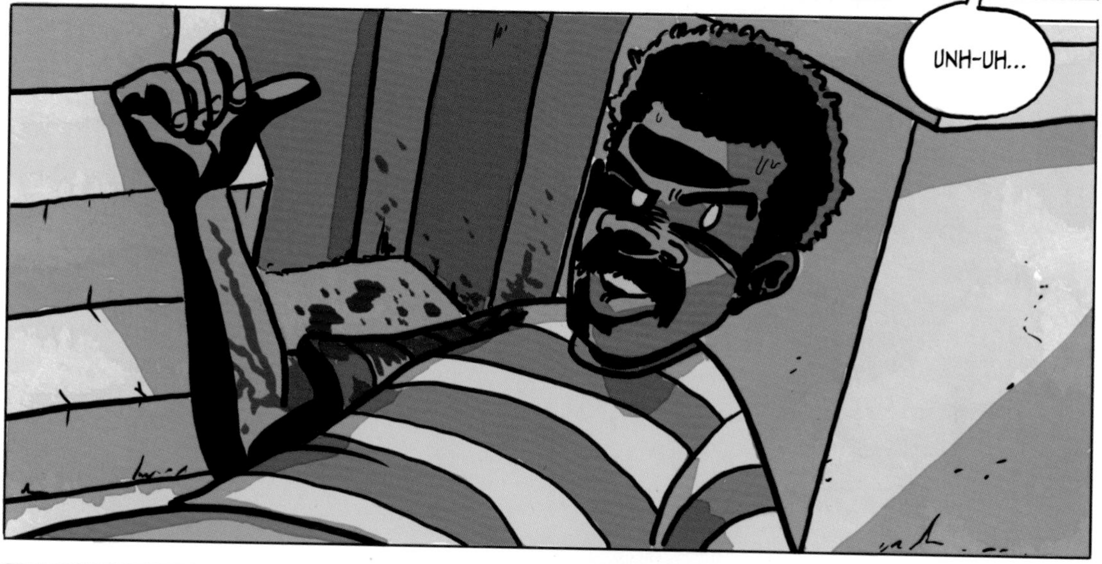
UNH-UH...

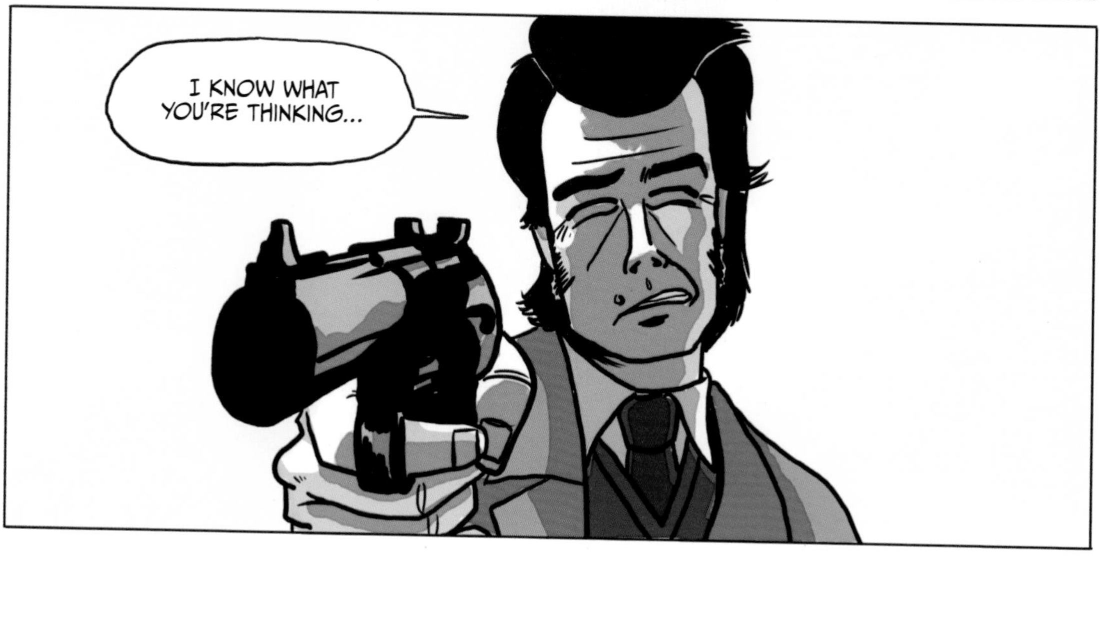
I KNOW WHAT YOU'RE THINKING...

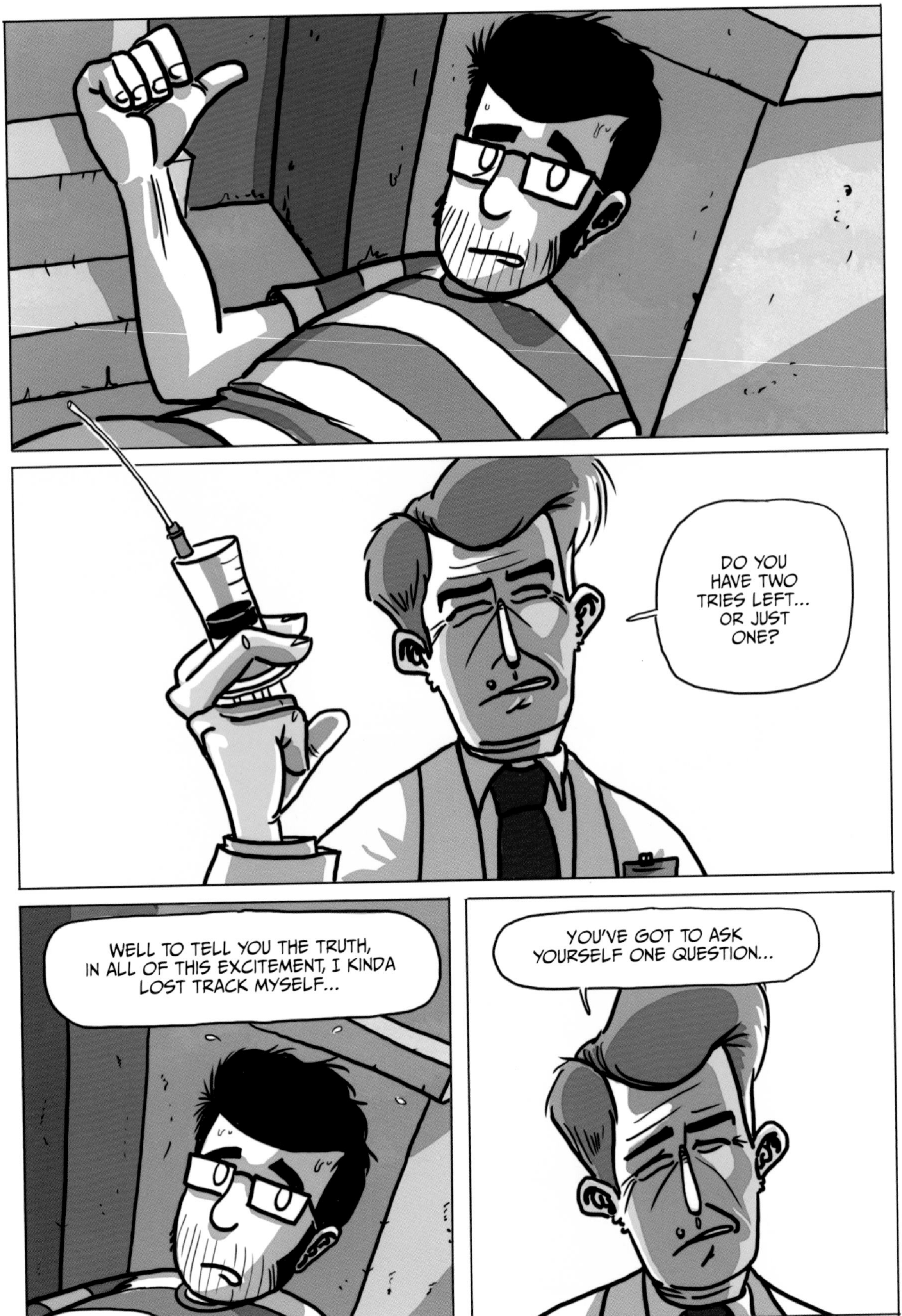
DO YOU HAVE TWO TRIES LEFT... OR JUST ONE?
WELL TO TELL YOU THE TRUTH, IN ALL OF THIS EXCITEMENT, I KINDA LOST TRACK MYSELF...
YOU'VE GOT TO ASK YOURSELF ONE QUESTION...

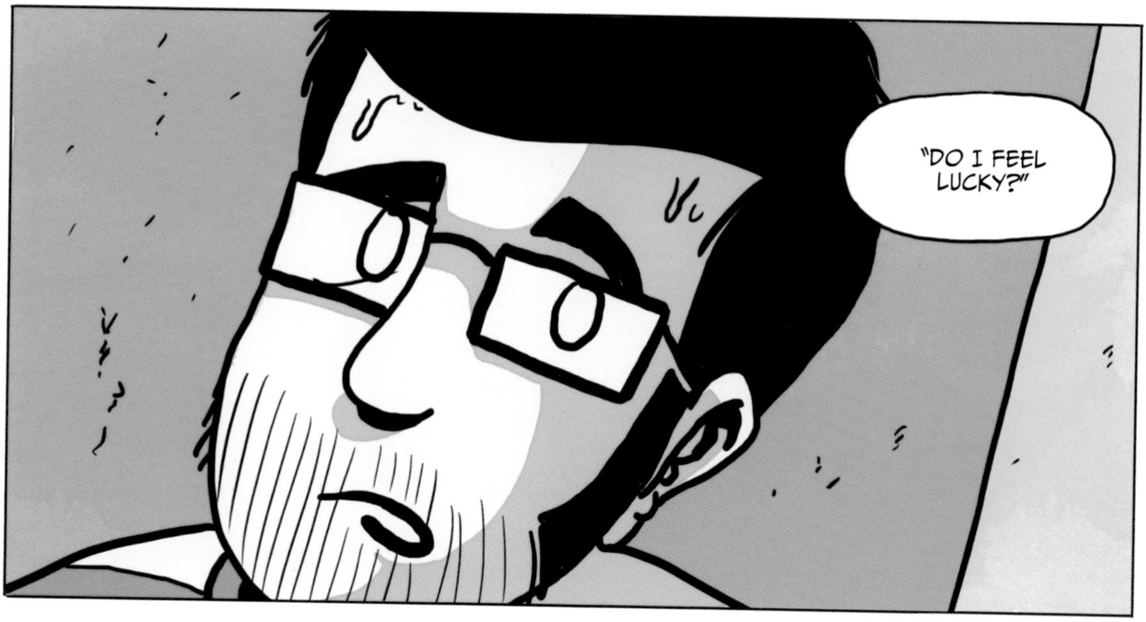
"DO I FEEL LUCKY?"

BEEP BEEP... BEEP BEEP... BEEP BEEP...

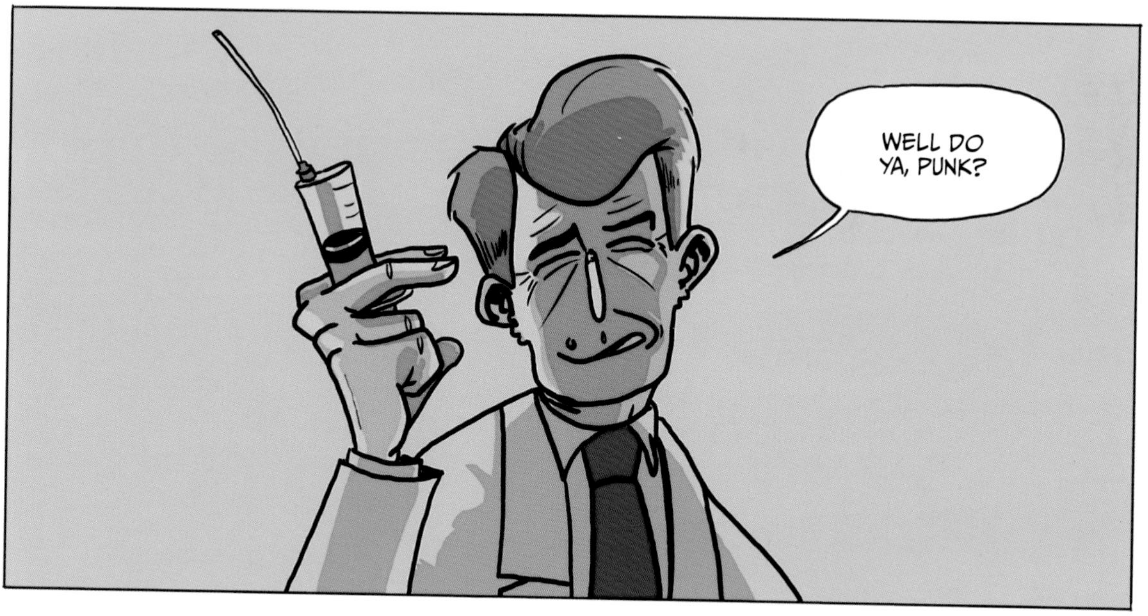
WELL DO YA, PUNK?

BEEP BEEP... BEEP BEEP... BEEP BEEP...

BEEP BEEP...

BEEP BEEP...

BEEP BEEP...

BAM

06:50

IT'S EARLY... WHERE ARE YOU GOING?

I HAVE TO TAKE THE KIDS OUT FOR A WALK, REMEMBER?

HELLO.... I'M MR. LEROY. I'M HERE TO PICK UP THE VIALS YOU PRESERVED.

YOUR I.D., PLEASE.

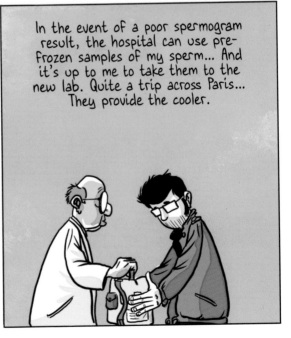

In the event of a poor spermogram result, the hospital can use pre-frozen samples of my sperm... And it's up to me to take them to the new lab. Quite a trip across Paris... They provide the cooler.

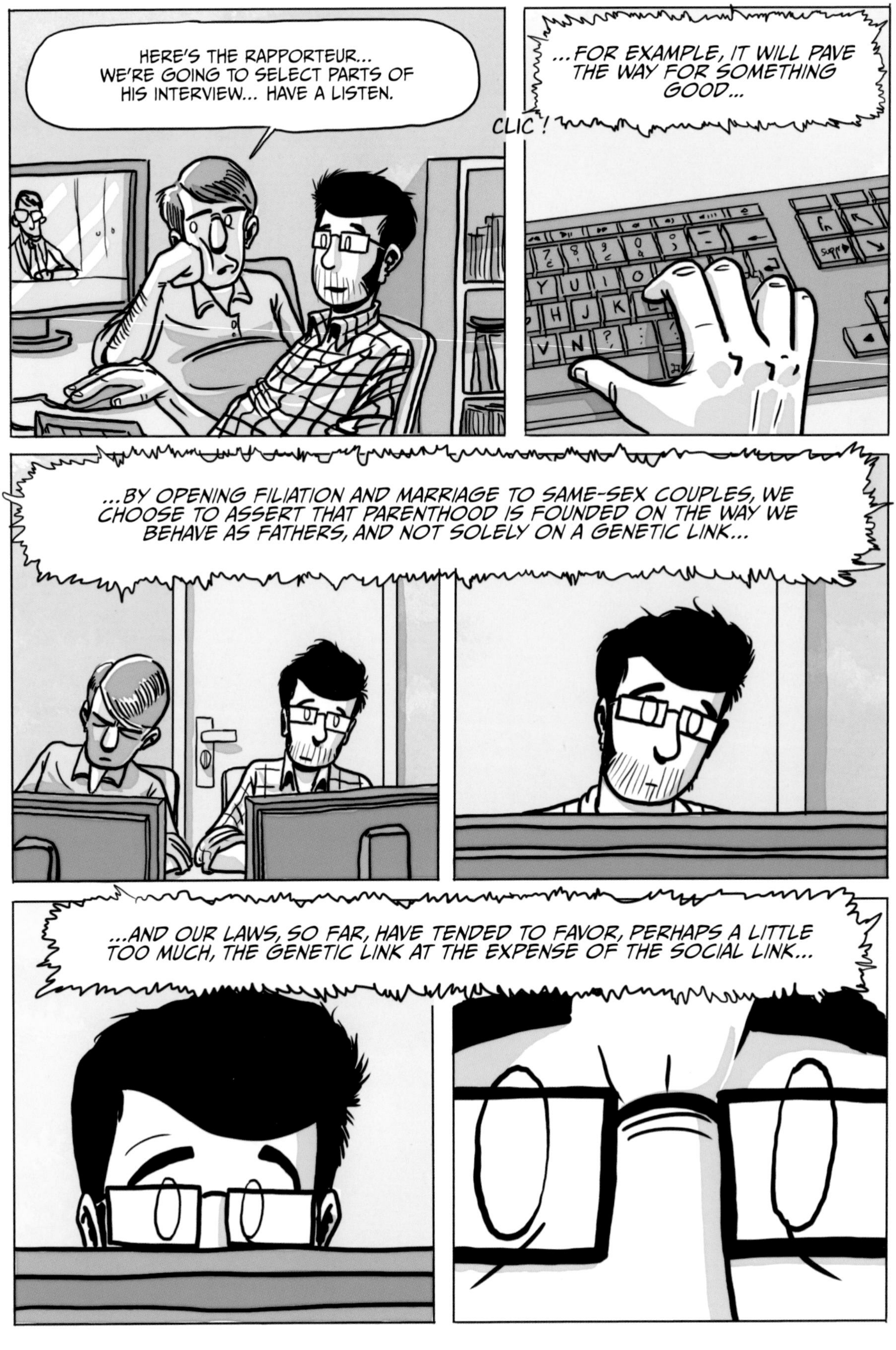
HERE'S THE RAPPORTEUR... WE'RE GOING TO SELECT PARTS OF HIS INTERVIEW... HAVE A LISTEN.
...FOR EXAMPLE, IT WILL PAVE THE WAY FOR SOMETHING GOOD...
CLIC!
...BY OPENING FILIATION AND MARRIAGE TO SAME-SEX COUPLES, WE CHOOSE TO ASSERT THAT PARENTHOOD IS FOUNDED ON THE WAY WE BEHAVE AS FATHERS, AND NOT SOLELY ON A GENETIC LINK...
...AND OUR LAWS, SO FAR, HAVE TENDED TO FAVOR, PERHAPS A LITTLE TOO MUCH, THE GENETIC LINK AT THE EXPENSE OF THE SOCIAL LINK...

From: Guillaume Leroy
Subject: Re: Re: Re: Re: Re: Re: Re: News?
Date: October 11, 2012 8:17:14 PM CET
To: Jean-Pierre Leroy

I have the feeling that instead of reviving our relationship, our exchange has only made things worse between us.

I have a fulfilling family life, many friends and a job I love: I no longer have the energy to sacrifice part of that life in order to let you into it.

I suppose both of us are clumsy and that we aren't intent on hurting each other, but I'd rather not go any further.

Maybe in the near or distant future, I will be able to agree to meeting you in person. For now though, I have to focus on other things that are more important to me.

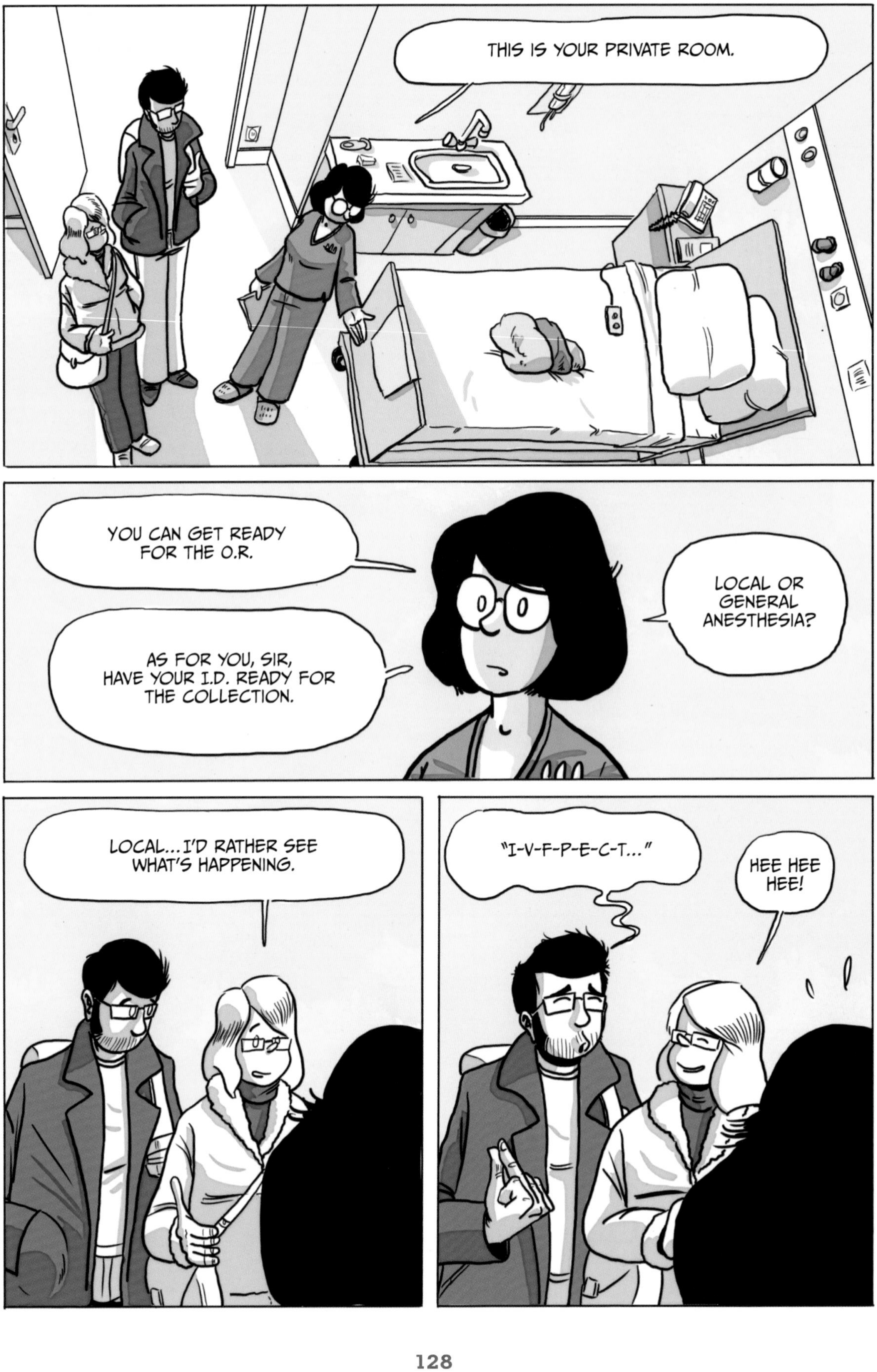
THIS IS YOUR PRIVATE ROOM.
YOU CAN GET READY FOR THE O.R.
AS FOR YOU, SIR, HAVE YOUR I.D. READY FOR THE COLLECTION.
LOCAL OR GENERAL ANESTHESIA?
LOCAL... I'D RATHER SEE WHAT'S HAPPENING.
"I-V-F-P-E-C-T..."
HEE HEE HEE!

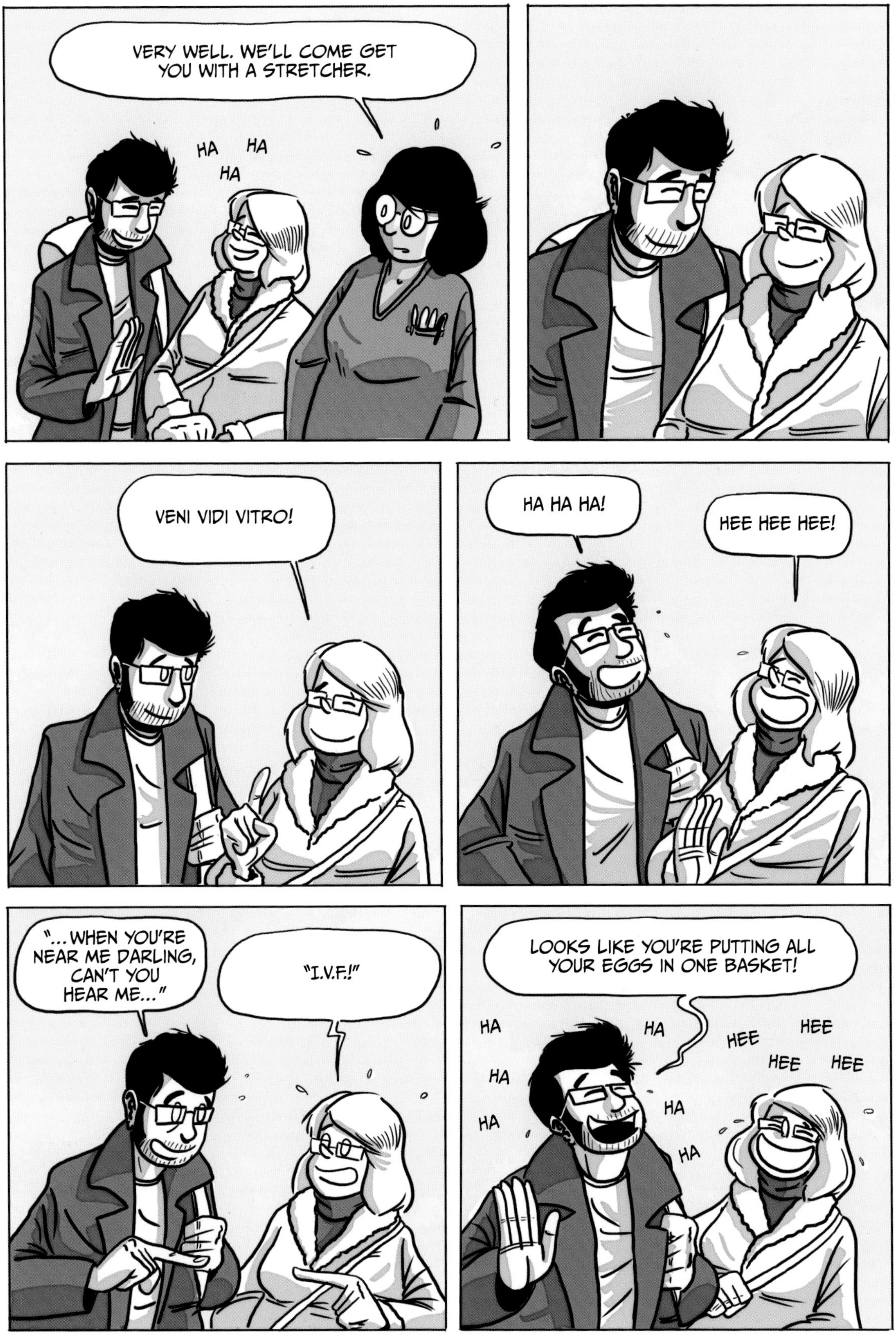
VERY WELL. WE'LL COME GET YOU WITH A STRETCHER.
HA HA HA
VENI VIDI VITRO!
HA HA HA!
HEE HEE HEE!
"...WHEN YOU'RE NEAR ME DARLING, CAN'T YOU HEAR ME..."
"I.V.F.!"
LOOKS LIKE YOU'RE PUTTING ALL YOUR EGGS IN ONE BASKET!
HA HA HA HA HA HA HA
HEE HEE HEE HEE

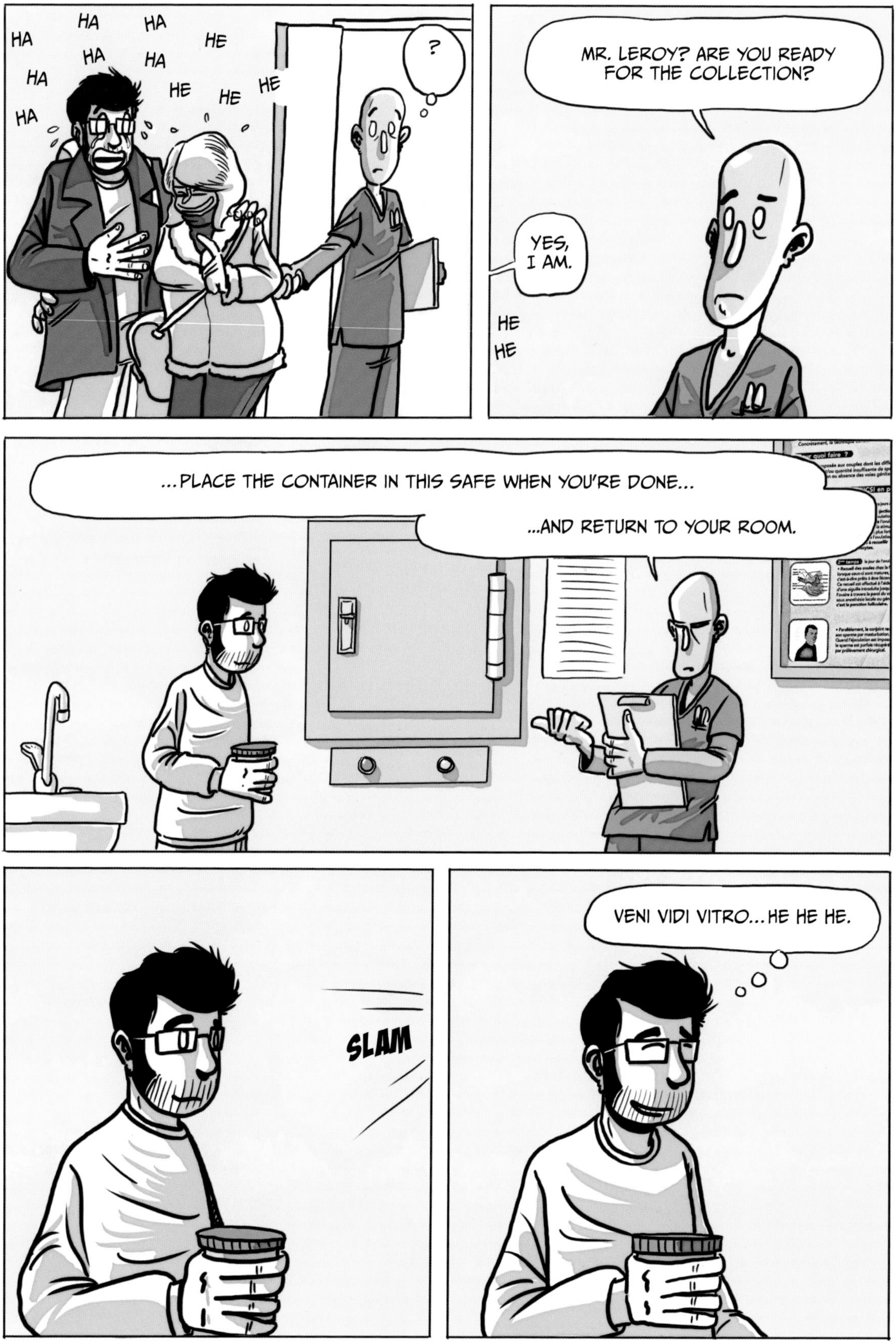
HA HA HA HA HA HA HA
HE HE HE HE
?
MR. LEROY? ARE YOU READY FOR THE COLLECTION?
YES, I AM.
HE HE
...PLACE THE CONTAINER IN THIS SAFE WHEN YOU'RE DONE...
...AND RETURN TO YOUR ROOM.
SLAM
VENI VIDI VITRO...HE HE HE.

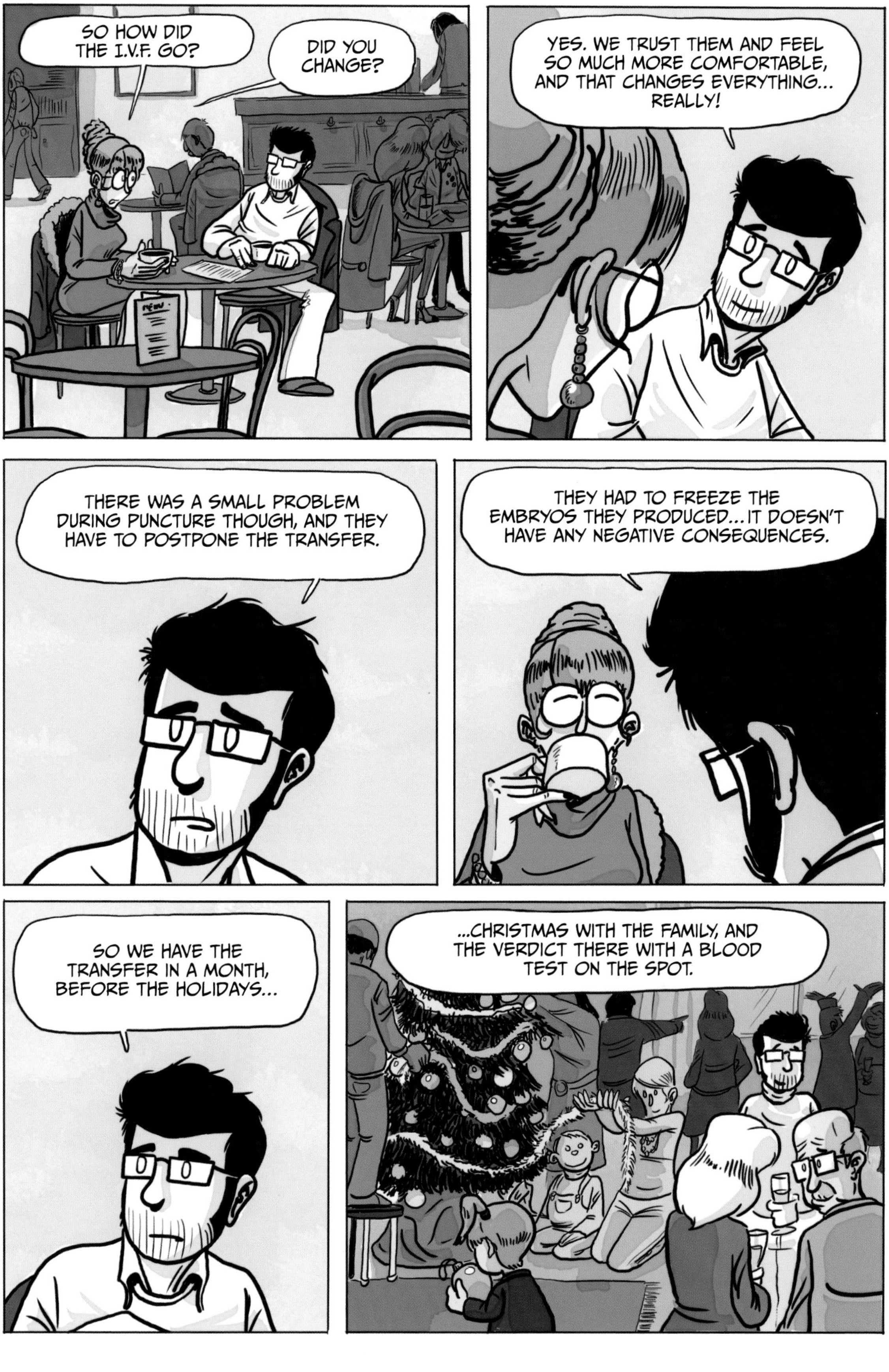
SO HOW DID THE I.V.F. GO?
DID YOU CHANGE?
YES. WE TRUST THEM AND FEEL SO MUCH MORE COMFORTABLE, AND THAT CHANGES EVERYTHING... REALLY!
THERE WAS A SMALL PROBLEM DURING PUNCTURE THOUGH, AND THEY HAVE TO POSTPONE THE TRANSFER.
THEY HAD TO FREEZE THE EMBRYOS THEY PRODUCED... IT DOESN'T HAVE ANY NEGATIVE CONSEQUENCES.
SO WE HAVE THE TRANSFER IN A MONTH, BEFORE THE HOLIDAYS...
...CHRISTMAS WITH THE FAMILY, AND THE VERDICT THERE WITH A BLOOD TEST ON THE SPOT.

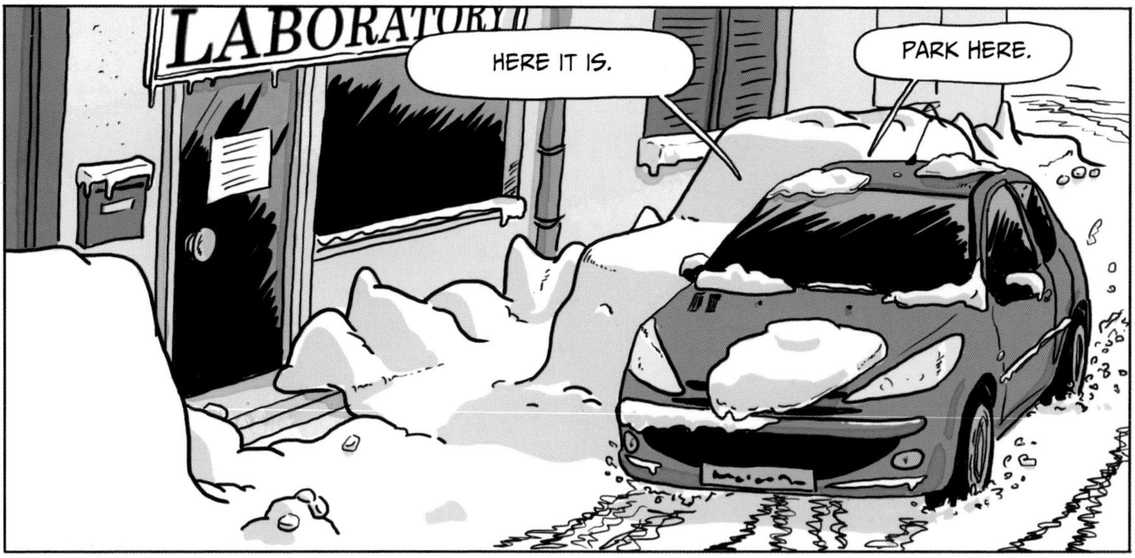
LABORATORY
HERE IT IS.
PARK HERE.

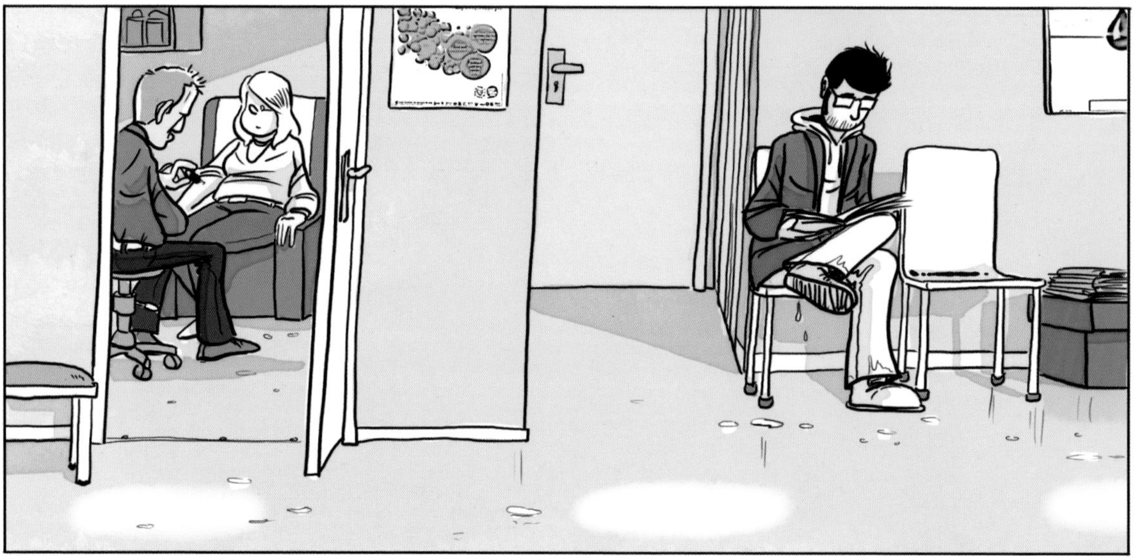

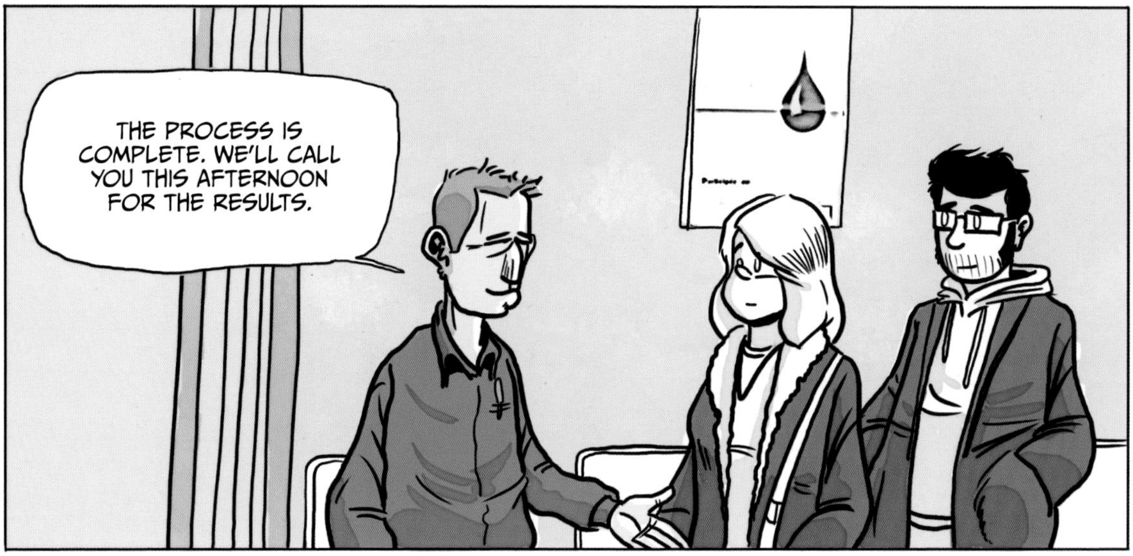
THE PROCESS IS COMPLETE. WE'LL CALL YOU THIS AFTERNOON FOR THE RESULTS.

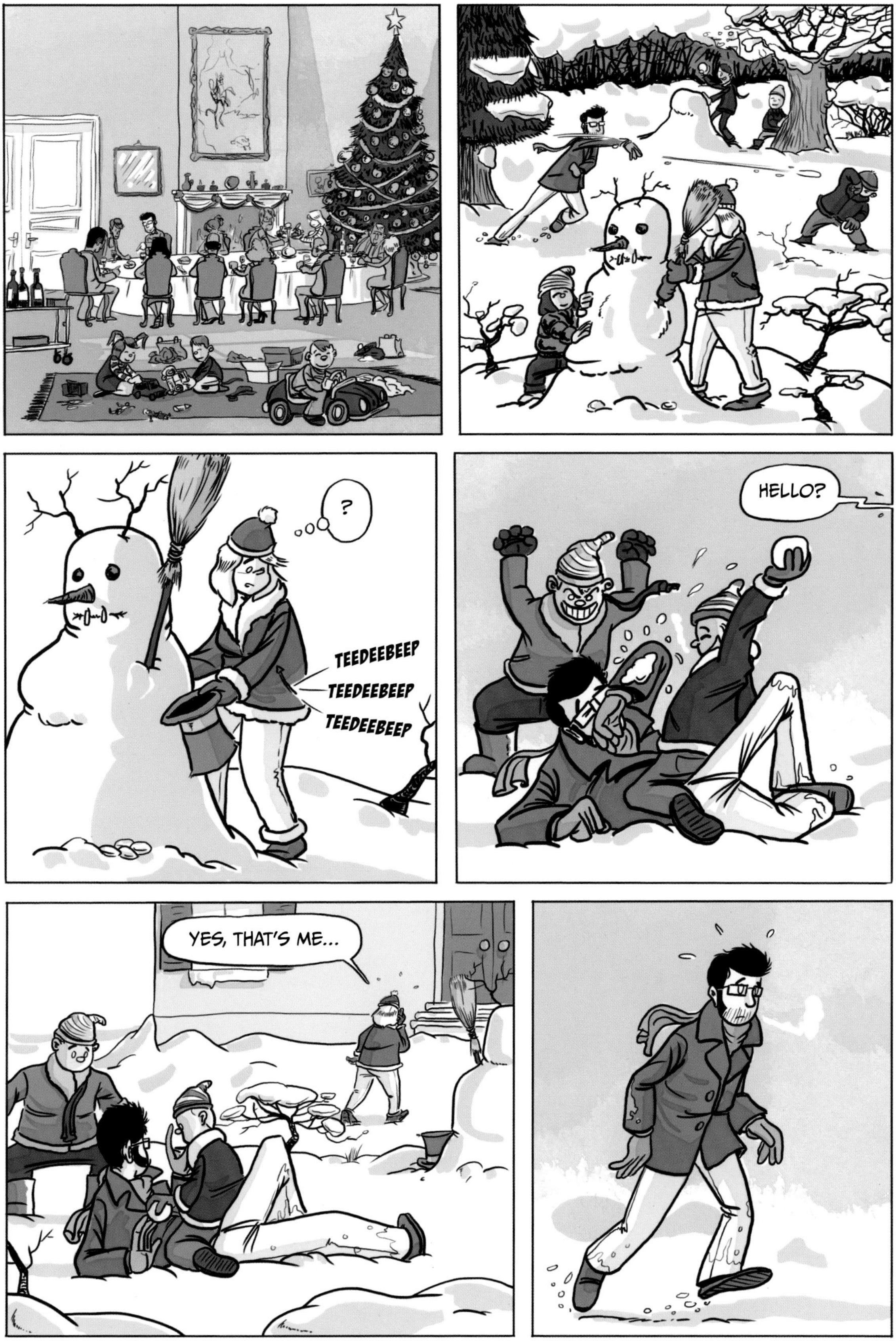
?
TEEDEEBEEP
TEEDEEBEEP
TEEDEEBEEP
HELLO?
YES, THAT'S ME...

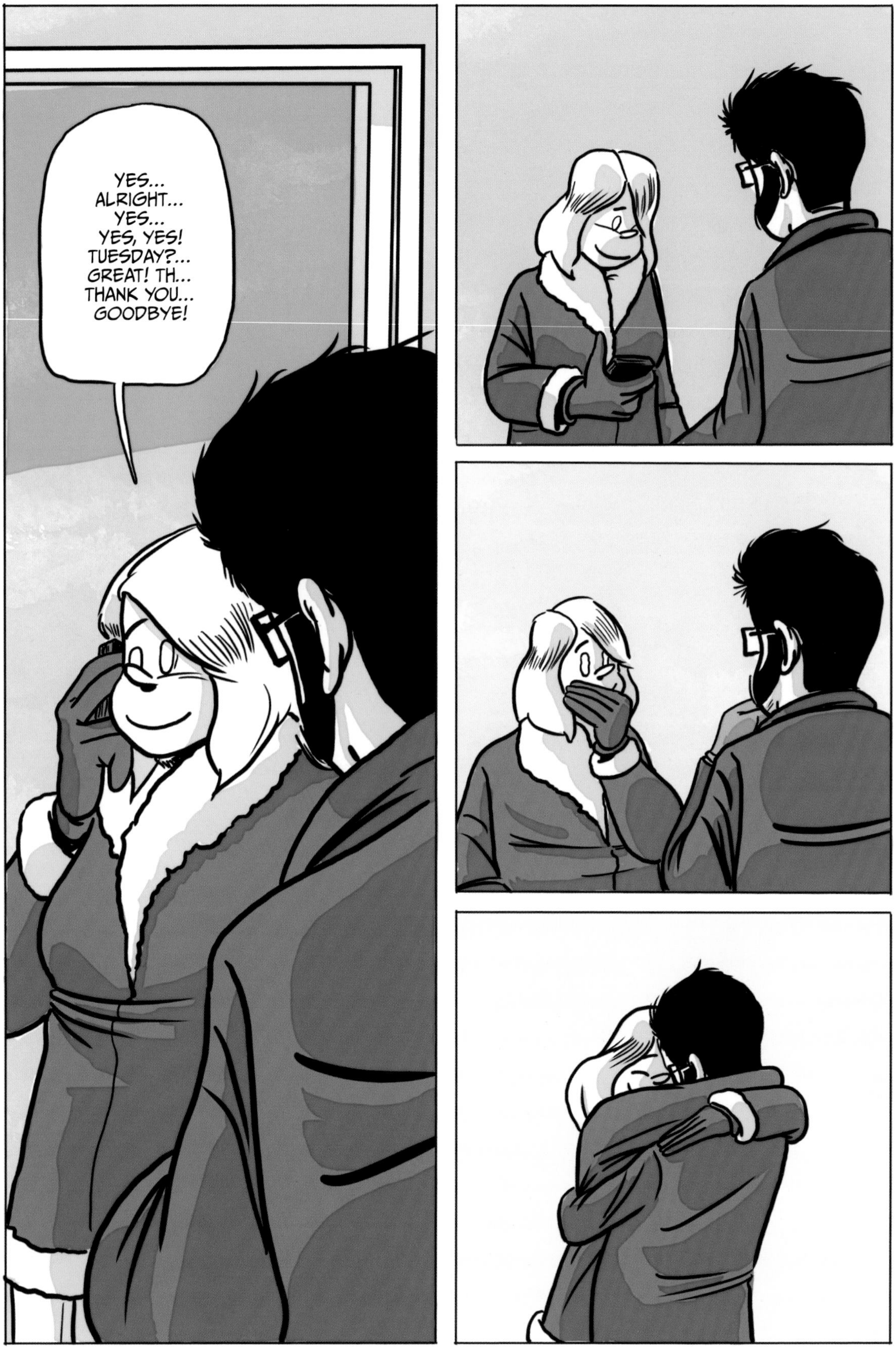
YES... ALRIGHT... YES... YES, YES! TUESDAY?... GREAT! TH... THANK YOU... GOODBYE!

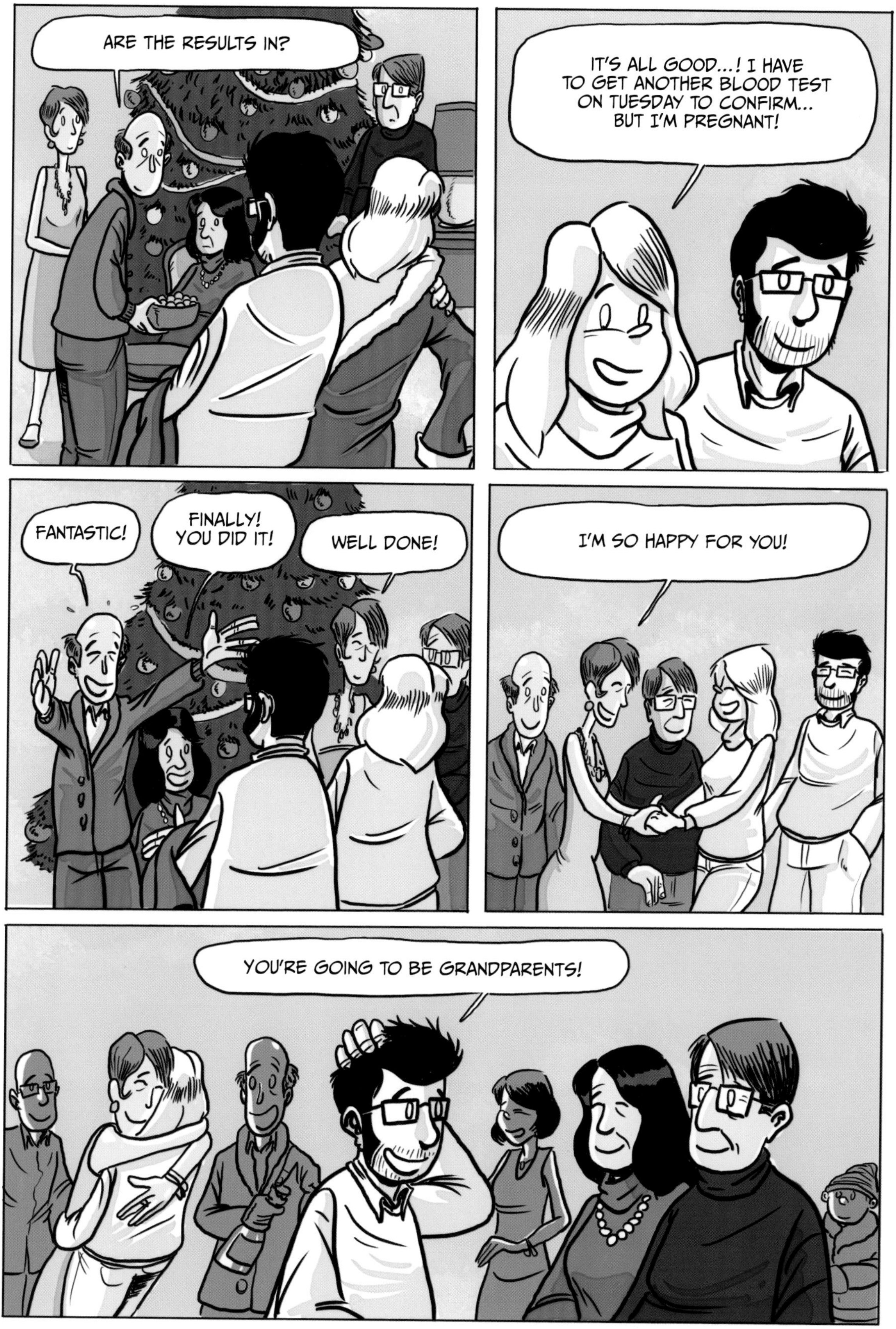
ARE THE RESULTS IN?
IT'S ALL GOOD...! I HAVE TO GET ANOTHER BLOOD TEST ON TUESDAY TO CONFIRM... BUT I'M PREGNANT!
FANTASTIC!
FINALLY! YOU DID IT!
WELL DONE!
I'M SO HAPPY FOR YOU!
YOU'RE GOING TO BE GRANDPARENTS!

SIR 153A482: LEROY Emma 28 F
01/12/2013 3:35:18pm
SA 5s2j
Aplio MX - 2010 US.7 gynecology
D1

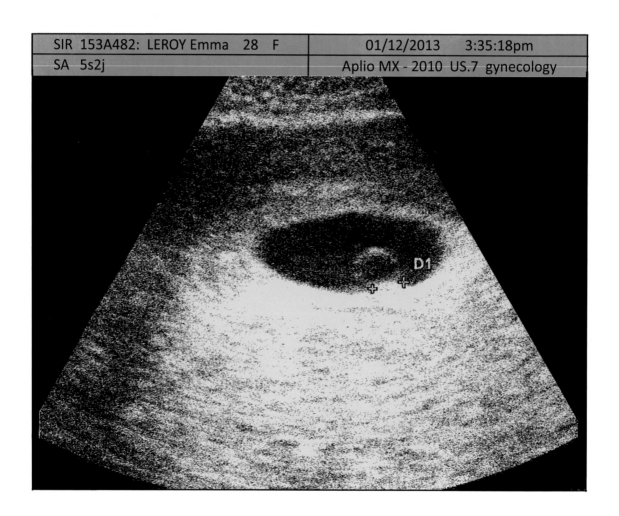

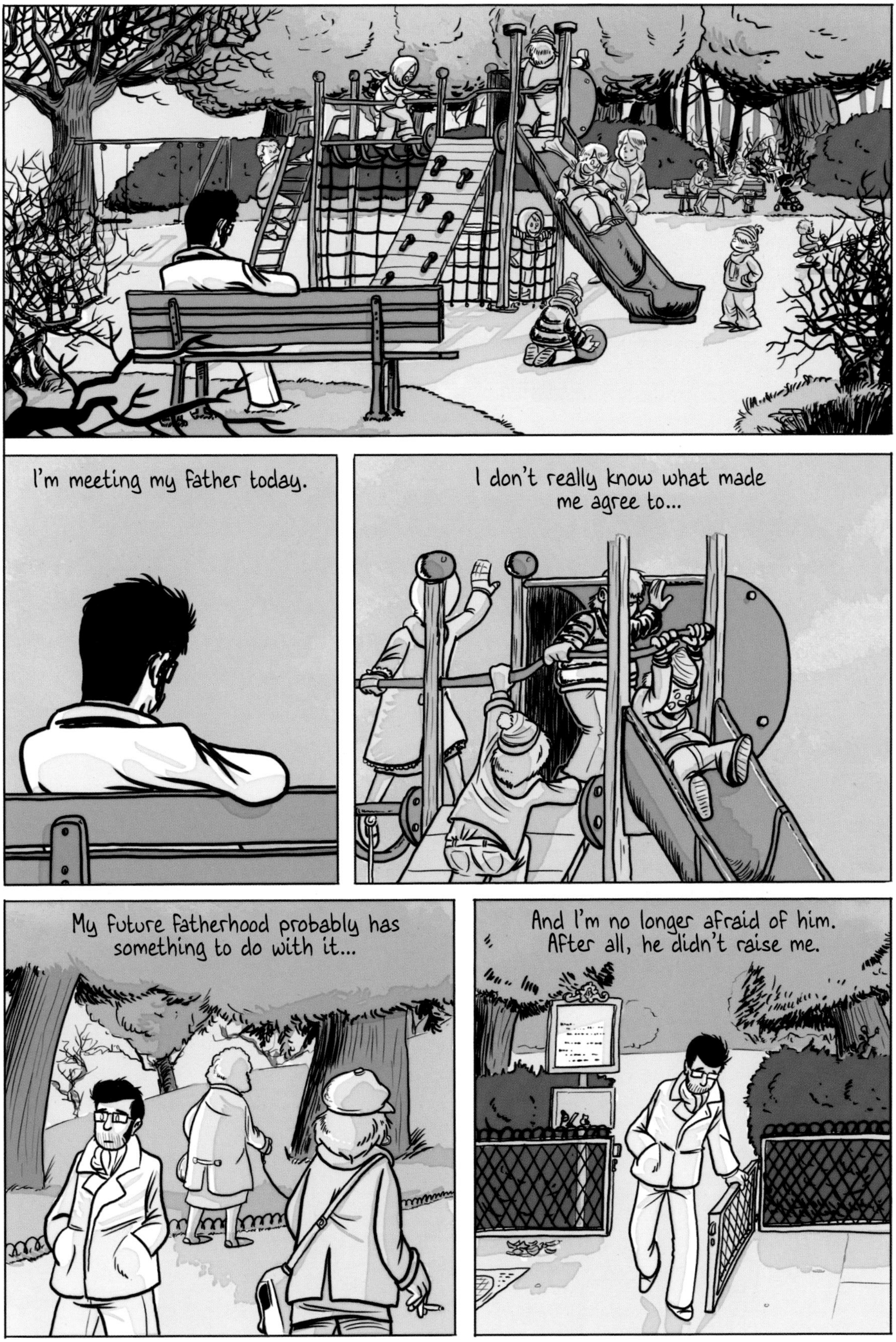
I'm meeting my father today.
I don't really know what made me agree to...
My future fatherhood probably has something to do with it...
And I'm no longer afraid of him. After all, he didn't raise me.

Yet I can't help but feel intimidated. I'm delaying the moment.

I'm half-an-hour late and I'm dragging my feet hoping to miss him.

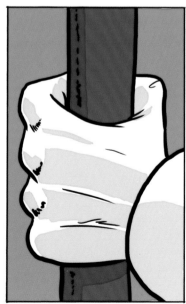

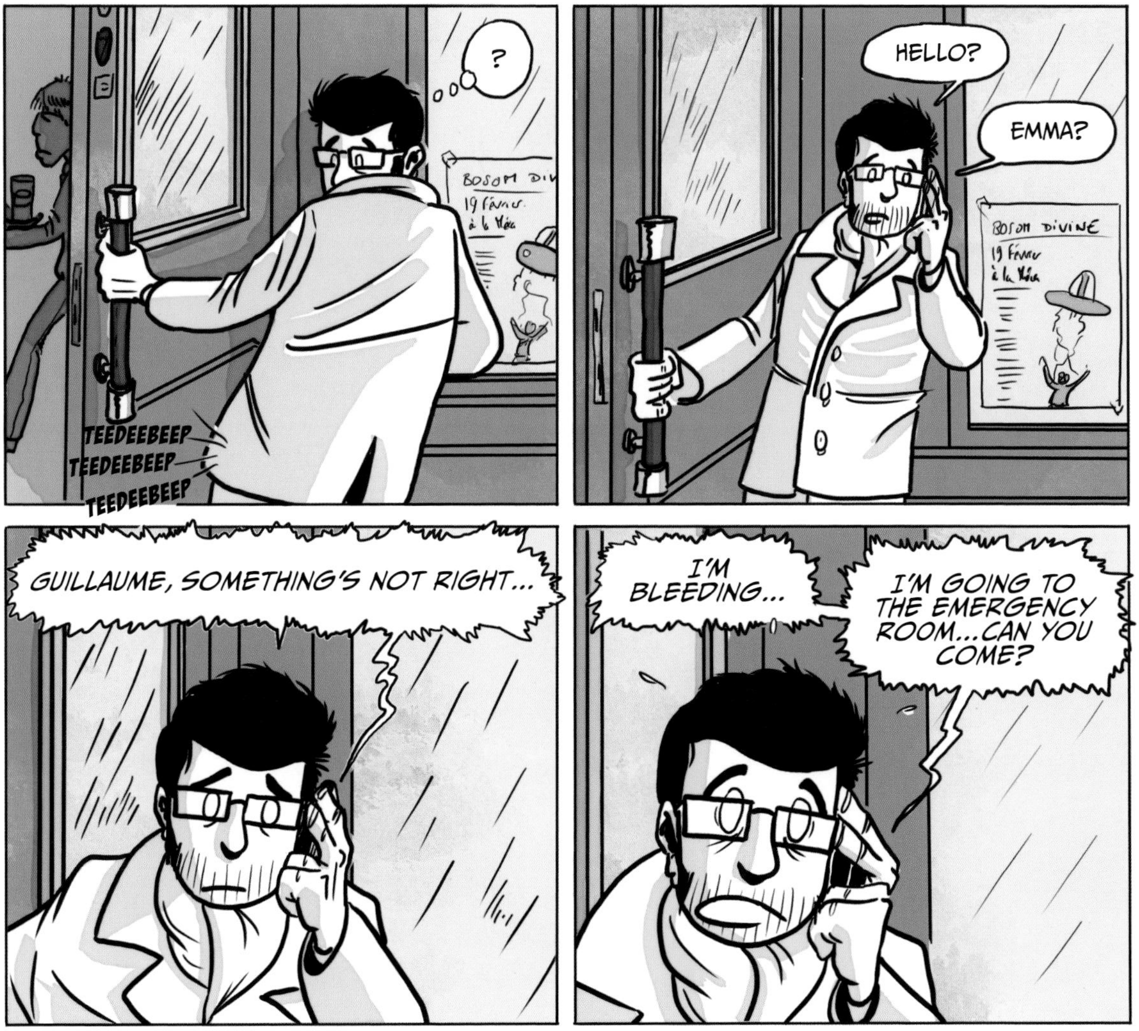
?
TEEDEEBEEP
TEEDEEBEEP
TEEDEEBEEP
HELLO?
EMMA?
BOSOM DIVINE
GUILLAUME, SOMETHING'S NOT RIGHT...
I'M BLEEDING...
I'M GOING TO THE EMERGENCY ROOM...CAN YOU COME?

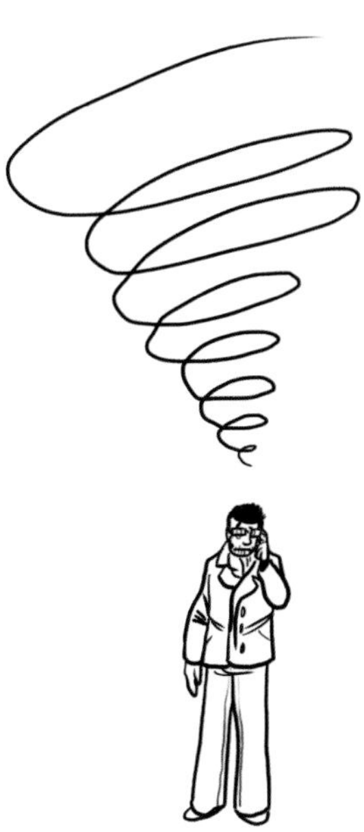

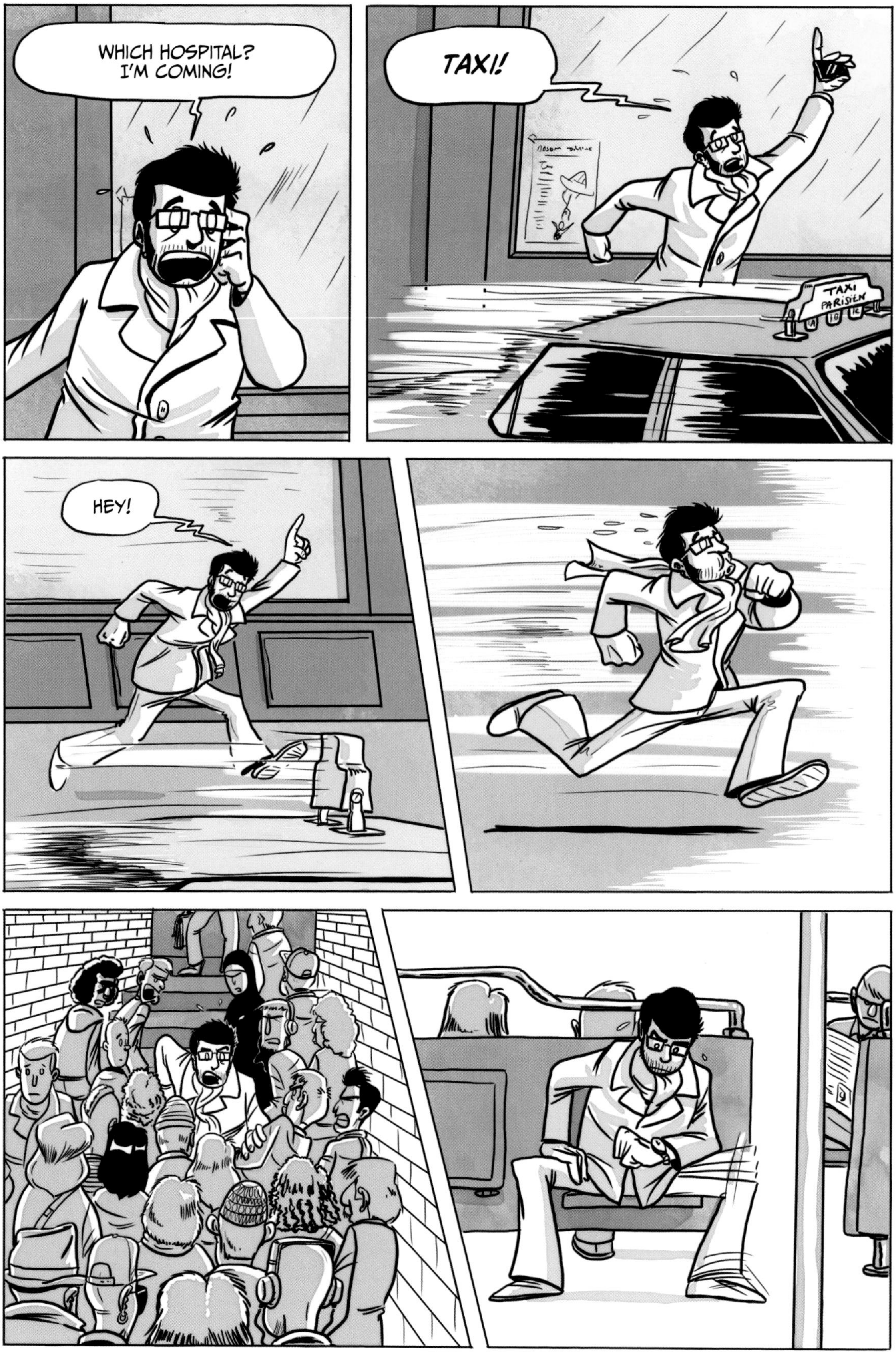
WHICH HOSPITAL? I'M COMING!
TAXI!
TAXI PARISIEN
HEY!

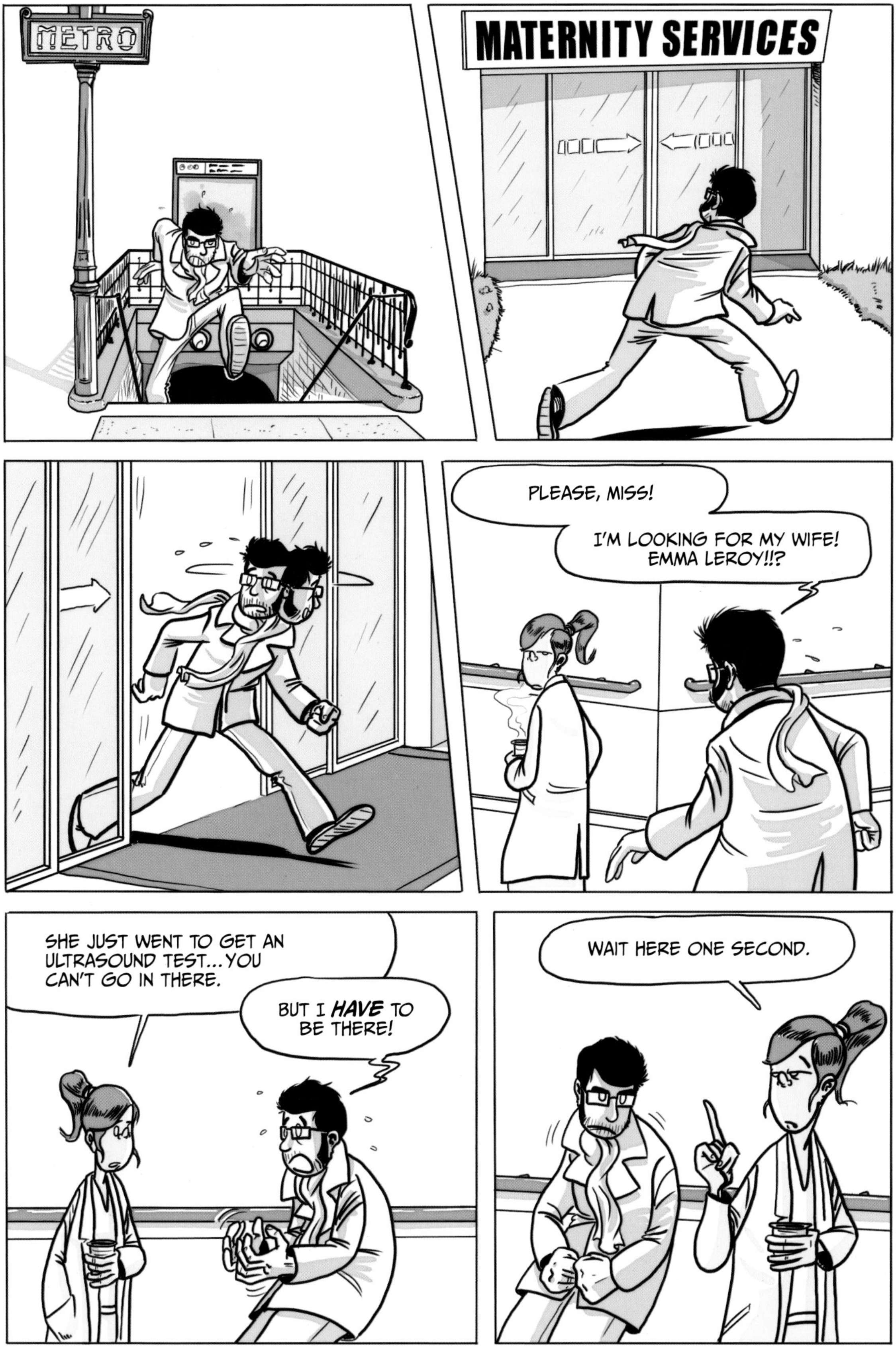
METRO
MATERNITY SERVICES
PLEASE, MISS!
I'M LOOKING FOR MY WIFE! EMMA LEROY!!?
SHE JUST WENT TO GET AN ULTRASOUND TEST... YOU CAN'T GO IN THERE.
BUT I ***HAVE*** TO BE THERE!
WAIT HERE ONE SECOND.

IT'S OKAY...FOLLOW ME.

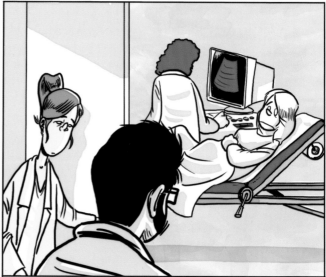

ARE YOU OKAY?

ALRIGHT, THE BLEEDING STOPPED A LITTLE WHILE AGO...I'M GOING TO DO AN ULTRASOUND.

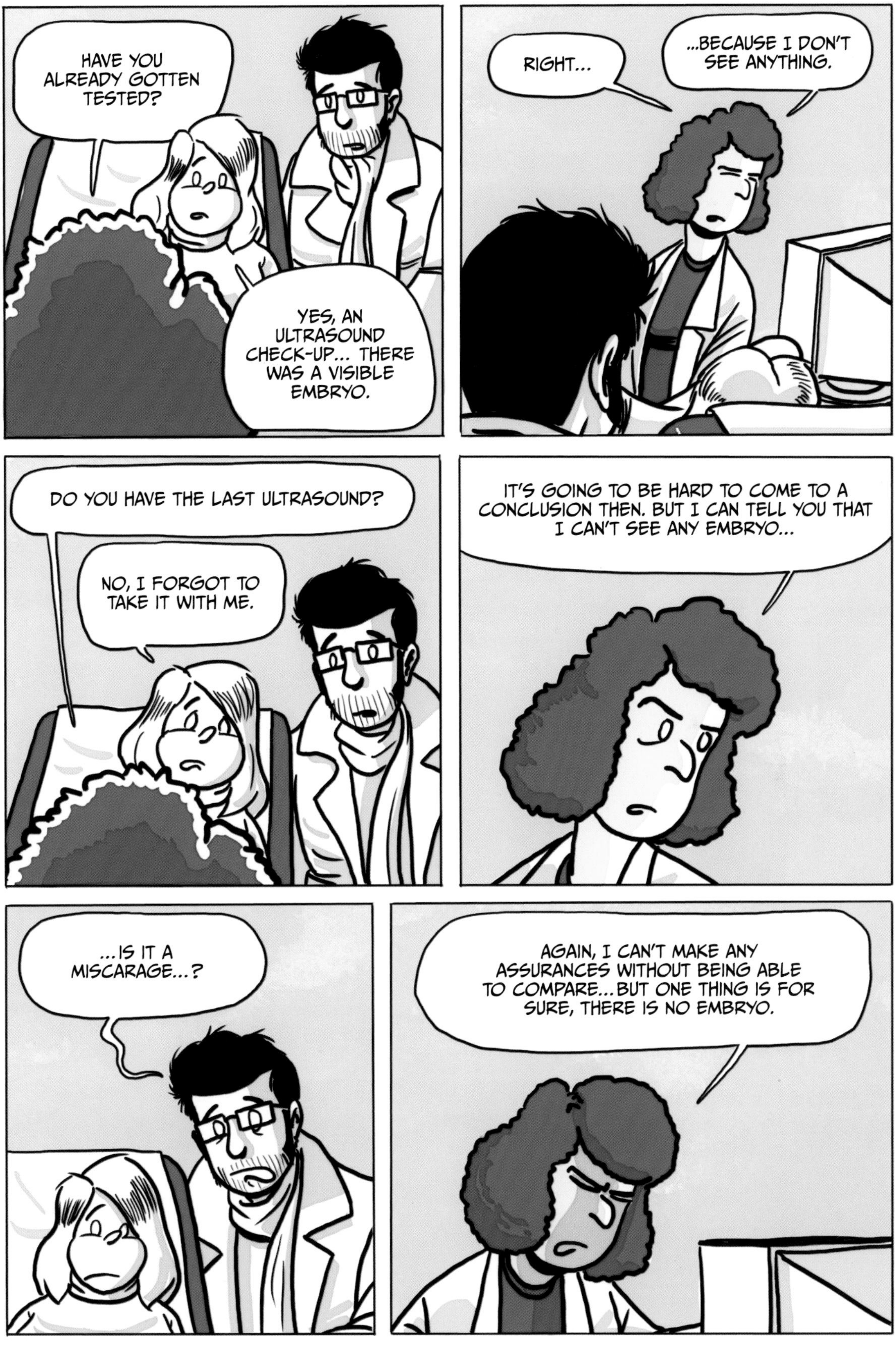
HAVE YOU ALREADY GOTTEN TESTED?
YES, AN ULTRASOUND CHECK-UP... THERE WAS A VISIBLE EMBRYO.
RIGHT...
...BECAUSE I DON'T SEE ANYTHING.
DO YOU HAVE THE LAST ULTRASOUND?
NO, I FORGOT TO TAKE IT WITH ME.
IT'S GOING TO BE HARD TO COME TO A CONCLUSION THEN. BUT I CAN TELL YOU THAT I CAN'T SEE ANY EMBRYO...
...IS IT A MISCARAGE...?
AGAIN, I CAN'T MAKE ANY ASSURANCES WITHOUT BEING ABLE TO COMPARE...BUT ONE THING IS FOR SURE, THERE IS NO EMBRYO.

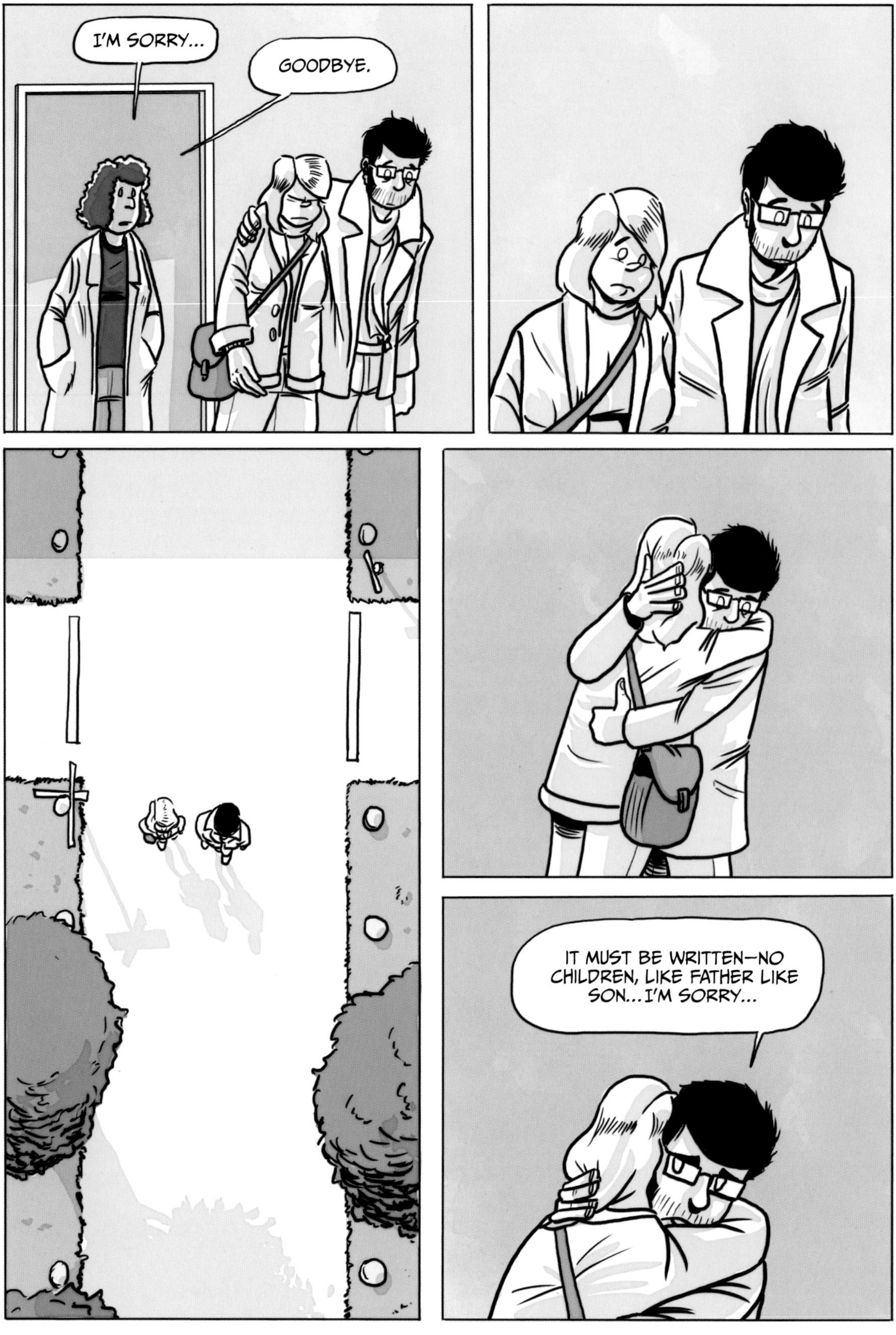
I'M SORRY...
GOODBYE.
IT MUST BE WRITTEN—NO CHILDREN, LIKE FATHER LIKE SON... I'M SORRY...

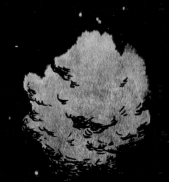

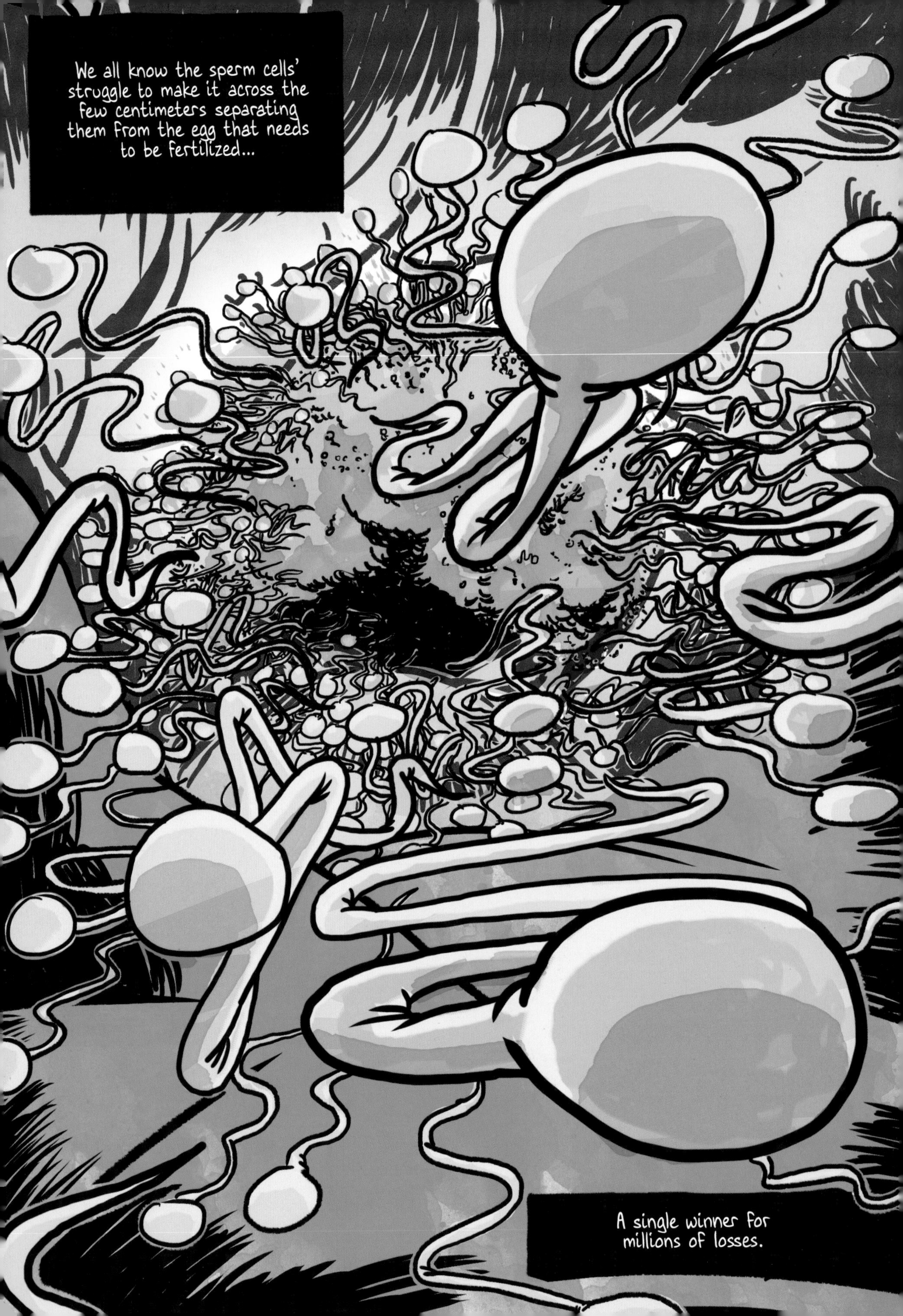
We all know the sperm cells' struggle to make it across the few centimeters separating them from the egg that needs to be fertilized...
A single winner for millions of losses.

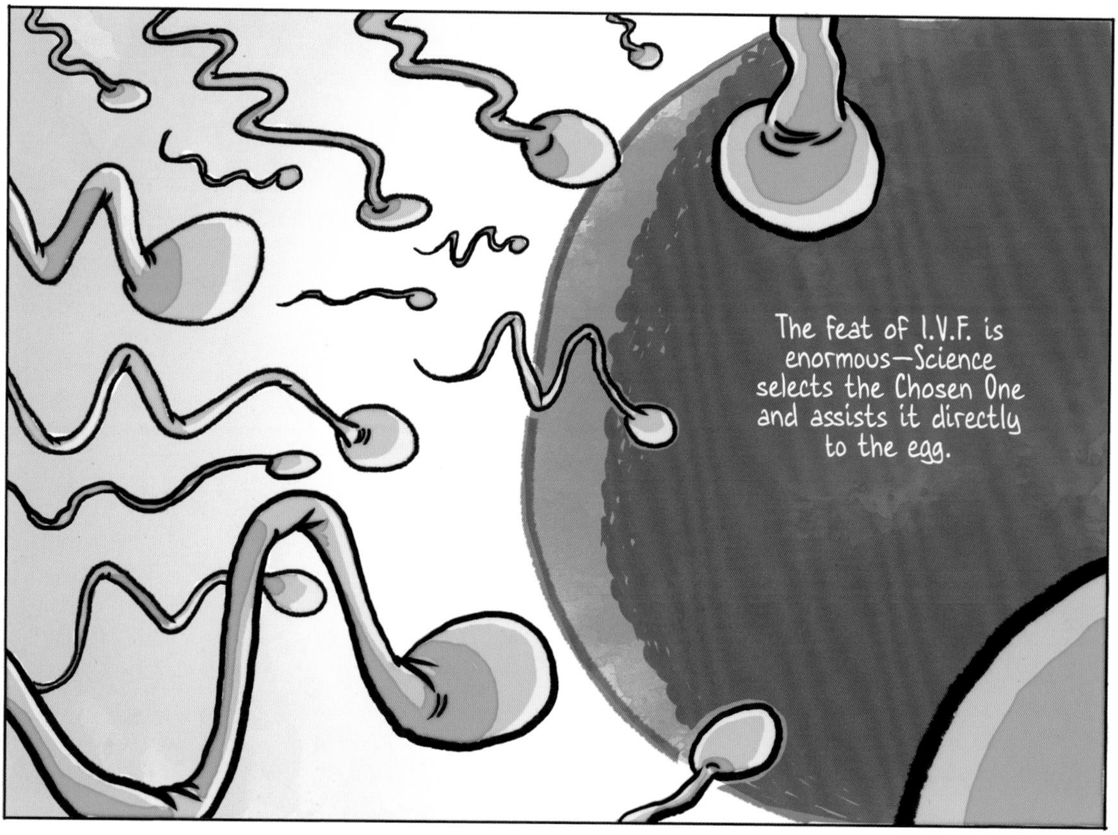
The feat of I.V.F. is enormous—Science selects the Chosen One and assists it directly to the egg.

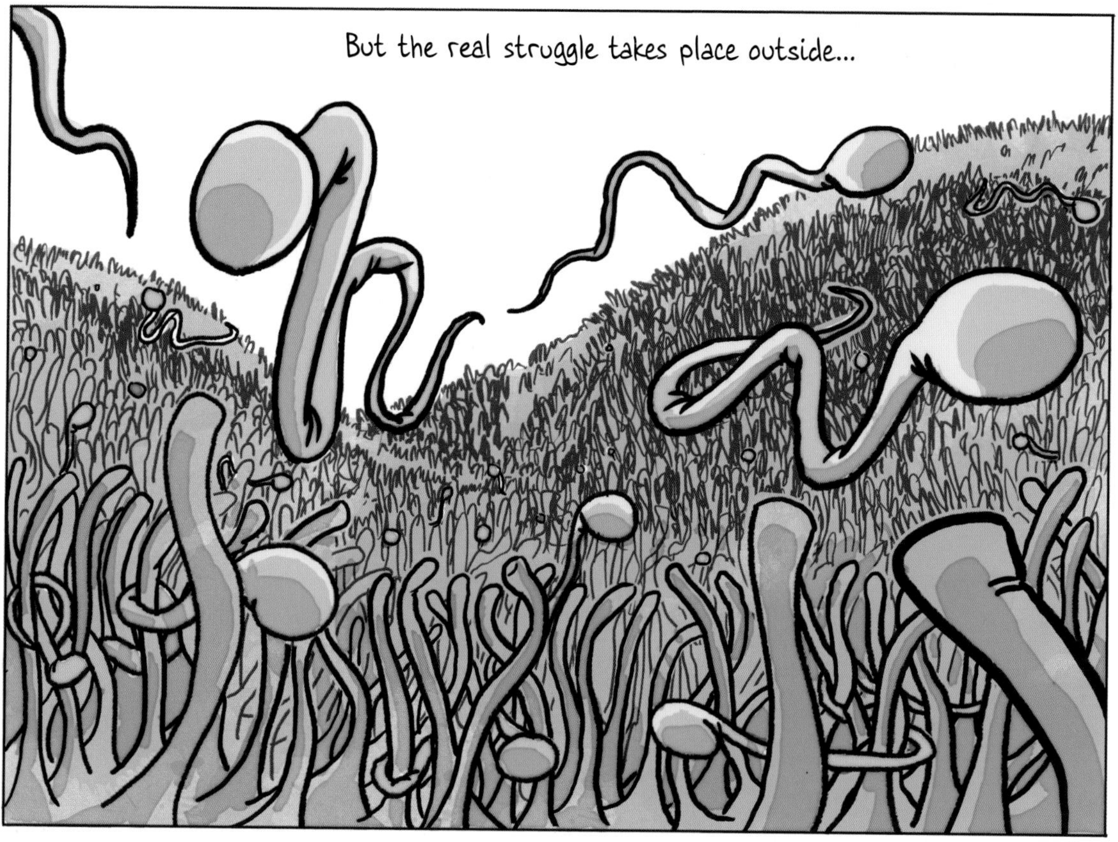
But the real struggle takes place outside...

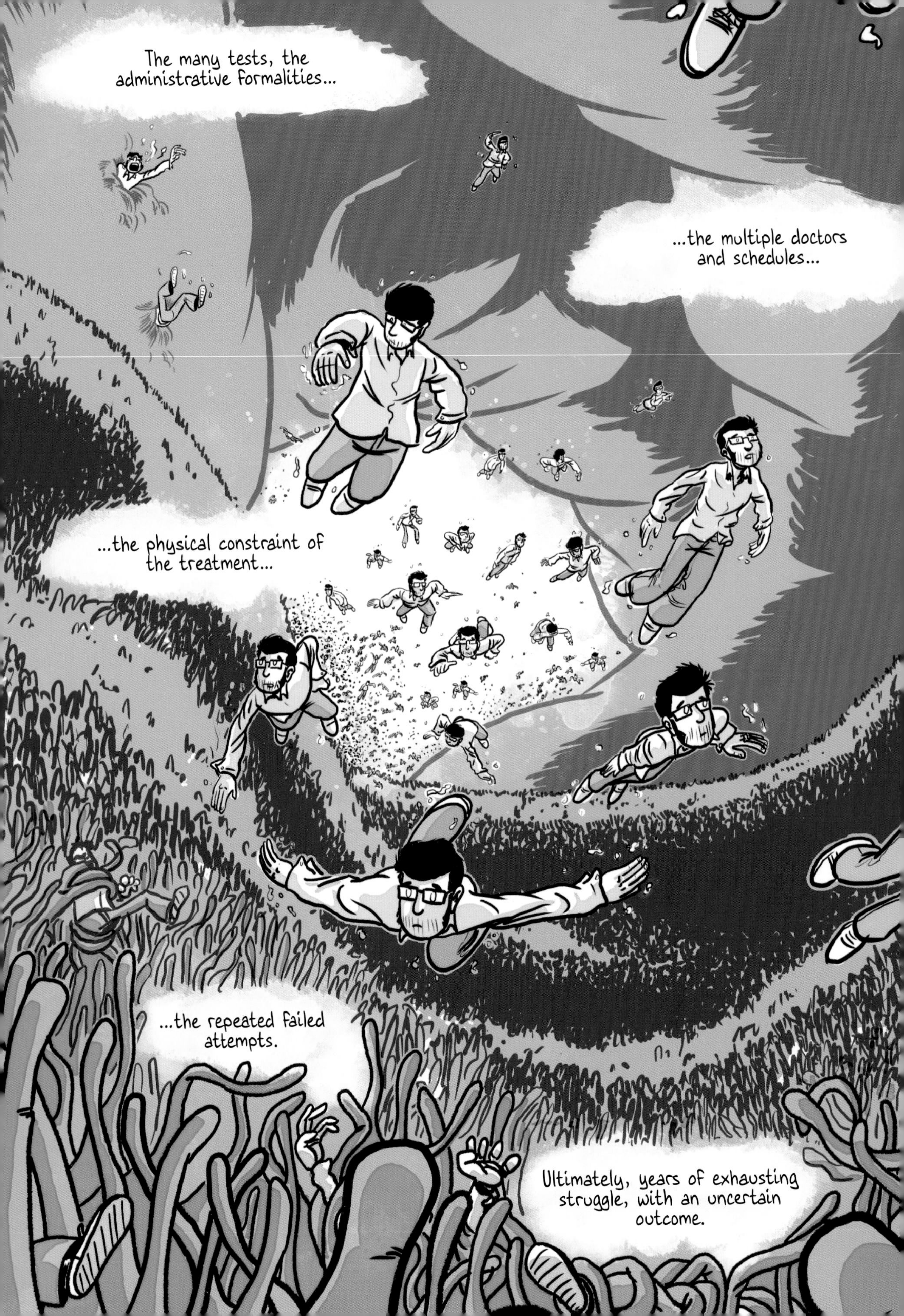

The many tests, the administrative formalities...
...the multiple doctors and schedules...
...the physical constraint of the treatment...
...the repeated failed attempts.
Ultimately, years of exhausting struggle, with an uncertain outcome.

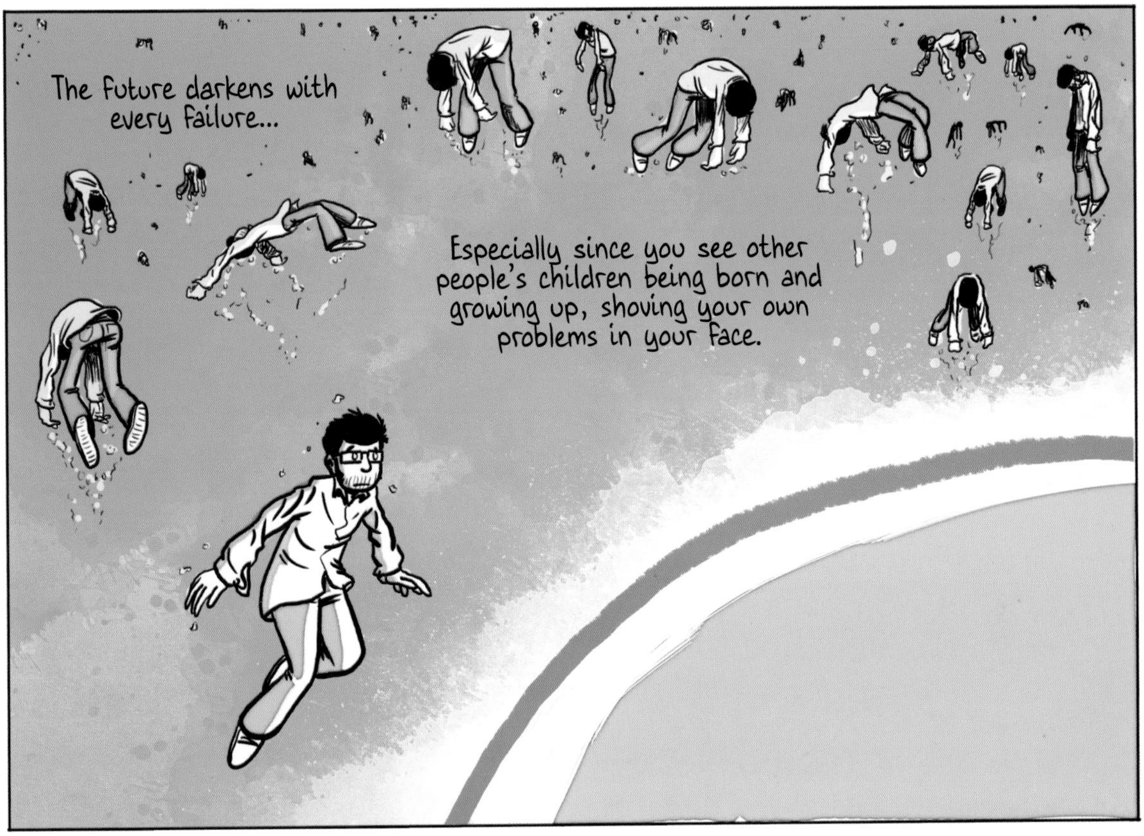
The future darkens with every failure...
Especially since you see other people's children being born and growing up, shoving your own problems in your face.

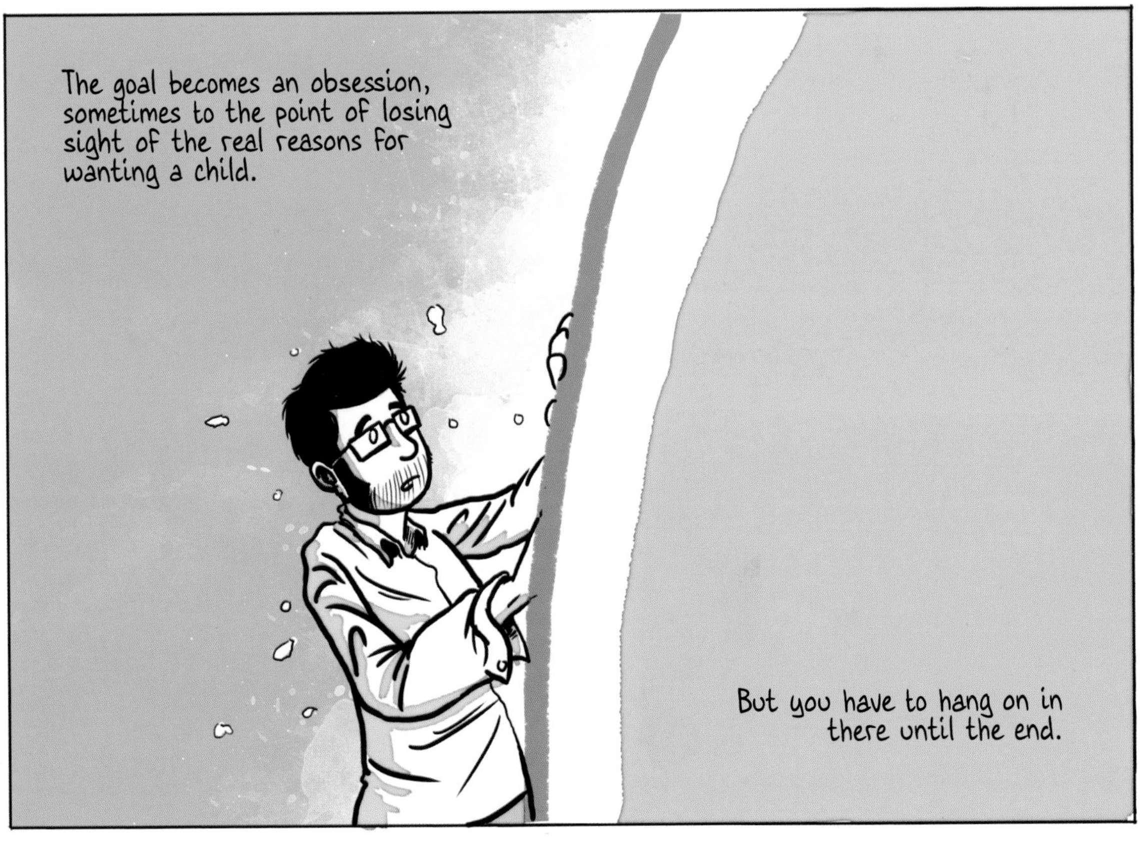
The goal becomes an obsession, sometimes to the point of losing sight of the real reasons for wanting a child.
But you have to hang on in there until the end.

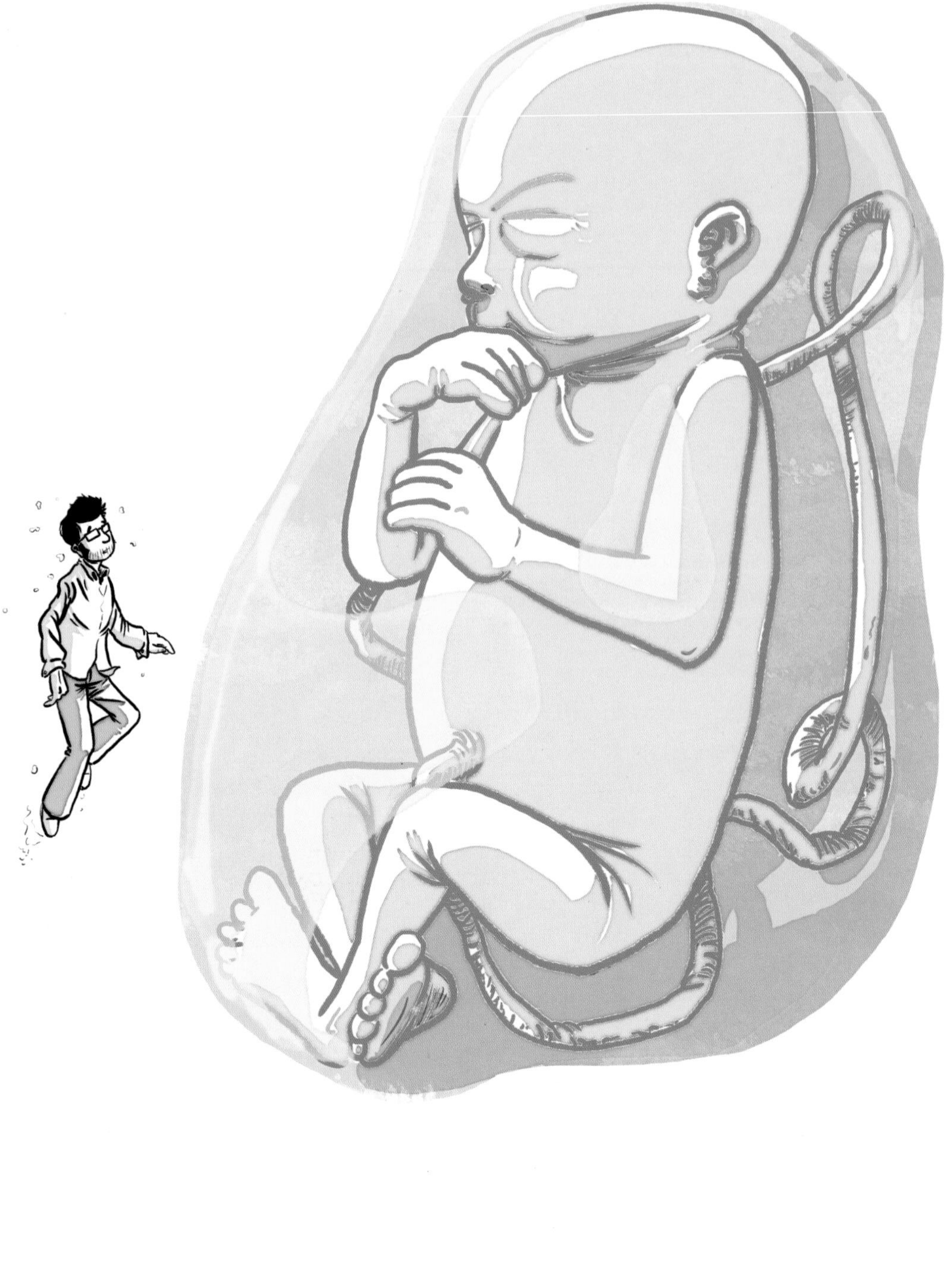

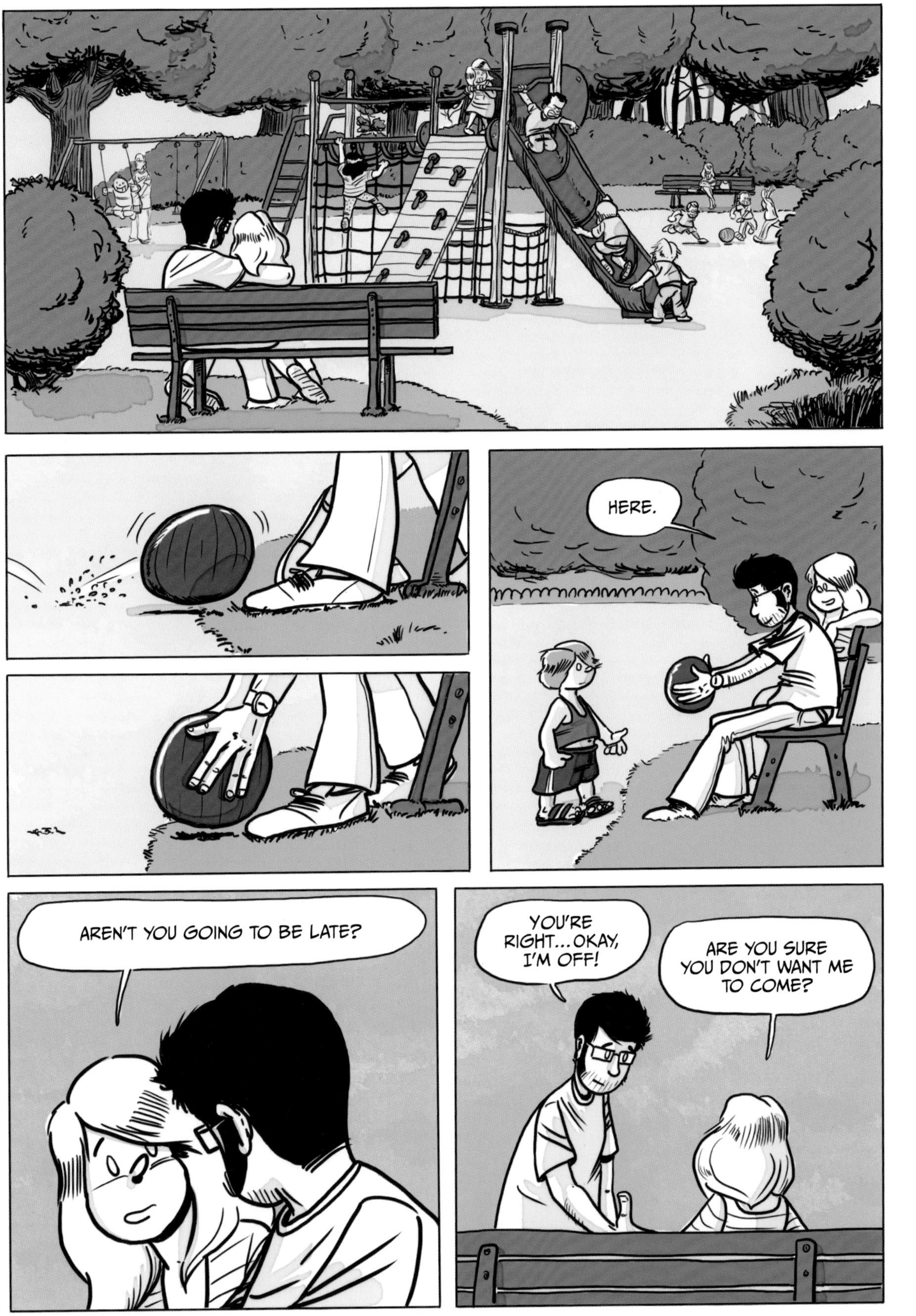
HERE.
AREN'T YOU GOING TO BE LATE?
YOU'RE RIGHT... OKAY, I'M OFF!
ARE YOU SURE YOU DON'T WANT ME TO COME?

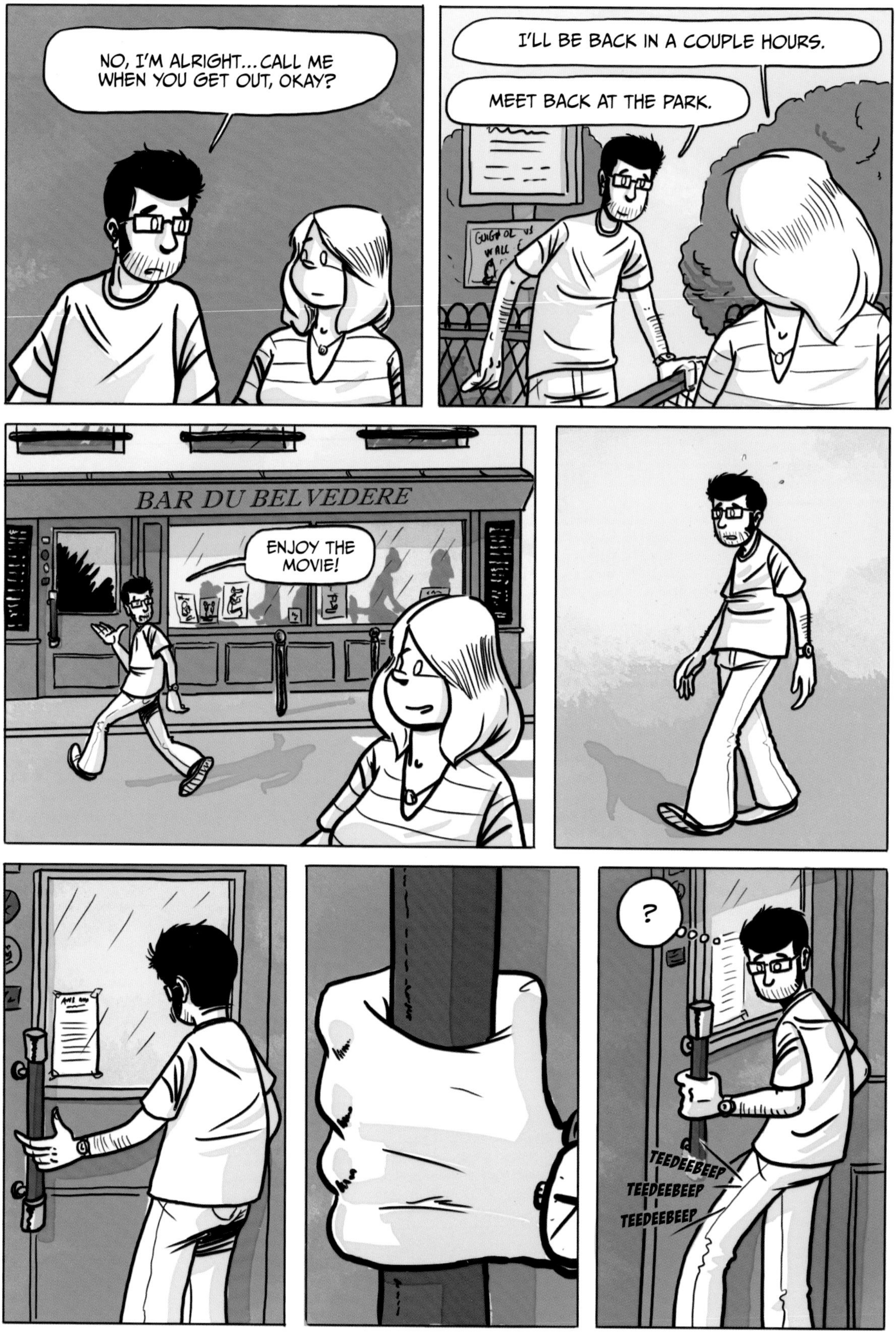
NO, I'M ALRIGHT...CALL ME WHEN YOU GET OUT, OKAY?
I'LL BE BACK IN A COUPLE HOURS.
MEET BACK AT THE PARK.
BAR DU BELVEDERE
ENJOY THE MOVIE!
?
TEEDEEBEEP
TEEDEEBEEP
TEEDEEBEEP

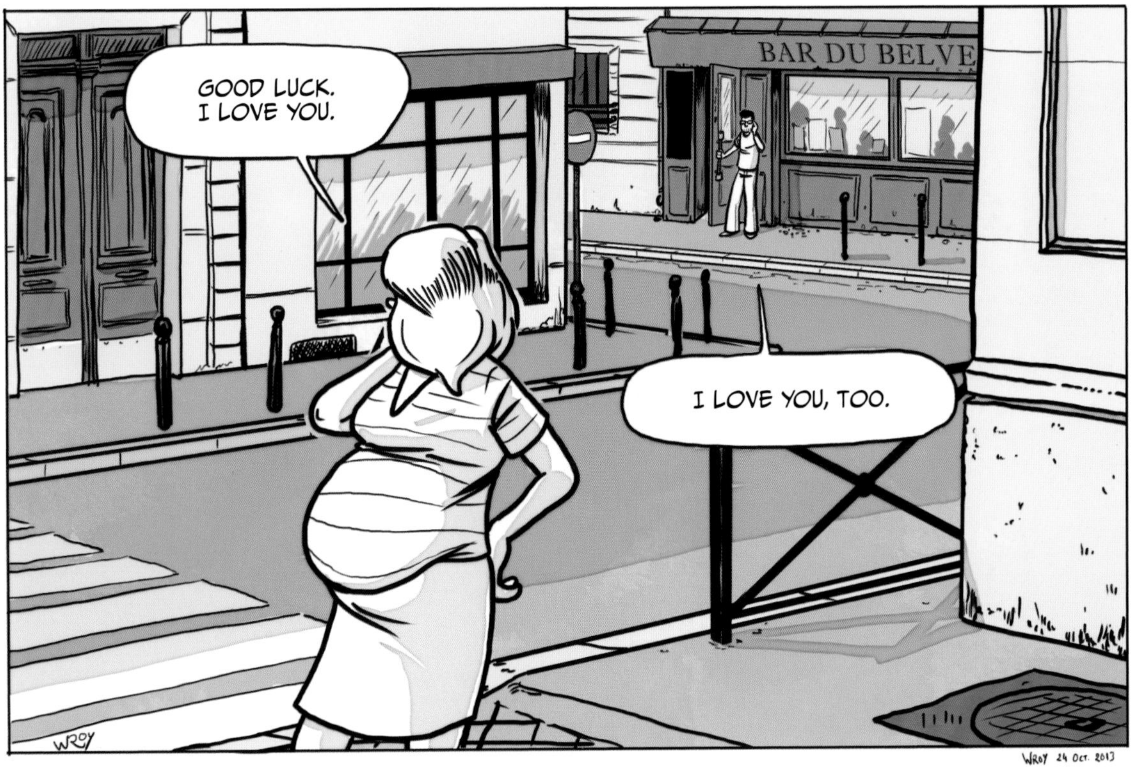
BAR DU BELVE
GOOD LUCK. I LOVE YOU.
I LOVE YOU, TOO.
WROY

WROY 24 Oct. 2013

To Anatole...
and, perhaps, future siblings.